KU-303-812
City and Islington College
BAT0966

FASHION

Front cover and slipcase
Paco Rabanne, Top, c. 1969 (cf. page 573)
Photo: © Takashi Hatakeyama/ © KCI

Back cover
Cristobal Balenciaga, Cocktail Dress, 1955 (cf. page 524)
Photo: © Takashi Hatakeyama/ © KCI

The Collection of the Kyoto Costume Institute

FASHION

A History from the 18th to the 20th Century

Volume II: 20th Century

TASCHEN

HONG KONG KÖLN LONDON LOS ANGELES MADRID PARIS TOKYO

III.

20th

CENTURY · FIRST HALF

World War I quickly and completely demolished the old social systems and values that had begun to crumble at the end of the nineteenth century. Society changed, and consequently the whole look of society changed too. The rise of a powerful middle class brought about a new lifestyle, and as women stepped out of the home to participate more fully in the world at large, they discarded the corset and sought more functional clothing. Fashion designers as well as artists thought hard about new types of apparel. While it is important to understand the impact that the two World Wars had on fashion, it is also true without a doubt that *haute couture* functioned as the central influence leading fashion in the first half of the twentieth century. Also during this period, various vital media systems were established which spread the fashions of Parisian *haute couture* around the world.

The Quest for a New Type of Clothing and The Escape from the Corset

World War I accelerated shifts in various aspects of society and culture. An increasing number of highly educated and professional women, the more frequent use of automobiles, and a growing fascination with sports were just some of the developments that resulted in a whole new lifestyle. Clothing, too, evolved to acquire the shape of the new epoch. For active women in this period, day-to-day clothing gradually achieved a certain degree of functionality in the form of tailored suits.

On the other hand, prominent dress designers such as Charles Frederick Worth, Jacques Doucet and Jeanne Paquin, who had all started *haute couture* houses during the previous century, still adhered to an *Art Nouveau* sensibility, aiming for ultimate beauty through a combination of elegance and opulence. Their ornate creations required long corsets to achieve the desired effect, an artificial S-curve silhouette. Long corsets distorted the natural body and hindered mobility so much that, although women followed such styles in public, they understandably sought release from such restrictive attire inside their own homes. The popular at-home garments were tea gowns with loose silhouettes, since they allowed women to loosen their corsets underneath.

It was Paul Poiret who first put forward a new line of fashion that did not require the use of a corset. His "Confucius Coat," with its straight cut and ample shape, first appeared in 1903. Next, in 1906, he created the "Hellenic Style," a corset-free and high-waisted design. With few exceptions, since the time of the Renaissance western women's clothing had required a waist-cinching corset as the main shaping element. Poiret rejected the use of a corset in female garments, shifting the supporting point of gravity from the waist to the shoulders. According to his autobiography, Poiret's designs arose not from a desire to release women from the centuries-old tyranny of the corset, but from an ardent quest for a new form of beauty. His garments, nevertheless, achieved something that even the disapproval of feminist activists and medical doctors during the late nineteenth century had failed to do: they liberated women from the corset. Consequently, fashion in the twentieth century evolved from a corseted, artificial form to a more natural shape supported by a brassiere.

Poiret's work was decorated in a splendidly exotic style, and employed strong, bold colors. He created harem pants, as well as the aptly named narrow-hemmed hobble skirt, and turbans inspired by the Orient. His designs fed into a nostalgia for foreign lands that characterized this period of the twentieth century. Orientalist painting, popularized in the late nineteenth century, and the publication of *A Thousand and One Nights* in translation in the early twentieth century fostered a yearning for the Orient. The sensational début of the *Ballets Russes* in Paris in 1909 was applauded for its exotic magnificence and certainly added to the trend. Attention turned increasingly to Japan, which opened its doors to the West in the late nineteenth century. By the time of the Russo-Japanese War (1904–1905), Japan's cultural influence had been dubbed "Japonism." Both Orientalism and Japonism made an impact on various fields of art and literature. Poiret and another fashion house, Callot Sœurs, found inspiration in exoticism and the sensuous beauty of the East. They were drawn to the patterns and colors of fabrics as well as the structure of garments such as loosely fitted harem pants and the exotic Japanese kimono. The flat shape and openness of the kimono, in fact, suggested one direction that the new relationship between the body and clothing would go.

The search for a new style in clothing was observed in other European countries aside from France. Spanish-born Mariano Fortuny, inspired by Greek shapes and forms, created a classically pleated dress and named it "Delphos." The "Delphos" was an innovative design combining functionality with decoration. Fine pleats gently encased the body, and ornamentation was supplied almost entirely by movement, as the slightest stir changed the glow and hue of the textile. The Wiener Werkstätte founded in 1903 by Josef Hoffmann and others also created new clothing. The Wiener Werkstätte started business mainly to engage in the production of architecture, craft works, and bookbinding, but it opened a fashion department in 1911 with its own clothing line, including such items as loose-fitting sack dresses.

Around the turn of the century, the media necessary to transmit fashion news were developed and their realm of influence spread rapidly. Fashion magazines such as *Vogue* (1892-, New York) and *Gazette du Bon Ton* (1912–1925, Paris) established a method of informing the world of fresh developments in fashion. Fashion pictures played a dominant role in such magazines; many new artists such as Paul Iribe and Georges Lepape caused this era to be known as the golden age of fashion illustration. Poiret was the first to use the fashion catalogue as a medium for individual designers to display their work to the world, publishing *Les Robes de Paul Poiret by Paul Iribe* (1908) and *Les Choses de Paul Poiret* (1911), illustrated by Georges Lepape.

Because buyers and fashion journalists from many countries subsequently began to crowd into Paris to obtain information on the latest fashions, the Chambre Syndicale de la Couture Parisienne was set up in 1910 to control the scheduling of collections and prevent the proliferation of unauthorized, imitation merchandise. Paris was then well on the way to establishing a system to maintain its dominance as the fashion center of the world.

The outbreak of World War I in 1914 halted much activity in the fashion world. Women, who found themselves taking on the responsibility of men's tasks in society and industry during the War, needed practical clothing rather than decorative and elaborate costumes. Simple designs and shorter skirts were in demand, and tailored clothing fit the bill. The functional tailored suit became an essential women's fashion item of the time. In contrast to the dramatic changes in women's clothing, men' s fashion saw only minor alterations, such as a slightly looser fitting jacket and narrow hemlines on trousers, both created to permit greater freedom of movement.

New Women

Although they lost their jobs when men were discharged from military service after World War I, nothing could turn back the tide for women who had acquired a taste for the excitement of the outside world. Jazz became popular. A dance craze for the tango and the Charleston boomed. Everyone seemed to be racing around in high-speed automobiles, getting suntans, and swimming. New rules were applied to a society that now included a burgeoning *nouveau riche* class alongside the old-money upper class, and an avant-garde sensibility alongside traditional ideals of elegance. Caught up in the dynamic energy of the time, the cycle of fashion trends grew shorter.

Female looks changed significantly. Hairstyles went from full, upswept arrangements to short bobs. Hemlines shot up from below the ankle to flirt with the knee. Since a youthful, slender style found more favor than a mature and voluminous one, women accordingly dressed up like boys. *La Garçonne*, from the eponymous novel by Victor Margueritte

(1922), was the symbolic image that women aspired to achieve. The new woman acquired a higher education, had a profession, and enjoyed romantic relationships without hesitation. She led society into new customs such as driving cars, playing golf and tennis, exercising, and even smoking.

The androgynous *garçonne* style, which eschewed any emphasis of the bosom or the waist, achieved general recognition at the Exposition Internationale des Arts Décoratifs et Industriels Modernes held in Paris in 1925, the exhibition that gave the style known as Art Deco its name. A short hairstyle with a close-fitting cloche hat and a loose-fitting drop-waist dress with a knee-length skirt characterized the *garçonne* look. The extreme simplicity of the dress was supplemented with surface decorations of spangled embroidery, a feather boa, and assorted bright accessories. Underwear consisted of a brassiere, teddy, and natural flesh-tone stockings; makeup included red lipstick, white powder, and blush; eyebrows were plucked into a fine line, and the eyes were accentuated with a dark line of kohl to complete the look.

With the boyish bent of the period, it was only natural that a demand for sports clothing emerged. French tennis champion Suzanne Lenglen also helped to foster the production of sports clothing by demonstrating her matchless strength in functional tennis wear. The bathing suit, exposing more of the body than ever before, appeared on beaches everywhere in the late 1910s. Beachwear was also introduced, and the fashion of wearing pants became popular at resorts.

Gabrielle ("Coco") Chanel played a decisive role in this new aspect of women's fashion. She designed clothing for comfort, simplicity, and chic appearance with an innovative combination of jersey material and shapes borrowed from men's clothing. After her jersey dress caused a sensation, she designed cardigan ensembles, sailor-style "yachting pants," beach pajamas, and the renowned must-have item, a simple black dress. Another of Chanel's contributions to fashion was the idea that fashionable, ostentatious costume jewelry could represent real wealth as surely as jewels. The perfect embodiment of both the *garçonne* style and the independent woman, Chanel created a whole new dress ethic and proposed a style for women who were ready to pursue their own active lives.

In the golden age of *haute couture* during the 1920s and 1930s, many rising names in fashion design such as Jean Patou, Edward Molyneux and Lucien Lelong actively worked alongside the older established houses of Paquin and Callot Soeurs. Female designers were especially influential, and in the 1920s Chanel and Madeleine Vionnet played the most important roles. While Chanel's role was that of a media-savvy stylist, Vionnet was more an architect of fashion. Her technique of cutting garments from geometrically patterned fabric with a superb sense of construction brought about genuine innovations in dressmaking. Vionnet invented a wide variety of detailed designs like the bias cut, circular cut, cut with slash or triangular insertion, halter neckline, and cowl neckline. Inspired by the plain construction of the Japanese kimono, she also created a dress constructed from a single piece of cloth.

The association between fashion and art gained an unprecedented intimacy in the 1920s. Designers teamed up with artists for inspiration. New movements in art like Surrealism, Futurism and Art Deco proposed that the entire living environment, including clothing, should be harmonized as a single artistic manifestation. Collaboration with avant-garde artists, and the influence of Surrealism and Futurism in particular, brought radical artistic design to clothing. The decorative accessories and textiles of Art Deco emerged from this rich collaboration, which included the adaptation of a number of artistic techniques such as Oriental lacquering.

But the Great Depression of 1929 brought an end to much of the postwar prosperity enjoyed during the 1920s. Many of *haute couture's* wealthy clients lost their assets overnight, and the streets thronged with homeless people. The middle classes who survived the worst of the period became much more interested in sewing at home.

Art and Fashion

These difficult economic circumstances meant that the abstract and straight silhouette favored in the 1920s gave way to a more natural form in the 1930s. The slim line of clothing remained, but the bosom was reasserted and the waistline was once again nipped into a standard position. Long dresses came back for eveningwear and hair regained a more traditional feminine length with a soft curl.

But not everything regressed. Day to day clothing continued to feature practical dresses with short skirts, and increasingly popular items of sports clothing. The rich spent long periods of time at resorts and common people also enjoyed vacations at the beach. As a result, fashion for outdoor activities gained in importance. Although the term *prêt-à-porter*, or "ready-to-wear," had yet to appear, *haute couture* houses had started to move in that direction by including sweaters, pants and bathing suits for sports in their boutiques.

Elsa Schiaparelli started her career as a designer of sportswear like sweaters and beach clothing. She gradually expanded her line to include town wear and evening dress, and established herself as one of the most important designers in the 1930s. Schiaparelli is known to have employed great wit to create her unique fashions, epitomized by the famous black woolen sweater with a *trompe-l'œil* white bow that launched her career in fashion.

Schiaparelli was the designer who most closely worked with artists during her time. She was influenced by Dadaism, and adopted ideas from Surrealism for the creation of her eccentric dresses and hats. But art for her was not simply a source of inspiration; she also integrated it directly into her designs. Original sketches by Salvador Dalí and Jean Cocteau were printed or embroidered on her dresses. She eagerly exploited new materials and experimented with rayon, vinyl, and cellophane. However, her intentions did not extend to reshaping clothing itself, and no dramatic new silhouettes figure in her work. The square shoulder and marked waist characteristic of her designs were the mainstream fashion in the 1930s, and remained the dominant style during World War II.

During the 1930s, such female designers as Gabrielle Chanel and Madeleine Vionnet, who had enjoyed international acclaim since the 1920s, as well as Schiaparelli, represented the vanguard of the fashion world. But a male designer, Cristobal Balenciaga, opened his Paris salon in 1937, offering designs with a completely modern structure that garnered much attention.

American films exerted a powerful influence on fashion during the 1930s. Famous Hollywood stars like Marlene Dietrich and Greta Garbo wore dresses made by costume designers such as Adrian. These costumes looked relatively conservative and simple in cut compared to *haute couture* fashion in Paris, but they appeared magnificent on the screen because of their luxurious fabrics. The number of women in the general public who watched Hollywood films – with an eye out for fashion tips – gradually exceeded the number who read fashion magazines featuring Paris *couture*.

Photography, invented in the nineteenth century, grew in importance in fashion magazines. Fashion photos appeared in magazines at the turn of the century, and as the quality of images improved, they became more prevalent. Photographers like Adolphe de Meyer in the 1910s and Edward Steichen in the 1920s are credited with the invention of fashion photography. In the 1930s, when color photography first appeared, the key images in fashion magazines became photographs rather than paintings or drawings. Through the efforts of many photographers, individual expression thrived; George Hoyningen-Huene and Horst P. Horst expressed modernity with sharp images; Toni Frissell pioneered outdoor photography under natural light; Man Ray and others experimented with the various possibilities of photography techniques.

World War II and Fashion

The outbreak of World War II in 1939 caused significant damage to the Parisian fashion scene. Many *couture* houses were forced to close and the few salons that remained open suffered a shortage of material and the flight of clients. The intention of the Germans was to transfer the entire fashion industry from Paris to either Berlin or Vienna. The fashion industry found itself under great pressure in Paris, and Lucien Lelong, the president of the Chambre Syndicale de la Couture Parisienne, went to great pains to try to maintain the status quo of Parisian fashion under the Occupation. In 1940, The Limitation of Supplies Order was enforced. This order regulated the quantity of cloth to be used in clothing manufacture, so that a single coat for example could use no more than four meters of material. Coupons were necessary to purchase rayon, which was one of the few materials available during the time. Many people had to make do with refashioning their own old clothing at home.

In England, The Incorporated Society of London Fashion Designers was commissioned by the British Board of Trade to create a range of prototype clothing to meet the requirements of the Utility Clothing Scheme, enforced in 1941. Thirty-two types of Utility garments designed by Edward Molyneux, Hardy Amies and Norman Hartnell among others, were selected and mass-produced. The United States entered the war in 1941, and the following year, the U. S. War Production Board issued General Limitation Order L-85, which regulated clothing in minute detail, stressing conservation of fabric; the slim and straight skirt without pleats was encouraged, and the flared skirt was completely forbidden.

Because of the shortage of material and the strict rationing systems, the slim silhouette with a skirt of shorter length became dominant in fashion. With the world's attention drawn to those engaged in military service and national defense, an interest in military fashion developed. The look of the time embraced uniform-styled tailored suits and jackets with square, padded shoulders, a pronounced waist with a belt, and large versatile pockets.

Since materials for making hats were not rationed, large hats and turbans in bold designs became characteristic of the period, as did platform shoes with cork soles that emerged as an answer to the shortage of leather.

The decline of Parisian fashion brought about the rise of American fashion. The United States, which had been the most important client for Parisian *haute couture* before the War, developed its own fashion industry at a comfortable distance from the fighting in Europe. Although the United States had its own *haute couture*, before the war it had relied on Parisian houses for high quality and elegant clothes. The field in which the United States was first to make its mark was not, however, in high fashion, but in casual wear for daily use and ready-to-wear clothing.

From the mid-1930s, a distinctively casual Californian style, a New York business style, and a functional, less expensive campus look all began to draw attention. The decline of Parisian fashion authority stimulated American fashion designers to be more creative and active. Claire McCardell, with her free sense of inspiration, designed a line of practical and innovative sportswear with simple construction in cotton or wool jersey. Backed by a powerhouse of similar American designers, the basis of American style, a style which pursued functional beauty, was established.

After the Liberation of Paris by the Allied Forces in June of 1944, the Paris fashion industry immediately resumed activity. *Haute couture* started to show collections again, and new designers such as Jacques Fath and Pierre Balmain made their debut. In 1945, the *Chambre Syndicale de la Couture Parisienne* planned the "*Théâtre de la Mode,*" an exhibition of miniature mannequins seventy centimeters high, dressed in *couture* clothing from new collections. The exhibition, intended to display to the world the breadth of French culture and creativity in fashion, accomplished its purpose through a yearlong tour of nine cities around world. In 1947, Christian Dior launched his first collection, "The New Look," which had palpable impact on the world of fashion. The result was that *haute couture* regained a dominance in world fashion that surpassed even that of the prewar period. It is interesting (and ironic) to note that women were highly appreciative of the nostalgic "New Look" style – a narrow waist cinched with a corset and a full and long skirt – as they simultaneously achieved various freedoms and civil liberties, including suffrage.

Reiko Koga, Professor at Bunka Women's University

The S-curve silhouette was most popular around 1900. To achieve a flowing line, light and soft materials such as chiffon and charmeuse were often used. The severe tightening of the body by the corset reached its peak around this time, and this later led to the quest for a new style that resulted in liberation from corsets. These are typical of the Belle Époque style. The elegant dress on the left with overlaid decoration is a style characteristic of Doucet.

→ **Jacques Doucet**
Evening Dress
Label: DOUCET 21. RUE DE LA PAIX PARIS
c. 1903

Black silk lace with bead embroidery and velvet; silk chiffon sleeves with inset lace; belt of gold grosgrain ribbon.
Inv. AC9465 97-21-3AB

→→ **Anonymous**
Day Dress
c. 1903

White silk chiffon two-piece dress with S-curve silhouette; high-neck collar and yoke of bobbin lace.
Inv. AC3638 80-29-19AB

Hats were elaborately decorated in the early twentieth century. As hats became bigger, light-weight feathers were abundantly used. Hats decorated with whole stuffed birds became popular, threatening beautifully plumed species with extinction. A chorus of public criticism resulted, and in the United States, regulations were brought in to prohibit the killing, importing and selling of wild birds.

↓ **Anonymous**
Hat
1900s

Beige silk tulle with cotton lace; ornamentation of cotton tulle; buckle and ostrich feather.
Inv. AC1726 78-41-130

→ **Anonymous**
Hat
1905–1909

Straw hat with black velvet ribbon and stuffed bird.
Inv. AC4667 83-26-8A

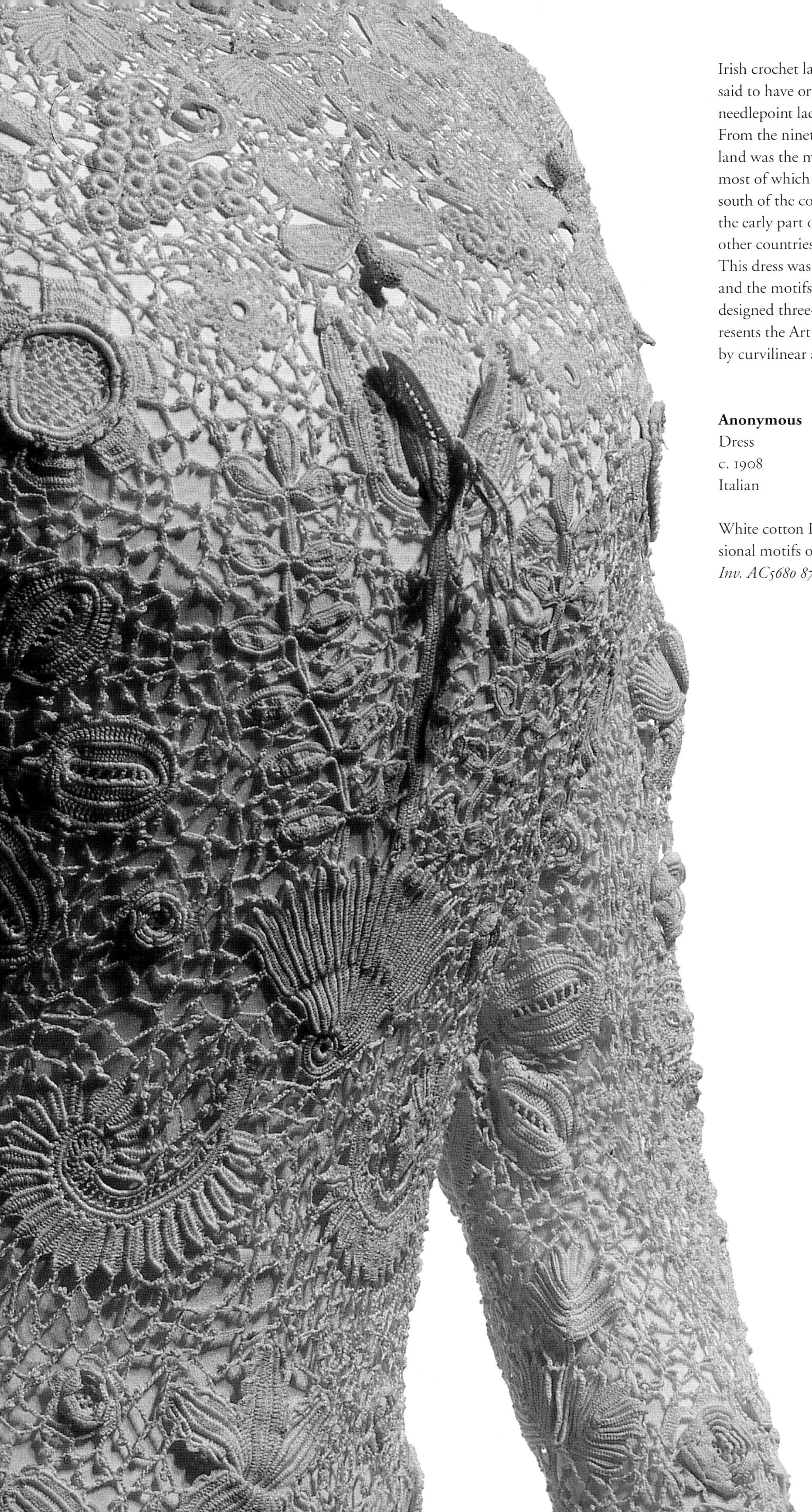

Irish crochet lace was knitted by hand. It is said to have originated from elaborate Italian needlepoint lace in the seventeenth century. From the nineteenth century onward, Ireland was the main producer of this lace, most of which originated in convents in the south of the country. It became popular in the early part of the twentieth century, and other countries began to produce it as well. This dress was knitted to fit the S-curve, and the motifs of the insects and plants were designed three-dimensionally. The dress represents the Art Nouveau style, characterized by curvilinear and organic forms.

Anonymous
Dress
c. 1908
Italian

White cotton Irish crochet; three-dimensional motifs of flowers and dragonflies.
Inv. AC5680 87-36-1

The female body was squeezed most tightly into corsets in the early days of the twentieth century. The body had to be forced to fit the artificial S-curve of the dress, which emphasized the bust and hips, while making the waistline as small as possible. Poiret introduced the corset-free dress in 1906, although women were not completely freed from the corset until after World War I. Both of these corsets are supported by a long straight steel busk at the front and solid boning around the body. These reinforcements were needed to suppress the abdomen and emphasize the hips.

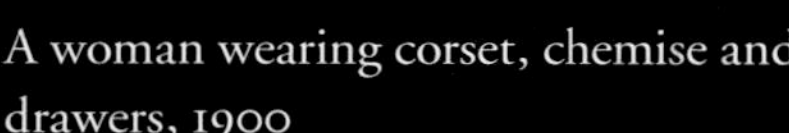

A woman wearing corset, chemise and drawers, 1900

← **Corset, Chemise and Drawers**
Label: VELVET GRIP (on corset)
c. 1900

Black corset of cotton brocade with small floral pattern; steel busk; garters at front; chemise and drawers of white linen.
Inv. AC727 78-20-50AB, AC4273 82-17-4A, AC4274 82-17-4B

→ **Corset**
c. 1907

Black cotton jacquard with small floral pattern; silk lace decoration with ribbon at top; garters at front.
Inv. AC4679 83-26-19AB

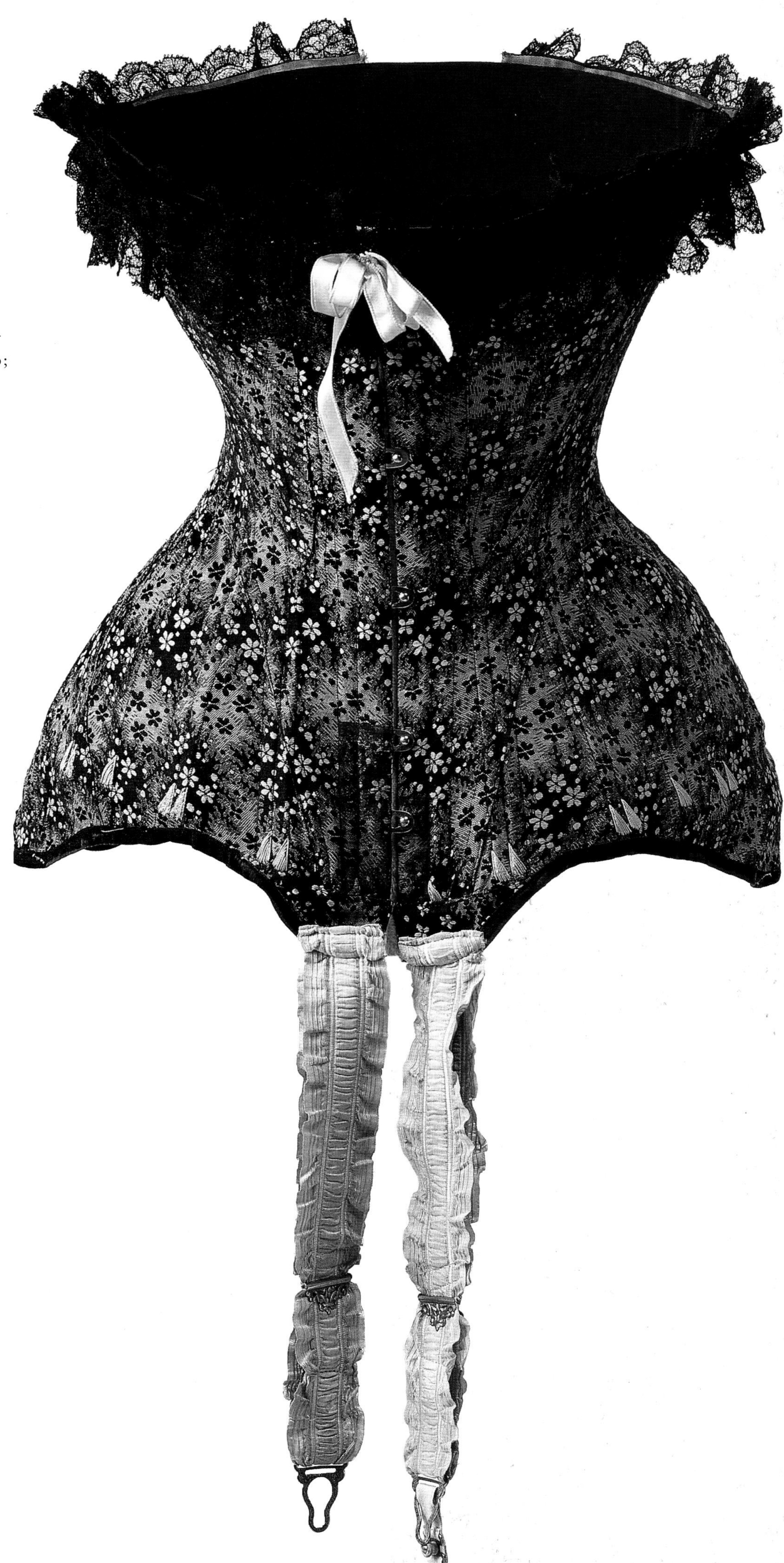

Poiret introduced the corset-free, high-waisted dress in 1906, when the S-curve-silhouette dress was still popular, thereby suggesting the shift from the ostentatious artificial forms of the nineteenth century to a revolutionary style that brought out the natural beauty of the body. The result was a great transformation in fashion. Although the corset did not disappear overnight, by the time of World War I Poiret's new style had totally supplanted the corset.

Paul Poiret
Evening Dress
Label: PAUL POIRET
1910–1911

Beige silk satin dress with silk tulle overdress; embroidery of polychrome beads and gold thread; gold tulle peplum.
Inv. AC2388 79-20

Orientalism was prevalent in Paris after the debut of the Ballets Russes in 1909. In 1911, Poiret held a fancy dress ball, *La 1002ᵉ nuit* where he showed his collection inspired by the Orient. The designs were adopted from the ethnic costumes of various Eastern countries such as India and China. The party was such a success that Poiret became known as a forerunner in dramatic and exotic fashion design. His dresses were illustrated in *Les Choses de Paul Poiret* by Georges Lepape.

→ **Paul Poiret**
Man's Party Costume
Label: PAUL POIRET-a Paris-Mars 1
1914

Gold lamé and purple silk satin jacket with fake pearls and black fur; kimono sleeves; gold lamé hat with fake pearls and aigrette plume.
Inv. AC9175 94-40-2AB

→→ **Paul Poiret**
Woman's Party Costume
Label: PAUL POIRET-a Paris-December 1913-31890
1913

Black silk gauze hooped over-dress with gold floral embroidery; gold lamé silk harem pants.
Inv. AC9330 96-15

Party costumes by Paul Poiret
Photo: Mario Nunes Vais

Between 1906 and 1909, Poiret's *maison* was located on Rue Pasquier, Paris. He suggested the corset-free dress in female fashion, introducing "Lola Montès" in 1906, and also created a dress in Directoire style in 1907. Both suggested an emancipation from the corset. He shifted the support point from the waist to the shoulder in a one-piece dress, and at the same time presented the loose-fitting coat shown here. Poiret named this straight-cut garment the "kimono coat".

→ **Paul Poiret**
Coat
Label: Paul Poiret. Rue Pasquier 37 Paris
c. 1909

Black silk satin; crochet and bobbin lace; black lace lapel with tassel; yellow silk *habutae* lining.
Inv. AC3777 81-8-3

→→ A group of Poiret's models in clothes designed by him.
Photo: Henri Le Manuel
L'illustration, July 9, 1910

→ **Anonymous**
Bags
c. 1910

Above: Polychrome beads with motif of cherry fruit and branch.
Inv. AC1430 78-38-10

Below: Polychrome beads with floral motif; fringe at hem; metal frame of floral openwork; pearls; chain strap.
Inv. AC1424 78-38-4

The popularity of Orientalism influenced the design of fans. Poiret and Paquin used fans as advertisements for their *maisons*. Paquin hired three talented illustrators of the time, Paul Iribe, Georges Barbier and Georges Lepape, to create artistic fans.

Above: **Anonymous**
Fan
c. 1910

Bordeaux leather and silk moiré; brass pivot and ring; silk strap with pom-poms.
Inv. AC438 77-14-38

Center: **Jeanne Paquin**
"L'OCCIDENTALE" Fan
Label: Edité par PAQUIN-Paris-PAUL IRIBE PINXIT
1911

Vellum; *pochoir* of woman holding flower in scene with ocean and mountain; illustrated by Paul Iribe.
Inv. AC9173 94-39-2

Below: **Jeanne Paquin**
"L'ORIENTALE" Fan
Label: PAQUIN 3-Rue de la Paix PARIS-Edité par PAQUIN-Paris- PAUL IRIBE PINXIT
1911

Silk *habutae*; *pochoir* of female nude in scene with ocean and mountain; illustrated by Paul Iribe.
Inv. AC9172 94-39-1

Worth, Poiret and many other *haute couture* designers created coats of *nukiemon* style, with a Japanese kimono-like open neckline and a loose silhouette in the back, from 1910 to 1913. The coat, which looked like a shawl, was created from a single piece of cloth, and it was simply cut in the center. When worn, the wide neckline resembles the *nukiemon* style in kimono dressing.

Jeanne Paquin
Evening Coat
Label: Paquin-Paris-LONDON ETE 1912
Summer 1912

Blue silk charmeuse satin and black silk chiffon; collar of silk chiffon; embroidery of Japanese-style flowers and waves.
Inv. AC9110 94-9

Page 349
The two dresses on the left of the right page are in the high-waistline style, and in the exotic colors popularized under the influence of the Ballets Russes, a style from the early 1910s. The Paquin dress on the right is characterized by the belt with an Egyptian scarab-shaped ornament, and the skirt in an asymmetrical silhouette.

Left
Jeanne Lanvin
Evening Dress
Label: Jeanne Lanvin PARIS
c. 1911

Green silk chiffon and tulle lace; floral embroidery; rose flower ornament.
Inv. AC5806 88-22-3AB

Center
Anonymous
Evening Dress
c. 1911

Beige silk tulle and pink silk chiffon; floral embroidery of beads and fake pearls; gold cord embroidery on skirt.
Inv. AC1000 78-30-14

Right
Jeanne Paquin
Evening Dress
Label: Paquin HIVER 1911-PARIS 3. Rue de la Paix LONDON 39 Dover Street 36193 Winter 1911

Off-white and silver silk jacquard with floral motif in Renaissance style.
Inv. AC4207 82-8-4AB

This dress was an interpretation of a Japanese kimono style by a Western designer. The influence of the Japanese kimono may be observed around the collar, the front neck opening in *uchiawase* style, and the straight-cut "kimono sleeves." The round cut from front slit to train evokes the beauty of a trailing kimono. The design of the embroidery and the style of the back of the dress demonstrate a Chinese influence as well.

Callot Sœurs
Evening Dress
Label: none
c. 1908

Black and purple silk charmeuse pieced together; *chinoiserie* floral embroidery; ribbons from shoulder stitched at back waist; tassels at ends.
Inv. AC7708 93-2-1AB

Woman in Beer's *forme Japonaise* dress
Photo: Paul Boyer
Les Modes, February 1907

Worth
Coat
Label: Worth
c. 1910

Dark red velvet; kimono neckline; looped *kumihimo* (Japanese cord)-like decoration; tassel with beading.
Inv. AC2880 79-27-1

Woman in Beer's Afternoon dress
Photo: Félix
Les Modes, May 1910

← **Amy Linker**
Coat
(Detail pages 354/355)
Label: AMY LINKER LINKER & Co.Sps.7 RUE AUBER PARIS
c. 1913

Black silk satin and light green silk crepe; black and green silk satin collar; floral and oriental motif bead embroidery; cocoon silhouette.
Inv. AC3775 81-8-1

→ Evening coat by Martial & Armand,
Photo: Félix
Les Modes, November 1912

Page 352, from top to bottom
Snapshots at Longchamp or Auteuil
1. 1911
2.–4. 1913
Martin Kamer Collection

In the early twentieth century, ostentatious *kabuki* costumes gained popularity around the time when the kimono style was popular in Western Europe. The bold stripe pattern and *date-eri* style of collar, and floral motifs similar to the patterns favored by *kabuki* actors, are all elements of *kabuki* costumes. The silhouette of *nukiemon*, the dropped collar at the back in kabuki dress, is also adapted to this coat.

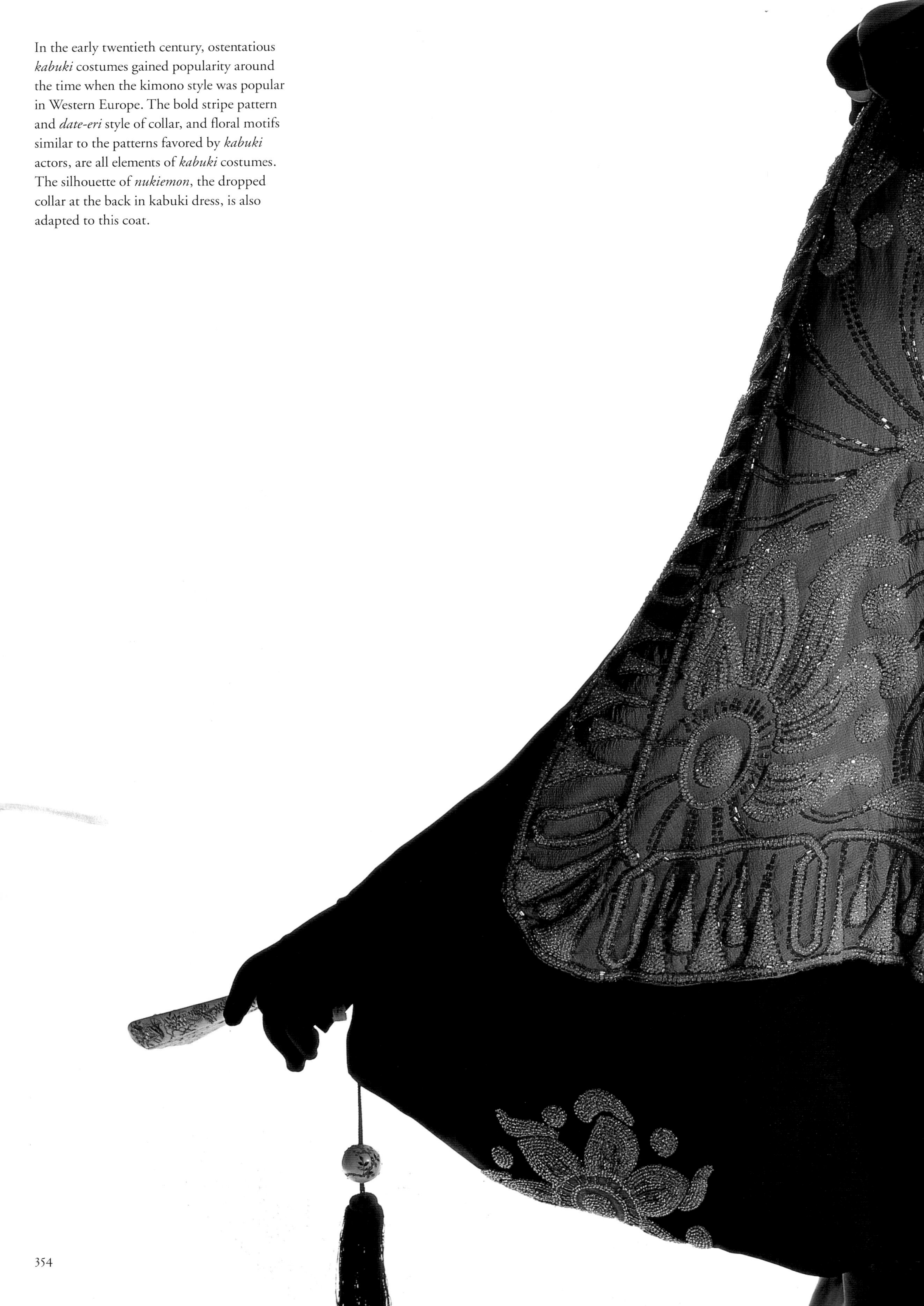

→ **Mariano Fortuny**
Coat
(Detail page 359)
Label: none, but there is a mark left by Fortuny's label (4.5 cm in diameter)
1910s

Light brown velvet with polychrome stencil print of Japanese traditional pattern; salmon-pink silk faille lining; straight-cut structure.
Inv. AC7771 93-19

← Evening dress and coat by Laferrière
Photo: Talbot
Les Modes, October 1912

From the end of the nineteenth century, the Japanese kimono was adopted as an at-home gown in the West because of its comfortable style. Kimono-styled indoor garments were even produced in the West. Mariano Fortuny took design ideas from many sources including Japanese kimono patterns. In this dress, he used butterfly and hollyhock motifs borrowed from a Japanese fabric. The original textile appeared in the second issue of the French journal *Le Japon Artistique* in 1888, and also in *Etoffes Japonaises* in 1910. The textile is currently in the collection of the Musée de la Mode et du Textile, Palais du Louvre.

↖ **Textile "Papillons et Feuilles de Mauve" by Bianchini Férier et Cie**
c. 1907
French
Musée de la Mode et du Textile, Paris, Collection UCAD

← **Textile**
Late *Edo* period (c. 1850–1867)
Japanese
Musée de la Mode et du Textile, Paris, Collection UCAD

The long and narrow collar and the sleeves, along with the kimono's *fuki*-like padded hem, cause this dress to resemble a kimono. The stencil-printed taffeta depicts traditional Japanese motifs. The garment underneath the gown is one of Fortuny's "Delphos" dresses.

Mariano Fortuny
Gown
Label: none
1910s

White silk taffeta stenciled with traditional Japanese motifs; pink silk taffeta padded hem and lining.
Inv. AC8934 93-26

Page 360
Japanese stencil-cutter from a book by Andrew W. Tuer, *The Book of Delightful and Strange Designs Being One Hundred Facsimile Illustrations of the Art of the Japanese Stencil-Cutter*, 1892

Tailored clothing, which was originally men's fashion, was worn as travel or sports attire by women from the late nineteenth century onwards. It became more popular in everyday life around 1910. On the left is a high-waisted dress in a simple silhouette made of soft material, a style typical of this period. On the right is a dress based on a tailored suit, made of soft material for a feminine look, a style especially common in the early twentieth century.

← **Anonymous**
Day Dress
c. 1909

Cotton tulle one-piece dress with floral pattern; cord embroidery; red rose corsage of silk satin.
Inv. AC9381 96-27-2

→ **Bulloz**
Day Ensemble
Label: PARIS Mon Bulloz 140 Champs Elysées
c. 1910

Deep purple silk satin; set of jacket, bodice and skirt; black silk faille belt; skirt with drapery; white cotton tulle jabot on bodice.
Inv. AC1910 79-10-2AC

Shown here is a dress with the high waistline and straight silhouette fashionable in the 1910s. However, this silhouette is still supported by bones inside the dress like those of the nineteenth century. This is a dress that appeared in the transitional period; throughout the previous century women's costumes were supported by layers of undergarments, but times were shifting to the revolutionary corset-free style of fashion.

Callot Sœurs
Evening Dress
Label: Callot Sœurs MARQUE MODE DÉPOSÉS. Paris
c. 1911

Black silk charmeuse, chiffon and lace; lace fabric hanging from shoulder; silk satin belt; fake jet ornamentation.
Inv. AC10339 2000-25-1AB

Westerners were interested in the family crest motifs used in kimonos and other decorative arts in Japan, and many armorial devices crossed over to Europe. On this dress, the roundels of Japanese family crests were embroidered with beads and paillettes arranged in a Western style. The Japanese influence can also be observed in the trailing train and bead decorations, which create an asymmetrical shape.

Anonymous
Evening Dress
c. 1913

White net with embroidery of beads and paillettes; Japanese family crest motifs; tunic-style double-layered front bodice; skirt with train.
Inv. AC7764 93-18-5

In this dress, Japanese *yotsukanawa* and *seigaiha* motifs are depicted on the train with metallic beads. The *seigaiha*, literally "blue ocean wave" in Japanese, represents a wave in China and a scale in Western Europe. This geometric design was often used in the Art Deco style, which was dominant in the 1920s. The almost-straight silhouette hinted at the Art Deco style, which was soon to become a trend.

Beer
Evening Dress
Label: Beer, 7 Place Vendôme, Paris
c. 1919

Black net with silver bead and rhinestone embroidery of Japanese traditional motifs; silver bead fringe; sash in green and gold stripes; silver lamé underdress.
Inv. AC7683 93-1

Japanese family crests from a book by T. W. Cutler, *A Grammar of Japanese Ornament and Design*, 1880

Mariano Fortuny was a versatile artist who showed talent in various fields such as painting, photography, stage design, lighting, textiles and clothing. "Delphos," his classical Greek-inspired pleated dress, dates from around 1907, and it is one of his most famous designs. The fine silk pleats flow from the shoulder and gently surround the body. This modern and body-conscious form was a clear indication of new directions in twentieth-century fashion. The pleats, which change color in accordance with movement and the reflections of light, are dazzling, and their timeless beauty still remains striking and influential today.

Mariano Fortuny
"Delphos" Dress
Label: none
1910s

Topaz-colored silk satin one-piece dress; thin pleats all over; glass beads at armholes and side seams.
Inv. AC5157 85-34-2

Mariano Fortuny
"Delphos" Dress
Label: MADE IN ITALY FABRIQUÉ EN ITALIE FORTUNY DEPOSE
1910s

Green silk satin one-piece dress; thin pleats all over; glass beads at armholes and side seams.
Inv. AC3189 80-8-3

Natasha Rambova wearing "Delphos" dress
Photo: James Abbe, 1924
Washburn Gallery, New York

The "Delphos" was not created for the artificial form outlined by a corset, but was intended to show the natural beauty of a body's shape; initially therefore, it was only worn as a gown at home. As previously illustrated, the "Delphos" as an indoor gown is very long and usually has a train. Venetian glass beads at the side seams and armholes function as weights for the dress. Details like the pleats and glass beads make the structure of the "Delphos" a decoration in itself. This innovative creation brought about a revolution in women's fashion of the time.

Pages 374/375
Mariano Fortuny
"Delphos" Dresses

Fortuny's dress-design began with the textiles he created himself. He dyed raw silk with a variety of products to produce delicate colors. For printing, he originally used wood blocks and later, influenced by the Japanese stencil-printing method, he developed a silk-screen printing technique with stencils that could print multiple colors, which he patented in 1909. Together with the "Delphos," these artistic textiles with their stencil prints became a hallmark of Fortuny's creations. On the left is a stencil-printed floral and plant design common in Cretan textiles. The design came from a painting by Bellini, a Venetian artist. On the right is a stencil-printed tunic with an Islamic design, making use of the full width of the fabric.

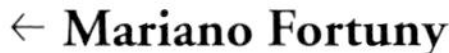

← **Mariano Fortuny**
Tunic and Pants
Label: none
1910s

Wine silk voile tunic stenciled with silver; glass beads; red pleated silk pants.
Inv. AC5076 85-8-2, AC5663 87-34-1

→ **Mariano Fortuny**
Tunic
(See also pages 378/379)
Label: none
1910s

Black silk gauze stenciled with gold Islamic pattern; glass beads.
Inv. AC5075 85-8-1

The movement to release the female body from the corset began in many parts of Europe, but was first proposed by artists of the Pre-Raphaelite and Aesthetic movements in the late nineteenth century. Their aim was the creation of a simple dress in a loose silhouette, which took its inspiration from the clothing of the classical Greek and medieval periods. Gallenga started out as a painter and joined the Pre-Raphaelites. She then became a costume designer who was strongly influenced by Fortuny, specializing in stencil-printed clothing and medieval-style dresses.
On the left is a dress with hanging sleeves made by Gallenga. The phoenix and griffin motifs in ancient oriental style give the dress the magnificent look of the Renaissance period. On the right is a dress with a Renaissance pattern made by Fortuny.

← **Maria Monaci Gallenga**
Dress
Label: Maria Monaci Gallenga
c. 1917

Moss-green silk velvet; oriental motif in silver-on-gold stencil print; belt of gold and green silk georgette cords.
Inv. AC3008 80-2-32

→ **Mariano Fortuny**
Dress
Label: MARIANO FORTUNY VENISE
1930s

Black silk velvet stenciled with gold Renaissance motif; black pleated silk satin insets at side and under arms.
Inv. AC688 78-20-13

→ **Mariano Fortuny**
Dress
Label: MARIANO FORTUNY VENISE
1930s

Blue-green velvet stenciled with gold; pleated silk satin insets at sides and under arms.
Inv. AC3839 81-15-4

← Catherine Hawley (dancer) wearing Fortuny's dress
Photo: Man Ray

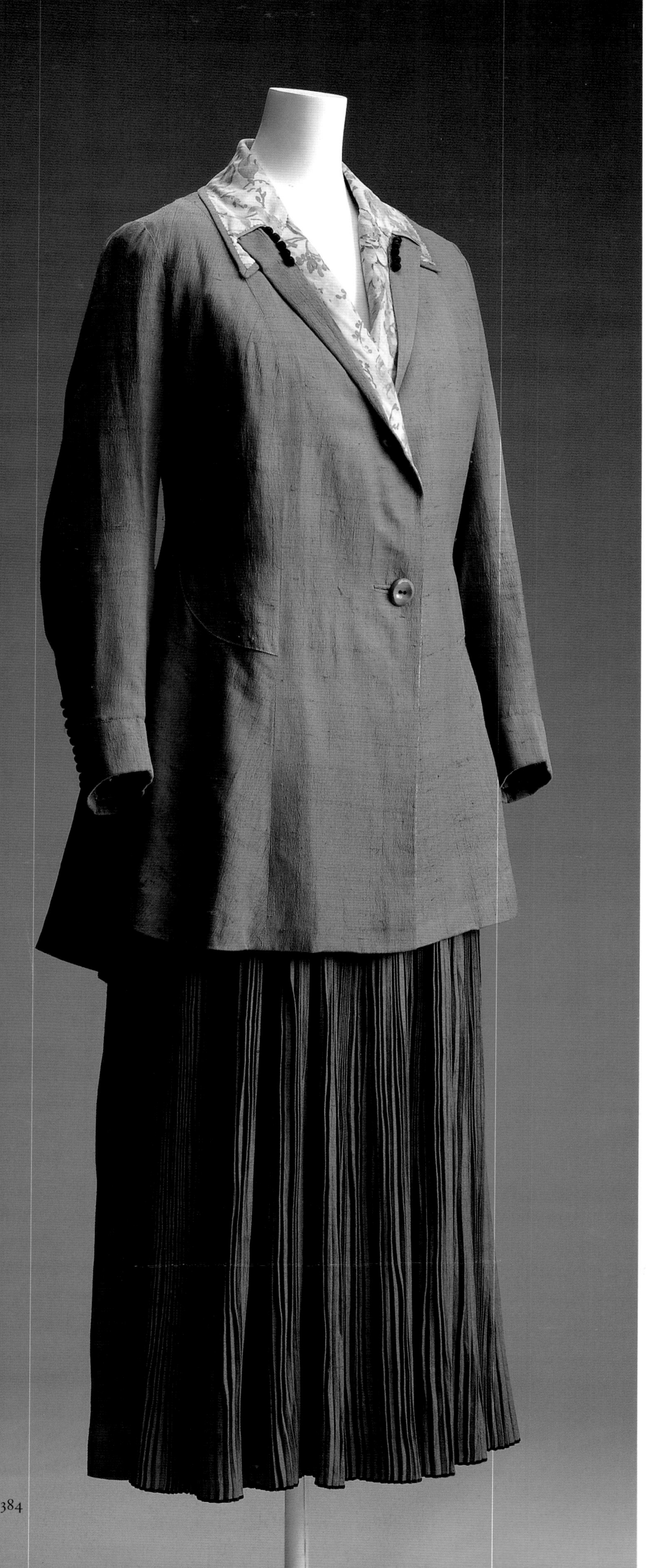

Redfern, which was originally based in London, became famous for its tailored suits and sportswear during the Belle Époque in Paris. To add a feminine touch to a tailored suit like this a floral print was applied to the jacket and lining, and other features such as skirt pleats were incorporated into the structure of the suit.
Lucile also originated in London, and later opened branches in Paris and New York. This dress, made in New York, with elaborate decoration in a nostalgic silhouette, resembles the Lanvin "*robe de style*." The short skirt, which allows the knee to show, was a characteristic of the transitional style moving into the 1920s.

← **John Redfern**
Day Ensemble
Label: REDFERN Paris
c. 1915

Set of jacket and skirt in green silk pongee; lining and collar in silk *habutae* with floral print; pleated skirt.
Inv. AC4801 84-90-4AB

→ **Lucile**
Evening Dress
Label: Lucile Ltd 37&39 WEST 57TH ST. NEW YORK
Autumn, 1916

Off-white tulle and silk satin; belt of *habutae* and satin; three-layered skirt with light-blue taffeta on top; corsage.
Inv. AC1900 79-1-52

Chanel thought that it was crucial for women's clothes in the twentieth century to have functional features. Discarding superficial decoration and adapting the essence of men's fashion, she created sporty, functional women's fashion that brought a new type of elegance. A working woman herself, Chanel embodied the "*garçonne*," the new model image of women after World War I, and wore her own creations. The dress shown here was made early in her career. The labels reading "Gabrielle Chanel," attached to the dress and coat, are among the few labels from this period to have survived.

← **Gabrielle Chanel**
Coat
Label: Gabrielle Chanel PARIS
c. 1920

Dark brown velveteen; stand-up collar; self-fabric panels at side; pin-tuck at low waist; tortoiseshell buttons with gold paint; metal beads; hat by Chanel (late 1910s).
Inv. AC3645 80-30-1

→ **Gabrielle Chanel**
Evening Dress
Label: Gabrielle Chanel PARIS
c. 1920

Brown silk charmeuse layered under silk tulle embroidered with floral motif; sash-like ornament at low waist, double-layered skirt of peg-top silhouette.
Inv. AC4339 82-21-2

Coco
SEM

→ **Labels of Gabrielle Chanel**
From top: 1921, c. 1930, 1930s

Shown on the right-top, the label with Chanel's full name "Gabrielle Chanel" is a rarity among her labels.
Inv. AC4339 82-21-2, AC4221 82-10-12, AC5506 86-51-2

← **Sem**
Chanel carried away by Arthur Capel as a Centaur, c. 1913

Two dresses that show the refined handcraft technique of *haute couture*. The clean and sleek image that resulted is typical of Chanel design.

← **Gabrielle Chanel**
Dress
Label: CHANEL 75476
c. 1926

Dress of off-white silk chiffon with cape-like piece; pin-tucks; skirt made of 15 panels; underdress of silk crepe de Chine.
Inv. AC6427 89-21-10AB

→ **Gabrielle Chanel**
Dress
Label: CHANEL 85123
c. 1928

Black silk charmeuse; skirt of silk chiffon and tulle.
Inv. AC4229 82-11-4
Gift of Mr. Martin Kamer

Page 392
Chanel created the simple "little black dress" in 1926. The dress on the left of the previous page is a good example. This dress had a sensational impact on women's fashion, and it has become one of the most indispensable outfits for women since then.

Gabrielle Chanel
Dress
Label: CHANEL
c. 1927

Black silk satin-back crepe; low waist, straight silhouette; creative use of different textures of fabric; ribbon decoration.
Inv. AC7605 92-26-1

Page 393
One of the main features of ensembles designed by Chanel is that the same silk fabric was used for the coat lining and the dress, and the same for the jacket lining and the blouse. This coat-and-dress ensemble is accented with an Art-Deco-style printed silk.

Gabrielle Chanel
Day Ensemble
Label: CHANEL
c. 1927

Set of coat and dress; dress in brown crepe de Chine with print, low waist; flounced skirt; shirring; coat in brown velveteen with lining of matching material with dress.
Inv. AC5304 86-6-9A, AC5305 86-6-9B

In 1916, Chanel designed cardigan suits made of wool jersey, which at the time was a fabric mainly used for underwear. This style, completed with elastic materials and a shorter skirt in a simplified silhouette, later became a prototype for the "Chanel suit." The dress on the right is an example of a cardigan suit from the 1920s. The knee-length skirt in simple silhouette and monotone colors makes the dress look modern. The carnation corsage is attached to the dress, although later on the camelia corsage was the one always applied to Chanel suits.

→ **Gabrielle Chanel**
Day Ensemble
Label: CHANEL
c. 1928

Jacket and skirt in black wool crepe without lining; white wool jersey sweater.
Inv. AC6301 89-9AC

Chanel wearing her wool jersey cardigan ensemble, 1928

Madeleine Vionnet came up with her own methods to maximize the beauty of the female body. For example, she invented the draping technique of cutting fabric on a torso with pins and scissors, and also used crepe fabric to gain a flowing line. This dress in a straight silhouette is a good example from her early career. The silk fringe, which swings with the movement of the person wearing the dress, functions as a decoration as well as lending weight to the dress. The diagonal cut of the square cloth later developed into the innovative "bias cut" technique.

Madeleine Vionnet
Dress
Label: Madeleine Vionnet
1921

Black silk georgette; bias cut; silk-thread fringes at armholes and skirt.
Inv. AC6590 90-4
Gift of Mr. Martin Kamer

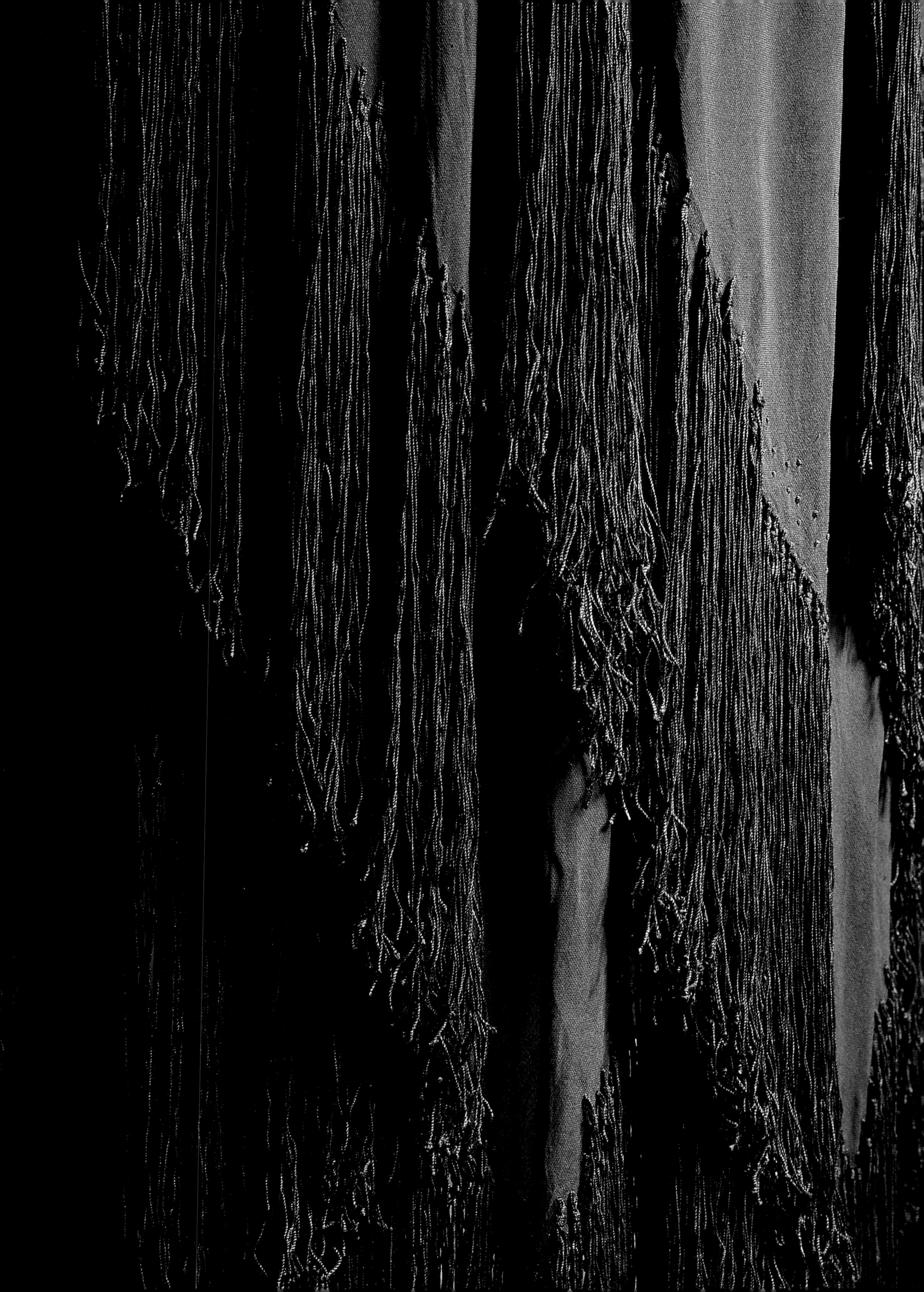

Vionnet reconstructed the female body with her designs and introduced a fundamental change in cutting techniques. For the skirt of the dress on the left, she used triangular fabrics folded alternately like *origami*, the Japanese art of paper-folding. Through this sewing process, the difference in texture between the surface and the back of the fabrics appears distinctly, creating an interesting effect in the appearance of the skirt. Although it looks simple, it is a complex construction that requires a superb cutting technique. The dress on the right is decorated with rose ornaments, which are common in her early works from the 1920s. These ornaments are placed only on the sides to highlight the simplicity of the bodice front.

Madeleine Vionnet
Dress
Label: Madeleine Vionnet
1918–1919

Black silk satin-back crepe one-piece dress; skirt constructed from 20 pieces.
Inv. AC6813 90-24-1

Madeleine Vionnet
Dress
Label: Madeleine Vionnet 12061
c. 1922

Black silk charmeuse and *habutae*; rectangular fabric used for front and back bodice; 271 rose ornaments on both side panels.
Inv. AC6423 89-21-6

The monastic style was fashionable in the early 1920s, and as this illustration demonstrates it was a clear influence on Vionnet. This cape with its large hood and thick tassels has an air of mystery thanks to its heavy materials and dark colors.

→ **Madeleine Vionnet**
Evening Cape
Label: none
c. 1923

Dark brown velvet; hooded; warp used in vertical orientation; red and brown lamé for lining; two cords with rayon tassels.
Inv. AC6814-90-24-2

Thayaht
La Gazette du Bon Ton, 1922

Inspired by Japanese lacquer products, decorative designers such as Eileen Gray and Jean Dunand created interior decoration with lacquer work in the 1920s. Dunand also created lacquered cloth. Lamé, which has a lacquer-like texture, has glitter and flexibility, and was frequently used in the 1920s. The dress on the left reflects the trend of the time. The dress on the right was worn as a wedding dress on June 27, 1922, in Paris. A picture of the marriage ceremony and the invitation cards both survive, and it was clearly a wedding of some style. Although the back seems to fasten in a bow, the dress consists entirely of straight-cut cloth. Vionnet was interested in Japanese *ukiyo-e* paintings and kimonos, and collected them under the influence of Mme Gerber, whom she knew when working at Callot Sœurs.

→ **Madeleine Vionnet**
Evening Dress
Label: Madeleine Vionnet 79531
c. 1922

Pink silk voile inset with warp thread of silver lamé; tubular-silhouette dress with over-bodice with kimono-like front and back; bow with bead embroidery.
Inv. AC6897 90-49-3AC

→→ **Madeleine Vionnet**
Wedding Dress
Label: Madeleine Vionnet 14053
1922

White silk faille and tulle; ankle-length with straight-cut hem, train; rose ornaments of silk faille by Lesage; set with headdress of wax flowers and belt.
Inv.AC7007 91-15-3A

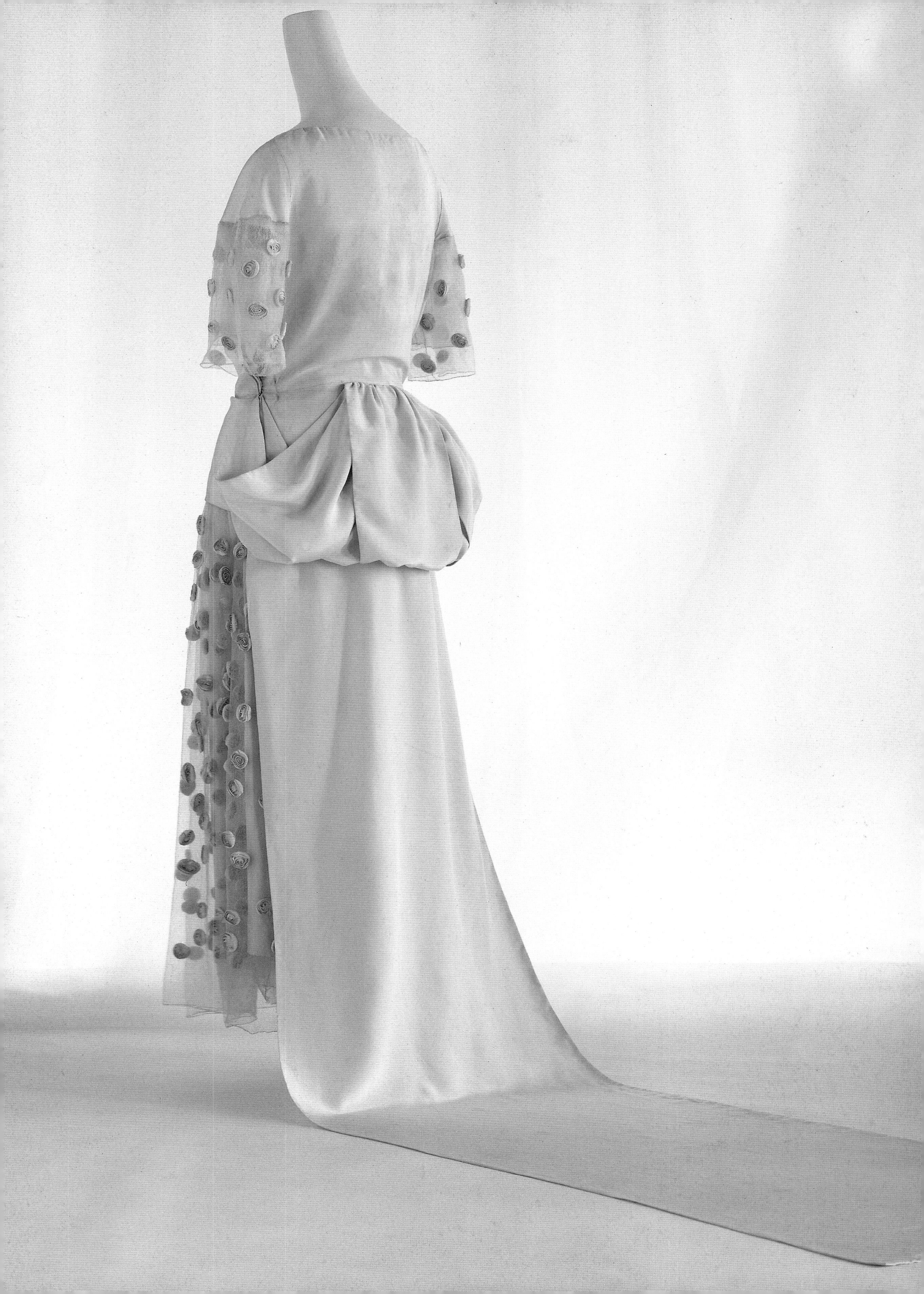

This dress looks simple in structure, but is a good demonstration of the high standard of *haute couture*. The pleats and tucks that Vionnet frequently used in her designs have both ornamental and functional effects. The pin-tucks placed all over the front of the body look like the mark of a rake in the sand garden of a Japanese Zen temple. This is a display of her superb technique, showing a perfect mastery of the fabric, and turning structural features into decoration.

Madeleine Vionnet
Dress
Label: Madeleine Vionnet 28693
c. 1925

Green silk crepe; straight silhouette; boat neck; all-over wavy pattern in pin-tucks.
Inv. AC8947 93-32-5

Woman in Vionnet's dress
Photo: Paul O'Doyé
Fémina, May 1927

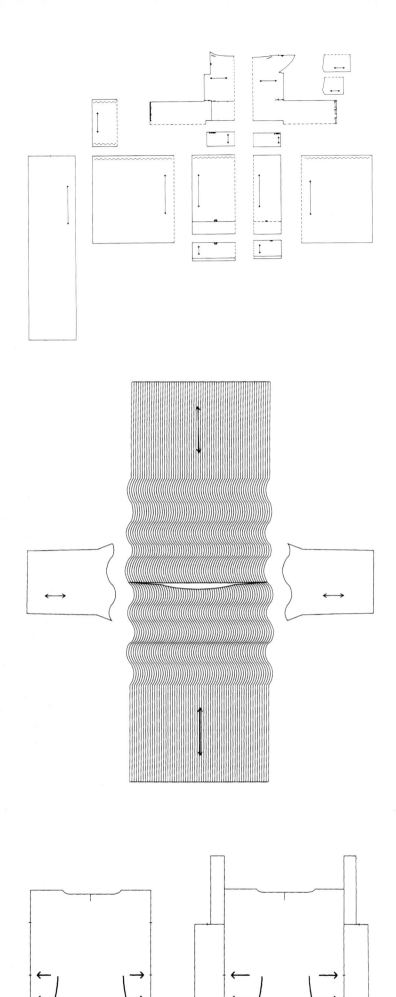

← **Pattern of Madeleine Vionnet's dresses**
From top: *Inv. AC7007 91-15-3A; AC8947 93-32-5; AC6423 89-21-6*

↓ **Label of Madeleine Vionnet**
(Detail page 407)
To prevent fraudulent copying, Vionnet's right thumbprint was added to her label from 1923.

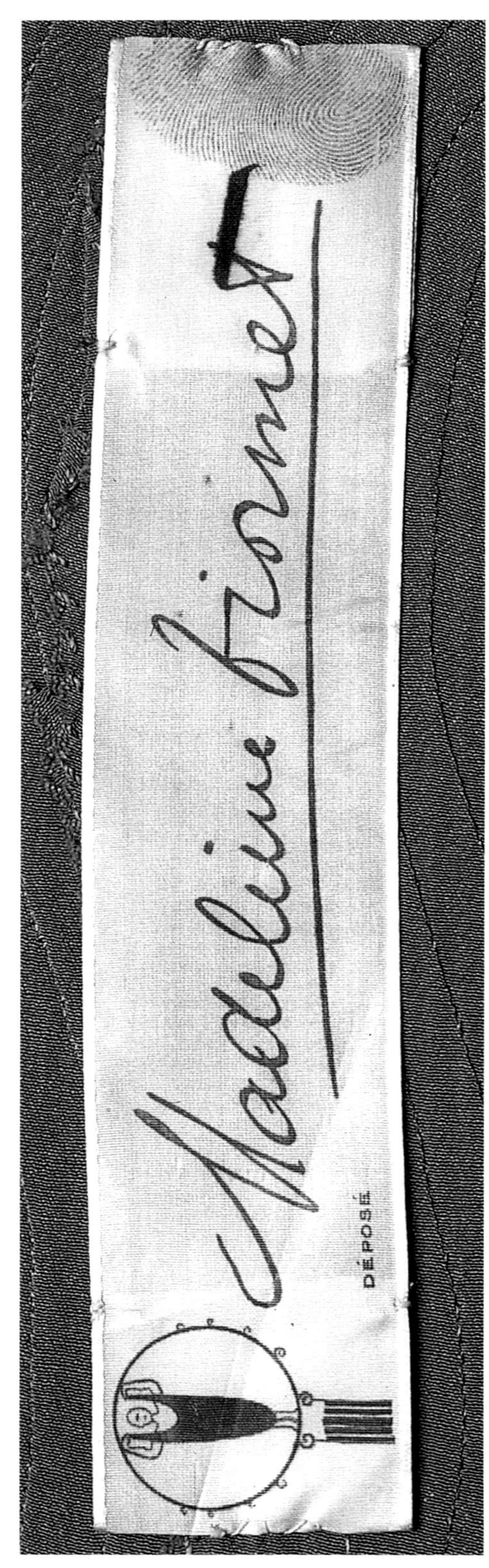

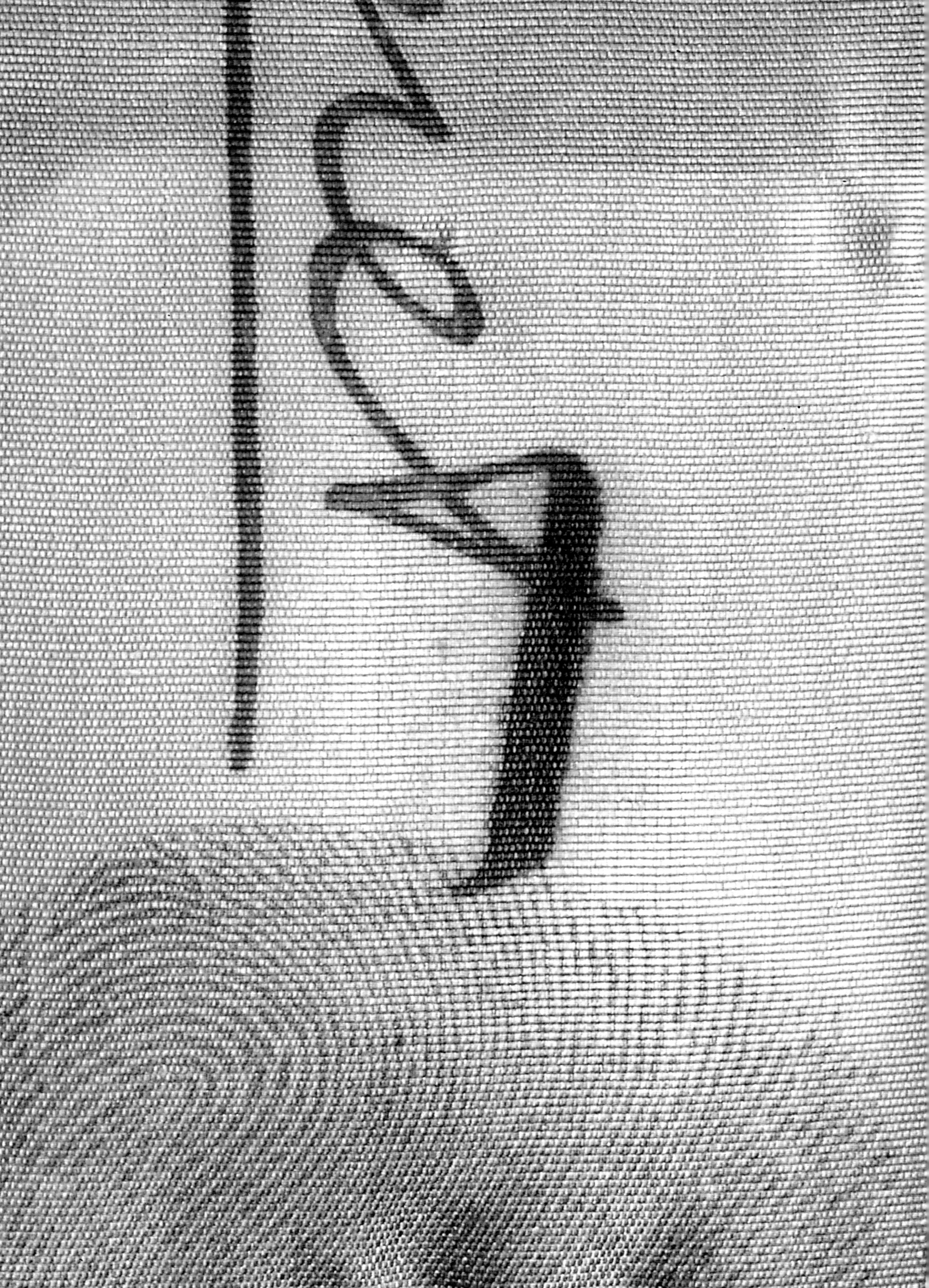

Through her patterns it is apparent that she was influenced by Japanese art, and by new art styles in the early twentieth century such as Cubism and Futurism. She established her design theory based on geometric form.

Madeleine Vionnet
"Henriette" Evening Dress
Label: Madeleine Vionnet 26288
c. 1923

28 pieces of gold and silver fabric pieced into two panels in checkerboard pattern.
Inv. AC6819 90-25AB
Gift of Mr. Martin Kamer

Woman in Vionnet's dress
Photo: Edward Steichen
Vogue (American), June 1, 1925

The exoticism of the 1920s was influenced by the many cultures that had reached Western Europe: Orientalism that had continued on from the 1910s, an Egyptian style spurred by the discovery of Tutankhamen's tomb (1922), and the Mexican craze influenced by Aztec art. Exotic influences are easily discernible in the fashion of the time. Vionnet introduced a classical Greek-inspired design in 1924; this dress was embroidered with gold thread using a similar technique, but depicts an Egyptian geometric pattern.

Thayaht
Vionnet's dress
La Gazette du Bon Ton, 1924

Madeleine Vionnet
Evening Dress
Label: none
1927

Black silk gauze with gold thread embroidery; Egyptian geometric pattern; strap with tassels.
Inv. AC6815 90-24-3

In the dress on the left, the Chinese letters, the embroidery of a peony motif and the colors in the whole suggest the strong influence of Chinese design. Egyptian embroidery was applied to the dress on the right. An article in the American edition of *Vogue* in April, 1923, introduced Egyptian fashion and dresses at Jenny's. The dress on the right dates from the same season.

← **Callot Sœurs**
Evening Dress
Label: Callot Sœurs PARIS ETÉ 192294681
Summer 1922

Orange silk tulle embroidered with floral and Chinese-letter motifs.
Inv. AC3701 81-30-3AB

→ **Jenny**
Evening Dress
Label: JENNY PARIS No.1126
Spring/Summer 1923

Black silk muslin; red, green and blue bead and gold thread embroidery of Egyptian motif.
Inv. AC9251 95-34
Gift of Ms. Mariko Fujita

While Chanel and other designers created dresses in avant-garde style, Lanvin had continued to make elegant and sophisticated *robes de style*, from the 1910s to the 1920s. Characteristics of her design were a billowing skirt and splendid decoration in a romantic style, overlaid with lace and embroidery. The response was favorable from conservative clients, who were not accustomed to the modern boyish fashion that was in style in the new age. This significant *robe de style* dress shows the exotic style of the 1920s, using an Aztec geometric motif patterned with silver and metallic materials.

Jeanne Lanvin
Evening Dress (Robe de Style)
Label: none
1920–1924

Black silk taffeta, lace and chiffon; embroidery of silver beads, rhinestones, sequins and green rhinestones; eight-paneled skirt; Aztec/geometric motif.
Inv. AC4139 81-27-1

The dress looks like a good example of fashion in the 1920s, although there is no trace of Poiret's signature style, such as the dramatic design and bold color contrasts which led to him being dubbed the "King of Fashion" during the 1910s. He lost his leading role in fashion, and gradually became a follower of the style led by other new designers.

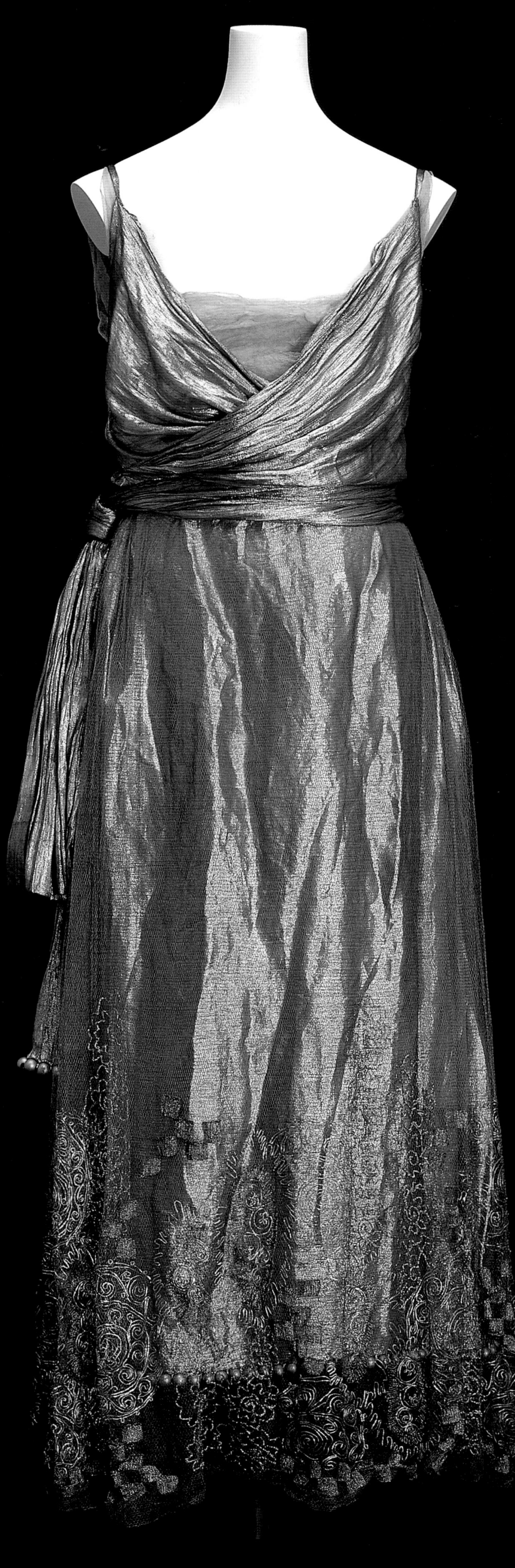

Paul Poiret
Evening Dress
Label: PAUL POIRET a Paris 375990
c. 1920

Silver lamé; silk tulle at bosom; overskirt of silk tulle with silver embroidery, floral and geometric motif; matching belt; wooden beads.
Inv. AC1090 78-32-1AB

← **Zimmermann**
Dress
Label: Zimmermann 10 Rue des Pyramides. PARIS
c. 1922

Silk crepe with rose print; panels of black crepe de Chine; black rayon fringe at hem.
Inv. AC9171 94-38-2

This dress, with light decoration on a flat and straight silhouette, exemplifies the style of the 1920s. Yet, already in this example, it is not possible to identify the impact Poiret had once had on the fashion of the 1910s, which he lost so abruptly.

→ **Paul Poiret**
Day Dress
Label: none
c. 1923

White linen embroidered with white thread and red beads; bird and floral motif, corsage ornaments.
Inv. AC6437 89-21-20

Poiret was a great eclectic creator. His oriental taste may still be observed in a coat of the 1920s.

Paul Poiret
Coat
Label: PAUL POIRET a Paris Mai 1923
33887
Spring, 1923

Dark rose silk jacquard with floral pattern; collar, yoke and sleeves of purple silk satin with gold embroidery; dolman sleeves.
Inv. AC2798 79-23-11

Robe "Paravent" by Paul Poiret, 1924

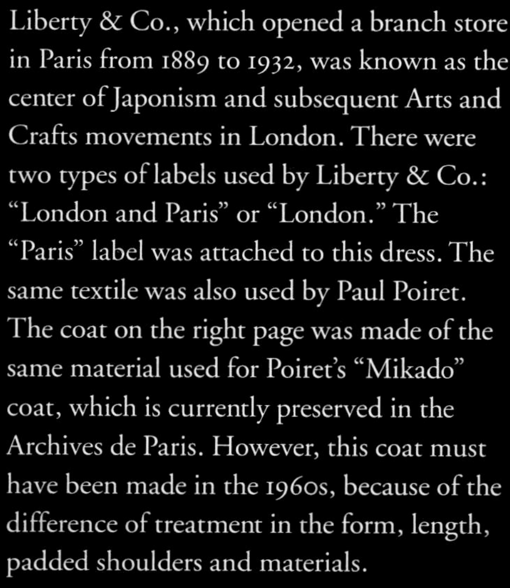

Liberty & Co., which opened a branch store in Paris from 1889 to 1932, was known as the center of Japonism and subsequent Arts and Crafts movements in London. There were two types of labels used by Liberty & Co.: "London and Paris" or "London." The "Paris" label was attached to this dress. The same textile was also used by Paul Poiret. The coat on the right page was made of the same material used for Poiret's "Mikado" coat, which is currently preserved in the Archives de Paris. However, this coat must have been made in the 1960s, because of the difference of treatment in the form, length, padded shoulders and materials.

←← **Liberty & Co.**
Evening Dress
Label: LIBERTY AND CO. PARIS & LONDON 18656
1921

Silk jacquard of lavender and silver lamé with scenic image; bead embroidery and fringe at hip; handkerchief hem.
Inv. AC3428 80-23-69

← **Anonymous**
Coat
c. 1923 (1960s)
French

Black and gold silk satin brocade; large scenic pattern matched when fabric is cut; gold lamé collar, cuffs and lining, wadded; knee-length.
Inv. AC6761 90-19-10

"Mikado" coat by Paul Poiret, 1923

Picturesque designs were applied to the dress in the 1920s, while the dress kept a simple silhouette. A snapshot showing this coat appeared in *Fémina* magazine in 1923. The title "Mandarin" meant a Chinese high official.

Paul Poiret
"Mandarin" Coat
Label: PAUL POIRET a Paris
c. 1923

Black wool twill with chain-stitch embroidery of chrysanthemum, bird and wave motifs; wing collar; lining of black crepe de Chine.
Inv. AC6382 89-18

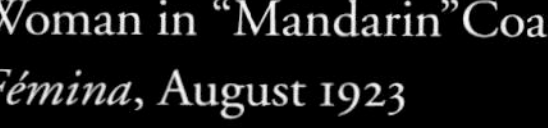

Woman in "Mandarin" Coat
Fémina, August 1923

Japanese lacquer was one of the media used to express Art Deco style in the 1920s. Surface decoration that had a quality similar to lacquer work was developed, and it was often used for textiles as well.

← **Anonymous**
Cape
c. 1925

Black lamé jacquard patterned with a natural motif; fur trimming; no lining.
Inv. AC112 77-9-1

→ **Paul Poiret**
Coat
Label: PAUL POIRET a Paris
c. 1920–1921

Brown lamé woven with warp of gold thread; polychrome pattern like a stencil print; green silk velvet at collar, cuffs and lining.
Inv. AC6279 89-1

The Japanese kimono was copied, adapted, and finally assimilated into Western clothing. On the left is an example of a coat with long sleeves inspired by the Japanese kimono. For surface decoration, an arabesque pattern in stencil-printing was applied.
An influence of Japanese design can also be seen in the coat on the right, in the embroidered motifs, wadded collar in kimono style, and blousing at the back of the body. There is no label, but its perfect form and elaborate decoration suggest that it was most likely made by an expensive Parisian *maison*.

← **Maria Monaci Gallenga**
Evening Coat
Label: Maria Monaci Gallenga
c. 1922

Black velvet with stencil of arabesque pattern; bodice with kimono-like over-sleeve; pillow-shaped collar; tassels; velvet lining.
Inv. AC1843 79-1-4

→ **Anonymous**
Evening Coat
c. 1925
French

White cotton voile; black and silver bead and paillette embroidery; lotus flower and wave motif; wadded collar; back blousing supported by another fabric from inside.
Inv. AC7037 91-25-1

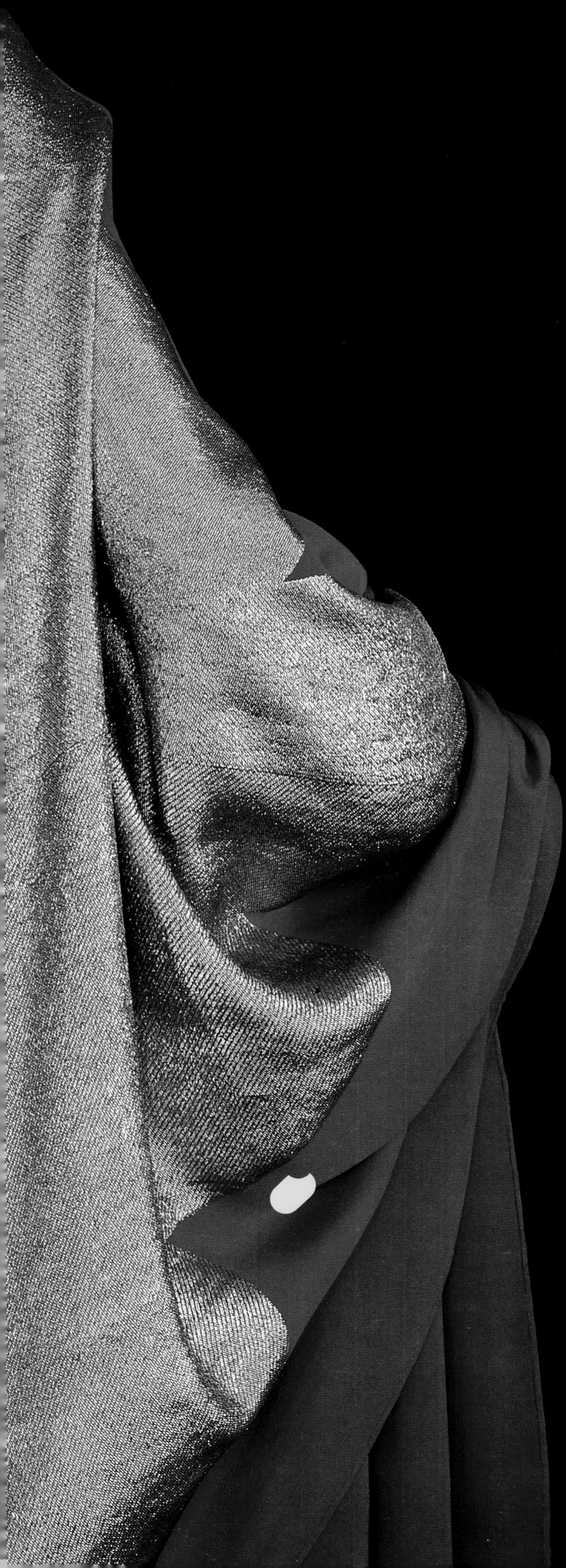

The same fabric used for this crepe de Chine shawl was also used by Paul Poiret for the dress "Insaalah." Caroline Reboux was one of the best millinery designers in Paris at this time.

Woman in "Insaalah" dress by Paul Poiret, 1923

Caroline Reboux
Evening Shawl
Label: Caroline Reboux
c. 1924

Red crepe de Chine woven with gold; motif at center.
Inv. AC7709 93-2-2

→ **Raoul Dufy**
"Amphitrite" Textile, 1925
Archives Bianchini Férier

Poiret's aim was to harmonize art and fashion. He thought that it was important to keep a close association with young artists, and supported them generously. Raoul Dufy started his work as a textile designer from his collaboration with Poiret, and became a forerunner in textile design done by artists. Dufy made this textile, based on his panel painting *Amphitrite*, in 1925 for Bianchini Férier in Lyons, and Poiret used it to create this cape.

← **Paul Poiret (Textile: Raoul Dufy)**
Evening Cape
Label: none
1925

Orange lamé jacquard with print.
Inv. AC9362 96-24-1

Page 434
This shawl has an elaborately ornamental jacquard woven with a dahlia pattern.

Anonymous
Textile: Coudurier-Fructus-Descher Lyon
Shawl
c. 1925

Gold and silver lamé silk jacquard
with woven pattern of dahlias;
color print over the pattern.
Inv. AC7763 93-18-4

Page 435
Woman in Vionnet's dress
Photo: Edward Steichen
Vogue, 1924

The house of Babani dealt in decorative arts, interior decoration, and silk fabrics from China and Japan. Liberty's textiles and the work of Fortuny were also sold there, and Babani created their own products influenced by Fortuny and Liberty.

← **Babani**
Cocktail Dress
Label: BABANI 98 Bd HAUSSMANN PARIS
c. 1925

Gold lamé jacquard; woven and printed with floral and geometric motifs.
Inv. AC6438 89-21-21

This coat was made of rayon, which was first invented in 1883 and then widely used after viscose-rayon was invented in 1905 in England. It used to be called "artificial silk", and gained great popularity in the 1920s.

→ **Liberty & Co.**
Evening Coat
Label: LIBERTY LONDON
c. 1925

Orange silk rayon jacquard with yellow chrysanthemum pattern; cuffs, front opening and hem in gold rayon; collar of beaver.
Inv. AC4210 82-10-1

There were enthusiastic crazes for new kinds of dance music like the tango and the Charleston from the 1910s onwards. Dancers reveled in the upbeat sound of this new music, and the 1920s came to be known as the "roaring twenties," or the "jazz age." Garments with materials shown off to their full effect by dance movements, such as sequins and fringes, became very popular.

↑ **Lucien Lelong**
Evening Dress
Label: LUCIEN LELONG 16 RUE MATIGNON PARIS
Mid-1920s

Pale pink silk chiffon; petal-shaped fabric sewn all over; embroidered with rhinestones, silver beads and gold leather; embroidery imitating a belt at low waist.
Inv. AC3753 81-6-3

→ **Worth**
Evening Dress
Label: WORTH
c. 1927

Beige silk tulle; silver bead fringe all over; underdress with silver floral embroidery and bead fringe at hem.
Inv. AC4857 84-19-3AB

Art Deco aimed for harmony between art and industry. Although Art Deco designers admired modernism, they tended to ignore modern methods of production, and one characteristic of the Art Deco style was the need for a considerable amount of handcraftsmanship to produce each object. Jean Dunand's works below show how he was influenced by Japanese lacquer products. The gloves on the right are good examples of Art Deco decoration, with their geometric pattern and strongly contrasted colors.

↓ **Jean Dunand**
Compact Cases and Buckle
Label: JEAN DUNAND (left and bottom of compact cases)
c. 1925

Brass bodies painted in red, black and metallic lacquer.
Inv. AC9322,23,24,25 96-11-1,2,3,4

→ **Anonymous**
Gloves
Label: GANT PERRIN
1925–1929
Chilean

Above: white and black kid; strap at wrist
Below: beige and black kid; strap at wrist
Inv. AC1099 78-32-10AB, AC1100 78-32-11AB

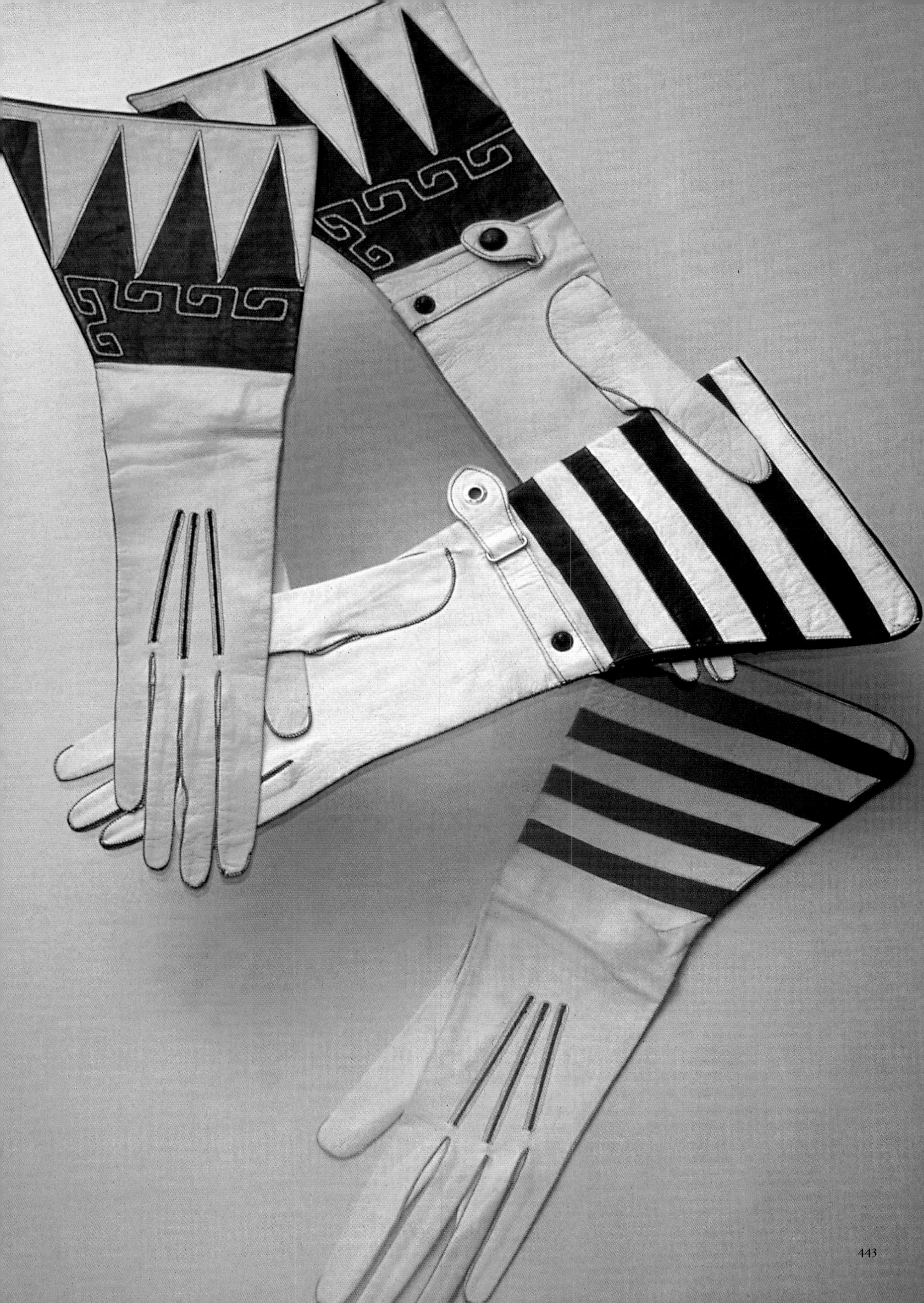

Skirt-lengths rose up to the knee and shoes played an important role in the fashion of the 1920s. Because of this trend, shoe designers who functioned differently from conventional shoe craftsmen became active. Perugia gained his fame making shoe designs for Poiret, and he was most active from the 1920s to the 1940s.

← **André Perugia**
Pumps
Label: Perugia BTÉS. G. D. G.21 AVEN. DAME.NICE 11.FAUBG ST HONORÉ PARIS
1920s–1930s

Above: silver and lamé brocade; t-strap; buttons.

Below: red and black silk satin; floral embroidery of metal beads; buttons.
Inv. AC8948 93-33AB, AC9039 93-50-1AB

↗ **Anonymous**
Heels
c. 1925

Wooden heels with enamel and resin paint; decorated with inset rhinestones.
Inv. AC7766 to 69 93-80-7AB to 10AB

→ **Faucon**
Evening Bag
Label: FAUCON 38 AVE DE L'OPÉRA PARIS
1910s

Gold lamé and black leaf-motif damask; brass frame with gilding; strap of silk cord; pocket.
Inv. AC4819 84-13-5AB

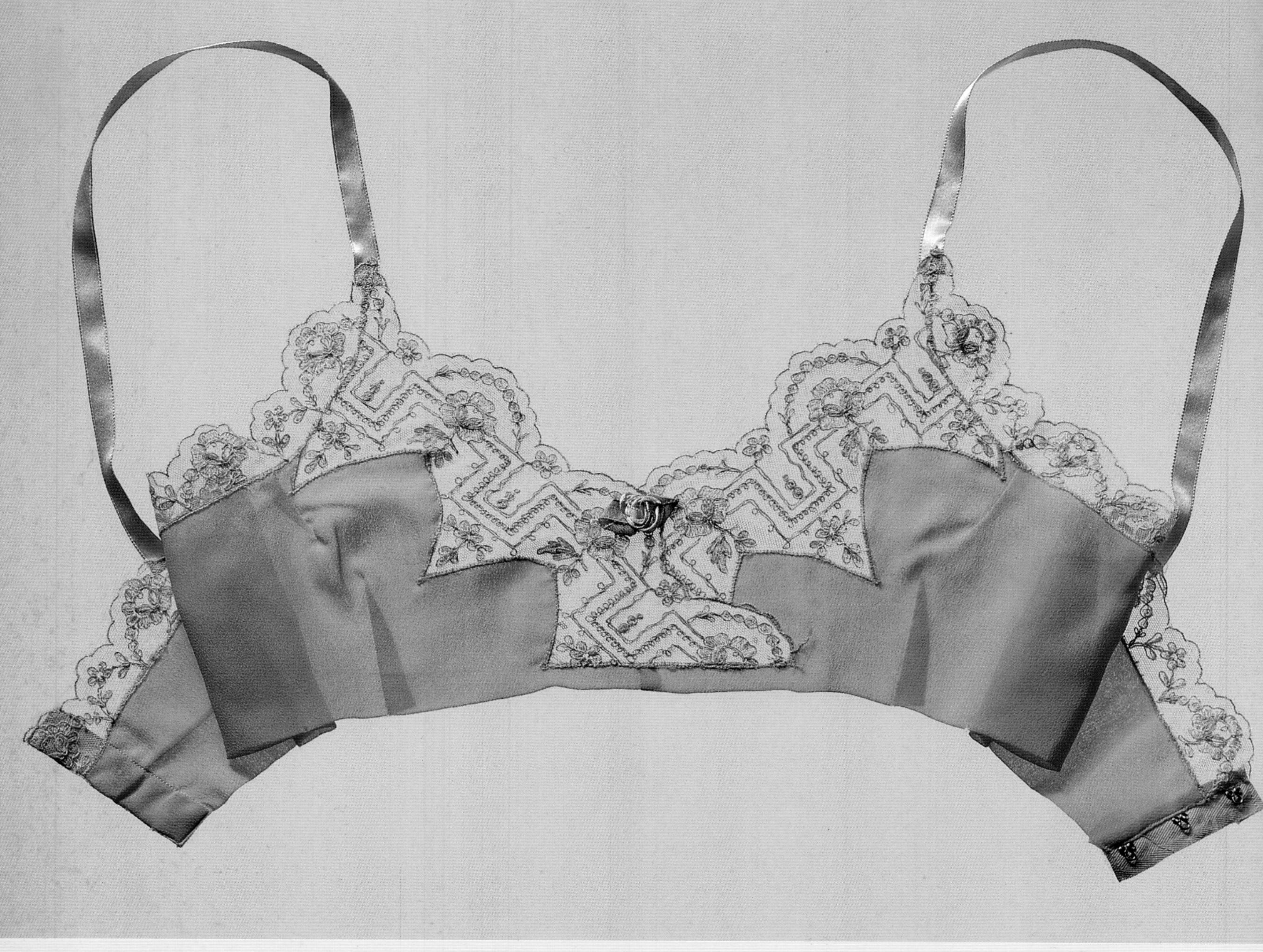

Twentieth-century fashion moved in a totally new direction. After World War I, the corset, which had constricted the female body for so long, was completely abandoned. The brassiere then replaced the corset as the supporting undergarment. The brassiere was more suitable for the free and active fashion of the *garçonne* in the 1920s, because of its less restrictive structure and flat silhouette. The slip, another piece of contemporary underwear, was also invented around this time to suit the one-piece dress then in fashion.

↑ **Anonymous**
Brassiere
1920s

Pink silk georgette with lace insertion; flower ornament.
Inv. AC1586 78-40-37

→ **Anonymous**
Chemise
1920s

Blue crepe de Chine with lace insertion.
Inv. AC1532 78-39-64

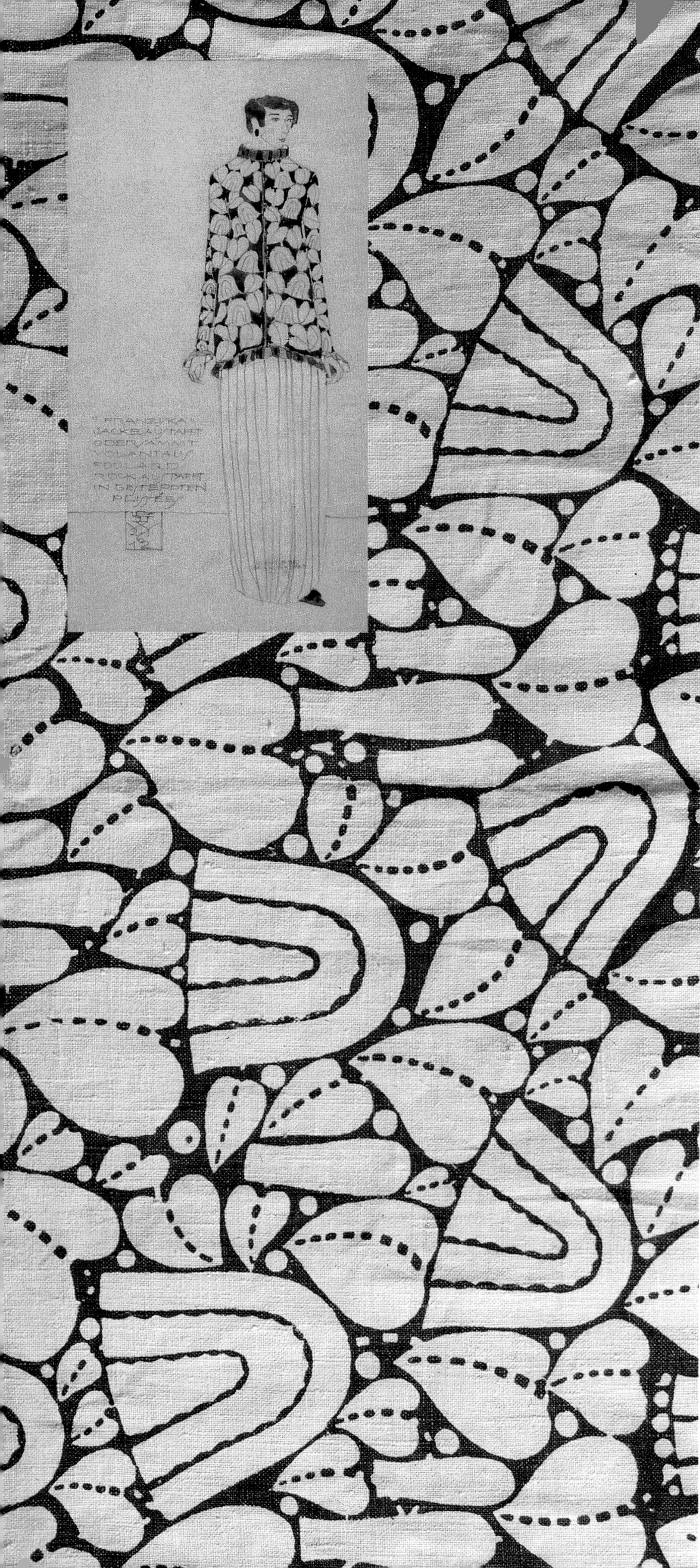

Josef Hoffmann was one of initiators of the Wiener Werkstätte in Vienna. On the left is "Franziska," a design drawing by Eduard J. Wimmer-Wisgrill of a single-textile coat from the collection of the Österreichische Museum für angewandte Kunst.

← **Josef Hoffmann**
"Jagdfalke" Textile
Label: none
1910–1911

White linen with black stencil print.
39 x 72.5 cm.
Inv. 7619 92-33
Gift of Mr. Wolfgang Ruf

This cape was made with the textile "Bavaria," designed by Carl Otto Czeschka around 1910. The cape was possibly made up in the fashion department at the Wiener Werkstätte. Using the same material, Eduard J. Wimmer-Wisgrill created a coat named the "Cresta" in 1913.

→ **Carl Otto Czeschka**
"Bavaria" Textile
Cape
Label: none
c. 1920

Black silk chiffon; print with plant pattern; marabou trimming.
Inv. AC10222 99-40-1

↖ **Eduard J. Wimmer-Wisgrill**
"Franziska" design with "Jagdfalke," a textile by Josef Hoffmann, 1912
MAK – Austrian Museum of Applied Arts/Contemporary Arts, Vienna

Maria Likarz: Design drawing
Mode Wien 1914–15, 1914–15, KCI

Dagobert Peche: Design drawing
Mode Wien 1914–15, 1914–15, KCI

← **Wiener Werkstätte: Felice Rix**
"Davos" Textile
Day Dress
Label: WIENER WERKSTÄTTE
c. 1920

Gray, black and purple striped silk pongee; white cotton collar and cuffs; black silk taffeta bow tie; wrapped buttons; four-paneled overskirt.
Inv. AC8945 93-32-3

→ Pajama ensemble in "Pan," a textile designed by Dagobert Peche, 1920
Photo: Madame D'Ora-Benda
Bild-Archiv der Österreichischen National-bibliothek, Vienna

Peche joined the Wiener Werkstätte in 1915. The textile "Pan" in different colors is in the collection of the Austrian Museum of Applied Arts/Contemporary Arts, Vienna. The design was used for pajamas, shawls and cushions.

→ **Dagobert Peche**
"Pan" Textile
Label: WIENER WERKSTÄTTE
1919

White silk with pastel-colored stencil print.
46 cm x 129.5 cm. Inv. AC7602 92-24A

Josef Hoffmann and Koloman Moser founded the Wiener Werkstätte in 1903. To achieve their goal that artistic endeavor should permeate all aspects of everyday life, they established a textile department in 1905 and a fashion department in 1911. The textile department aimed to create designs that were modern, but still had the warmth of hand-made products. The fashion department sought a new type of clothes, and made innovative dress designs such as the loose-fitting sack dress. The textile of this gown was designed by Mathilde Flögl, who was also a member of the Wiener Werkstätte. The stylized peacock feather looks distinguished on the black cloth.

Wiener Werkstätte: Mathilde Flögl
"Hoby" Textile
Gown
Label: WIENER WERKSTÄTTE
c. 1928

Black silk *habutae* printed with peacock motif, "Hoby"; kimono style; wrapped buttons; belt and bag in the same fabric.
Inv. AC9011 93-47

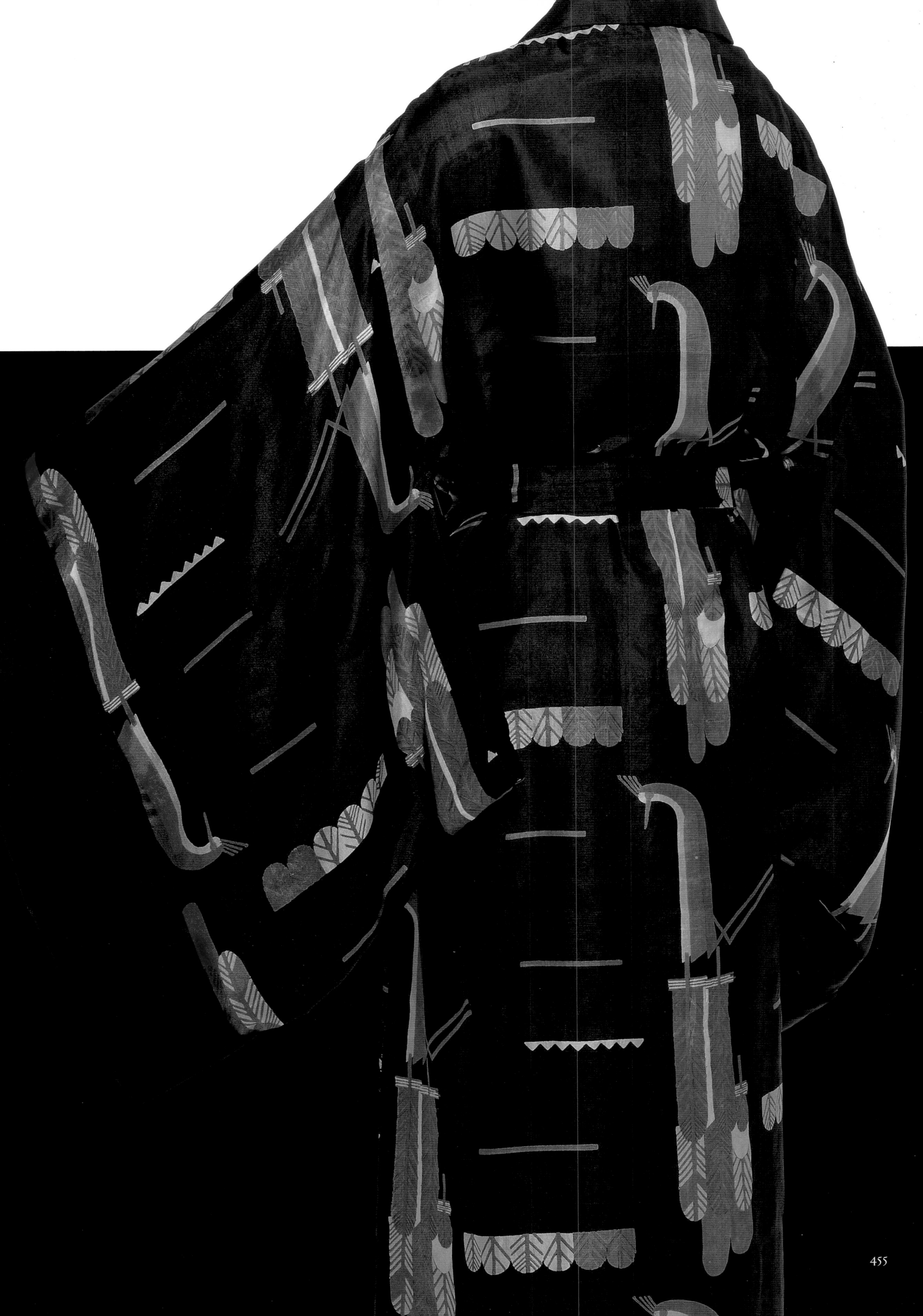

Filippo Tommaso Marinetti proclaimed "Futurism" in 1909 as an impetus to artistic reform. In its wake, poets, painters and architects in Italy tried to bring art into living spaces to achieve harmony in all aspects of everyday life. The term "Futurism" suggests a larger movement rather than a single style of art, and the Futurist movement involved a range of fields such as literature, music and fashion design.

The vest and hat on this page may have been made by a Futurist artist: the new design ethic, which tried to let the arts permeate all aspects of everyday life, is clearly visible here.

↖ **Anonymous**
Man's Vest
1920s
Italian

Canvas embroidered with polychrome wool yarn.
Inv. AC9719 98-35-1

← **Anonymous**
Hat
1920s–1930s
Italian

Beige and brown felt.
Inv. AC9720 98-35-2?

Sonia Delaunay created a range of designs including textiles and clothing. She created a dress as one medium of her artistic expression rather than seeking to achieve a trend in fashion. She adopted her vivid abstract paintings for her textile designs and simply-constructed dresses.

Sonia Delaunay
Coat
Label: none
c. 1925

Brown wool embroidered with yarn and silk thread; wave pattern in gradations of brown.
Inv. AC7038 91-25-2

Vionnet invented an innovative cutting technique, the bias cut. These two dresses are wonderful examples of the technique.

← **Madeleine Vionnet**
Evening Dress
Label: MADELEINE VIONNET DÉPOSÉ 64396
c. 1929

Pink silk voile embroidered with star pattern; bias-cut bodice; cowl neck; skirt with nine panels; matching belt.
Inv. AC6419 89-21-2A,CD

→ **Madeleine Vionnet**
Evening Dress
Label: MADELEINE VIONNET DÉPOSÉ 64397
1929

Ivory silk chiffon; appliqué of circle motif; cowl neck; bias-cut skirt with seven layers of the same fabric.
Inv. AC6420 89-21-3AB

The bias cut became a useful technique in the 1930s, when consciousness of body line was revived in fashion. Vionnet created unique dresses using original design techniques; she first divided up the body along anatomical lines, and then united the lines with the bias cut.
The dress on the left looks very minimal, thanks to her calculated design theory. The effect is created by bias cutting, where different textures result from sewing some pieces of fabric vertically and others horizontally. The dress on the right was made of elastic rayon jersey, treated in bias cut to fit around the body. The surrounding bow has the effect of highlighting the sleek body. The dress is from Vionnet's personal wardrobe.

← **Madeleine Vionnet**
Evening Dress
Label: none
1932

Black silk satin; two pieces used for bodice and five, in various sizes, for skirt; bias cut.
Inv. AC3700 81-3-2

→ **Madeleine Vionnet**
Evening Dress
Label: none
c. 1933

Black rayon jersey; vermilion silk crepe bow; bias cut.
Inv. AC7652 92-43-2

Lightweight material gained in popularity in the 1930s, as it was useful for achieving the flowing line fashionable at the time. Prints with varied colors and patterns were an efficient method for decorating dresses while keeping the sleek line.

→ **Gabrielle Chanel**
Dress
Label: CHANEL 24128
c. 1935

Bordeaux silk chiffon with white print; cape; underdress of same color crepe de Chine.
Inv. AC5506 86-51-2

→→ **Madeleine Vionnet**
Dress
Label: none
c. 1933

White silk chiffon with red and yellow shaded print; bias cut; long sash twisted and crossed at bodice front, then extended and sewn on neckline as collar.
Inv. AC9170 94-38-1

Woman in Vionnet's dress, 1936
Photo: Horst P. Horst

Chanel had a striking impact on fashion from the 1910s, adopting an underwear material, wool jersey, for *haute couture* dresses. On the left, this elegant evening dress from the 1930s has an insertion of lace, which was frequently used for lingerie during the Belle Epoque period.

← **Gabrielle Chanel**
Evening Dress
Label: CHANEL CANNES-31, RUE CANBON PARIS-BIARRITZ
c. 1930

Beige silk satin and lace; pieced alternately.
Inv. AC4479 83-11-15

With the growing popularity of sports in the 1920s, the pajama as beachwear became fashionable. The pajama, which had been worn as men's sleeping wear, was adapted for women's beachwear and hostess dresses on informal occasions and at resorts. The culotte dress on the right has elements of the pajamas created in the 1920s. The black lace pattern looks intricate over the pink underdress.

→ **Madeleine Vionnet**
Culotte Dress
Label: MADELEINE VIONNET DÉPOSÉ
1937

Pink silk chiffon culotte dress; overskirt of black net with lace appliqué; velvet bow; undergarment of crepe de Chine.
Inv. AC6817 90-24-5AB

While fashion underwent dramatic changes in the 1920s, the world of Parisian *haute couture* also shifted from old to new. The emerging talents were Edward Molyneux, Jean Patou, Maggy Rouff and Jacques Heim, who replaced the *maisons* that had been active before the war. Molyneux, who established his house in 1919, made the dress shown on the left at the height of his career. The bias-cut fabric encases the body closely, and the gathers at the seams create a beautiful drape. The dress on the right is a good example of the simple, fresh structures that are characteristic of Patou. Fabrics of two different colors are sewn together alternately, in pleats that spread at the bottom with the movements of the wearer.

→ **Edward Molyneux**
Evening Dress
Label: MODÈLE MOLYNEUX 5, Rue Royale
Autumn/Winter 1935

Green velvet one-piece dress; bias cut.
Inv. AC9463 97-21-1

→→ **Jean Patou**
Evening Dress
Label: Jean Patou PARIS
c. 1930

Black and green silk crepe; skirt pleats pointed at hem; belt.
Inv. AC10215 99-38-004

The elaborate long dress came back into fashion in the 1930s, despite the serious social conditions caused by the Great Depression of 1929. Since Lanvin always kept her very elegant design line, she was very much in tune with the atmosphere of the 1930s. These two dresses made by Lanvin exhibit the silhouette typical of the 1930s. The dress on the right has detachable sleeves. The shimmering velveteen brings out its beautiful line. The dress on the left, of mermaid line, shows Lanvin's fine technique which enabled her to give an impression of lightness in spite of the long train.

← **Jeanne Lanvin**
Evening Dress
Label: Jeanne Lanvin Paris UNIS FRANCE ÉTÉ 1934
Summer 1934

Black linen organdy; plaid pattern with paillette embroidery; underdress of crepe de Chine.
Inv. AC7583 92-17-17

→ **Jeanne Lanvin**
Evening Dress
Label: none
Autumn/Winter 1937

Black velveteen; bow on sleeve; wrapped buttons on back opening, sleeves and strap-neckline.
Inv. AC5551 87-14AD

Christian Bérard
Vogue (American), September 15, 1937

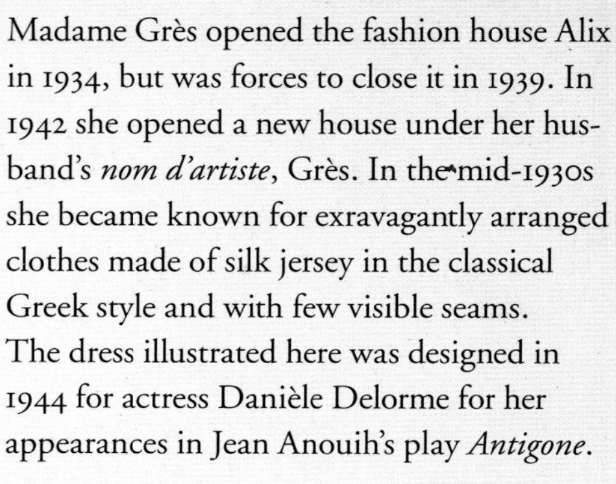

Madame Grès opened the fashion house Alix in 1934, but was forces to close it in 1939. In 1942 she opened a new house under her husband's *nom d'artiste*, Grès. In the mid-1930s she became known for exravagantly arranged clothes made of silk jersey in the classical Greek style and with few visible seams. The dress illustrated here was designed in 1944 for actress Danièle Delorme for her appearances in Jean Anouih's play *Antigone*.

Madame Grès
Evening Dress
Label: none
c. 1944

White silk jersey; finely pleated.
Inv. AC5664 87-34-2

Elsa Schiaparelli led fashion in the 1930s with a keen eye on new developments in the arts and in technology. She worked closely with Dadaist and Surrealist artists, and tried to use the artificial materials that were being newly produced. The design on the left shows a figure in a celestial chariot – the Greek God Apollo. The motif was designed by Christian Bérard, a painter and stage designer from Paris. Lesage, an embroidery workshop founded in 1924, was responsible for the embroidery, which shows the high standard of the Parisian *haute couture*. The cape on the right was trimmed with cellophane in "shocking pink," a color that was Schiaparelli's signature. She found artificial fabrics very valuable, not regarding them just as supplements for natural materials, and proposed a shift in conventional ideas of high and low classes through the use of artificial materials.

← **Elsa Schiaparelli**
Evening Cape
Label: none
1938

Black velvet embroidered with gold thread, sequins and beads.
Inv. AC9227 95-19-1

→ **Elsa Schiaparelli**
Evening Cape
Label: Schiaparelli London
Spring/Summer 1937

Silver lamé net trimmed with "shocking pink" cellophane.
Inv. AC792 78-22-41

Print dresses, a trend in the 1930s, became humorous and unique in the hands of Schiaparelli. The print on the left was possibly designed by a popular illustrator, Marcel Vertès. There is a column motif with her logotype in the print design. The column motif is a symbol of the Place Vendôme, where Schiaparelli's *maison* was located, and appeared in the advertisement for her perfume illustrated by Vertès shown on the following pages. On the right, she applied matches, objects from everyday life, to her dress. As artists were challenged to employ everyday utilitarian objects as their main subject, Schiaparelli brought such items to *haute couture*, where dignity and elegance had been considered important.

← **Elsa Schiaparelli**
Evening Dress
Label: none
c. 1937

Black silk crepe; printed, pleated; with matching belt.
Inv. AC9470 97-23-1AB

→ **Elsa Schiaparelli**
Evening Dress
Label: Schiaparelli 21 Place Vendôme Paris ÉTÉ 1935
Summer 1935

Black silk with print.
Inv. AC8936 93-27-2

Pages 476/477
Marcel Vertès
Advertisement for Schiaparelli perfume

Sleeping de Schiaparelli
Vertès

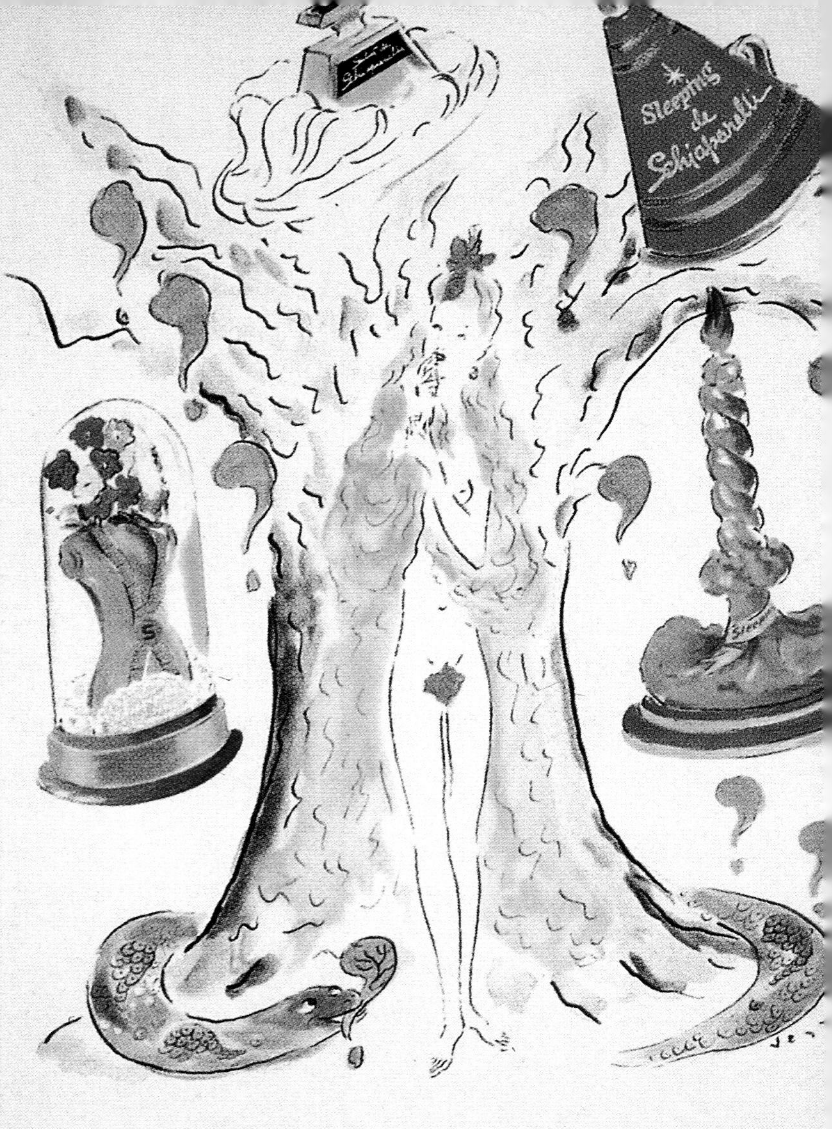
Sleeping de Schiaparelli
Sleeping
parfums de schiaparelli—shocking · salut · sleepin

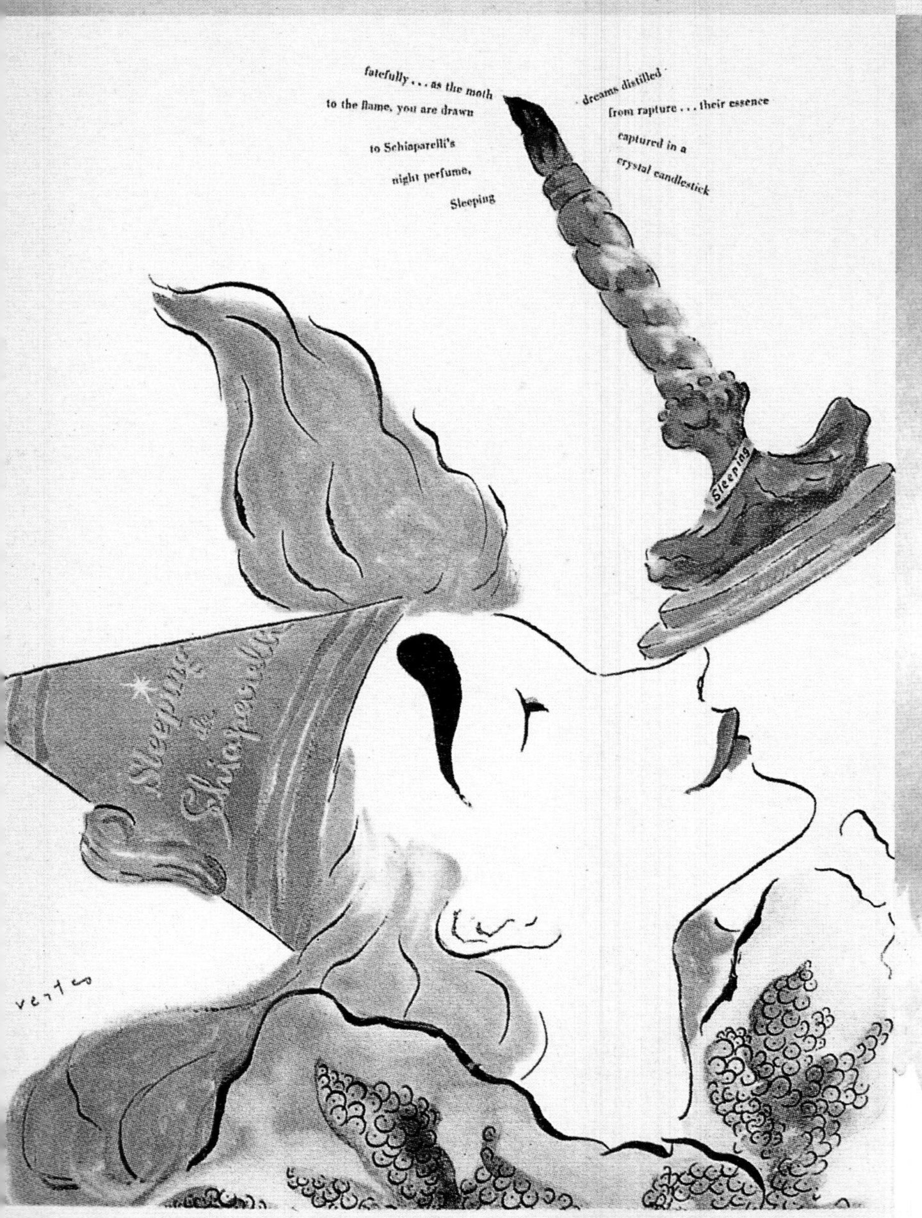
fatefully . . . as the moth
to the flame, you are drawn
to Schiaparelli's
night perfume,
Sleeping
dreams distilled
from rapture . . . their essence
captured in a
crystal candlestick
Sleeping
Sleeping de Schiaparelli
vertes
parfum sleeping de schiaparelli

Shocking de Schiaparelli

Sleeping
de
Schiaparelli
Sleeping
Sleeping
de Schiaparelli
IT LIGHTS THE WAY TO ECSTASY . . .
Schiaparelli's own interpretation of
a night perfume, caressing,
intoxicating, lingering.
parfums schiaparelli . . . . made in france

Schiaparelli was the first designer who used a zipper for a haute couture dress in 1935. This coat also has a zipper inside.

Elsa Schiaparelli
Evening Coat
Label: Schiaparelli London 4136
Autumn/Winter 1936

Wine-red wool; collar of velvet appliquéd with gold leather and beads.
Inv. AC7681 93-1-3

After World War II, Schiaparelli returned to Paris from New York, where she had spent the war. Her attempts to re-establish herself as a designer were unsuccessful, so she retired in 1954. Her efforts to integrate art and fashion were later taken up by Yves Saint Laurent.

Giorgio De Chirico
Vogue (American), January 1, 1937

← **Elsa Schiaparelli**
Evening Dress
Label: Schiaparelli 21 Place Vendôme Paris
HIVER 1939–40
Winter 1939

Wine-red velvet; silk satin striped bow.
Inv. AC2014 79-3-3

→ **Elsa Schiaparelli**
Evening Dress
Label: none
c. 1947

Black silk satin-back georgette; sleeves and ribbon of "shocking pink" velvet.
Inv. AC798 78-22-47

In 1924, the first Winter Olympics were held in Chamonix, France, and the following edition took place in Saint Moritz, Switzerland in 1928. Skiing became popular, and upper-class people enjoyed spending vacations at beaches on the Riviera in the summer, and skiing in Chamonix in the winter. This ski suit is pants-style, but women continued to ski in skirts until the mid-1920s.

→ **Anonymous**
Ski Suit
c. 1930

Set of sweater and pants of black and off-white wool jersey; rib-knit turtleneck and cuffs; matching belt with pom-poms at ends.
Inv. AC4641 83-24-1AC

Jean Pagès
Vogue (British), 1928
The Condé Nast Publication Inc., New York

The *garçonne*, a new style for women popular after World War I, aimed at the elimination of the gender division in dress. Women started wearing pants, which had formerly been a symbol of men's attire, although they were only worn inside the house or at resorts. The regular appearance of trouser-wearing women in public only came about after World War II. During the 1920s, spending time at resorts and suntanning became trends. Sports clothing became increasingly important, and sports clothes by Patou, as seen on this page, Schiaparelli and Hermès became popular among the upper class.

← **Jean Patou**
Beachwear
Label: Jean Patou SPORT ET VOYAGE 21719
c. 1929

Black rayon knit jump-suit with cape.
Inv. AC9247 95-30AB

→ Simone Demaria in beachwear by Schiaparelli
Photo: George Hoyningen-Huene
Vogue (French), 1930

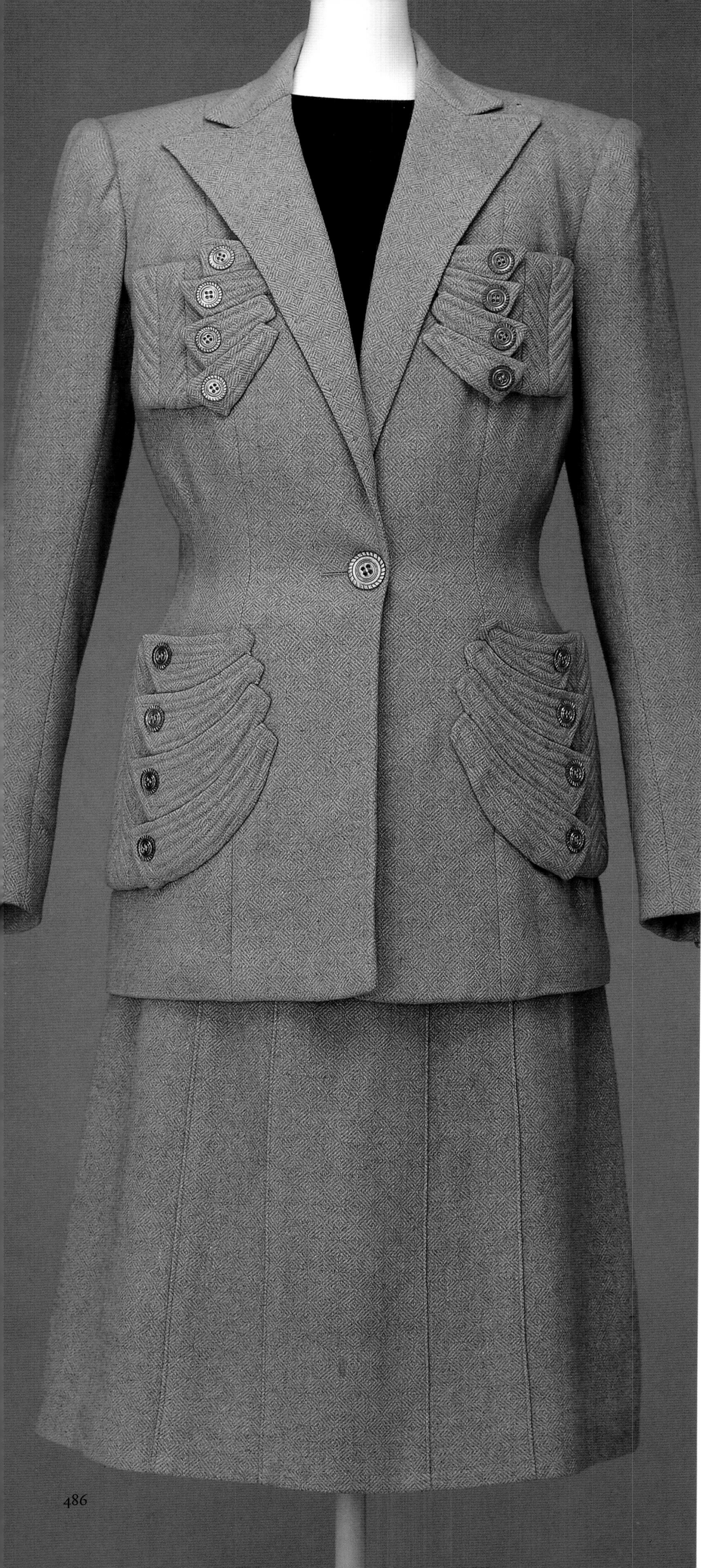

In 1944, Paris was freed from the Occupation. Many Parisian fashion houses had closed or moved to other cities during the war, and few remained. The serious shortage of materials had entailed a massive curtailing of production.

The pre-war style of square padded shoulders and a slim line remained fashionable during the war, as this suit demonstrates. Lanvin took pride, as an established *haute couture* house, in producing the highest quality creations even in a regulated time, as may be observed in the elaborate quilting work and the beautiful seams of the skirt.

Jeanne Lanvin
Day Ensemble
Label: JEANNE LANVIN PARIS 22 Frg St HONORÉ
1940–1944

Set of jacket and skirt; beige-pink wool tweed; quilted pocket with buttons.
Inv. AC4786 84-4-6AB

During the war period in London, the regulations of the Utility scheme stipulated that only functional clothing with minimum decoration should be made. The dress on the left was made by the London branch of Callot Soeurs, which had been open since 1917. The square shoulders, padded and tucked sleeves and knee-length skirt are all typical of the style of the 1940s. On the right is the simple silhouette of an airy knee-length coat made by Fath. Fath created youthful, energetic designs, while maintaining the traditional elegance of the post-war style. The swinging pleats at the back created an appearance that constantly changed with the wearer's movements.

→ **Callot Sœurs**
Day Ensemble
Label: Callot Sœurs Ltd LONDON
c. 1940

Set of top and skirt; yellow wool; leopard fur on detachable collar and breast; matching belt; padded shoulders; box-pleated skirt.
Inv. AC1851 79-10-11AC, AC1853 79-10-11E

→→ **Jacques Fath**
Coat
Label: JACQUES FATH PARIS 10092
Spring/Summer 1949

Beige cotton; large pleats at back; 3/4 sleeves with double cuffs; large patch-pocket; front opening; hook closure at collar.
Inv. AC6703 90-16-6

The wide shoulders and pockets extended to the sides create a horizontal outline, while a tight waistline highlights the parallel lines. These effects are a result of Fath's precise cutting technique. During the regulated period, when clothing had to be simple and modest, women tried to be fashionable by wearing large and decorative hats or turbans to spice up such sober clothing.

Jacques Fath
Day Ensemble
Label: JACQUES FATH PARIS
1940–1944

Set of jacket and skirt; navy wool flannel; velvet trim; pleats at front of skirt.
Inv. AC 6702 90-16-5AB

→ "Fashion is Indestructible"
Photo: Cecile Beaton
Vogue (British), 1941

← **Anonymous**
Gloves
1930s

White cotton crochet.
Inv. AC35 77-7-2AB

↓ **Anonymous**
Hat
1930s

Black wool felt with pink ostrich feathers.
Inv. AC1773 78-411-77

Page 494
Left
Anonymous
Hat
1940s

Black aigrette feathers with comb.
Inv. AC5428 86-31-11

Right
Anonymous
Hat
1940s
Brown aigrette feathers with comb.
Inv. AC5429 86-31-12

Page 495
Left
Marthe Schiel
Hat
Label: Modes Marthe Schiel 13, LOWER GROSVENOR PLACE S.W.I.
1930s

Black felt with feather-shaped ornaments in leather.
Inv. AC1771 78-41-175

Right
Anonymous
Hat
1930s

Black silk faille with matching ribbon; white fur.
Inv. AC1770 78-41-174

Regulations that came into force during World War II combined with a serious shortage of materials meant that Parisian *haute couture* had to slow down its activity. Even hairpins disappeared from the market, so women could not put up their hair. Large hats became popular because they could cover undressed hair and bring quick elegance to plain clothing; in addition, they were not regulated items. Elaborate hats such as high-rising turbans and straw hats with plenty of floral ornament were an effective contrast to the restricted dresses in Paris.

From left to right
1. Marie-Louise Bruyère
Hat
Label: BRUYÈRE 22, PLACE VENDÔME, PARIS
c. 1945

Beige straw with silk faille ribbon and hatpin.
Inv. AC5992 88-56-68AC

2. Helen & René
Turban
Label: Helen & René
c. 1945

Brown silk georgette, padding at top.
Inv. AC5948 88-56-24

3. Caroline Ranchin
Turban
Label: Caroline Ranchin 10 RUE DUPHOT PARIS
c. 1943

Pink velvet, with hatpin.
Inv. AC6046 88-56-122AB

4. Albouy
Turban
Label: ALBOUY 49, RUE DU COLISÉE ELYSÉE 91–23 PARIS
c. 1943

Red velvet padded tube.
Inv. AC6060 88-56-136

5. Marie-Louise Bruyère
Turban
Label: BRUYÈRE 22, PLACE VENDÔME, PARIS
c. 1944

Pale gray wool jersey with padding at top.
Inv. AC5993 88-56-69

6. Janine
Turban
Label: JANINE Opé 27–92 S4 Rue Vignon. PARIS
c. 1945

Silk crepe printed in navy, white and red, padding at top.
Inv. AC6062 88-56-138

IV.

20th

CENTURY · SECOND HALF

After the confusion caused by the aftermath of World War II in the 1950s, society entered an era of mass consumption in the 1960s. The dynamics of mass production were everywhere evident in the world of fashion. Perhaps best symbolized by space exploration, technological innovations proliferated, and this hastened the development of manmade fibers. As a result, reasonably priced and good quality *prêt-à-porter* (ready-to-wear) clothing came into existence. *Haute couture*, the accepted fashion authority up to this point, no longer seemed to offer designs that fitted the ordinary and practical lifestyle of people in the new, post-World War II era. During the 1970s, as social aesthetics went through a drastic transformation, there was a demand for new clothing for the masses. *Prêt-à-porter* proposed everyday outfits for active, working women, and brought fashion to a new level of popularization. Street fashion also proved to be an important inspiration for the creation of *prêt-à-porter*.

From the 1970s on, *prêt-à-porter* made it possible for the fashion industry to develop and diversify. Paris had long been the capital of mode and refined craftsmanship, but now various cities joined the ranks and became thriving centers of distinctive new trends. The 1980s saw a return to traditional style, but in the 1990s, people began to consider the meaning of clothing once again, and to search for an idealistic system for the fashion industry of the twenty-first century. At the turn of the twentieth century, fashionable clothing could be seen, ordered, and sent anywhere in the world instantly thanks to media such as television and the Internet. Consequently, fashion at present appears to be headed toward a universal uniformity.

The Revival of Parisian *Haute Couture*

Parisian *haute couture* suffered much during World War II, but started work again when Paris was liberated from the Occupation in 1944. Although the war was over, confusion reigned, and people seemed unable to completely enjoy the peace.

It was Christian Dior who stimulated the Parisian *haute couture* revival. In February 1947, Dior's first collection was heralded as the "New Look," which determined the direction of fashion for the 1950s. The "New Look" was a nostalgic and elegant style, characterized by rounded shoulders, a high and emphasized bust, a tiny, cinched waist, a longish and bouffant skirt, gloves, a hat, and high-heeled shoes. To make a "New Look" dress required dozens of meters of fabric. For women, who had been forced to dress in a simple and austere manner during the Occupation, this luxurious use of material was confirmation of the fact that the war really was over. During the 1950s, Dior presented a consecutive string of new designs each season and his output had a tremendous impact on world fashion.

Spanish-born Cristobal Balenciaga was another great designer in the 1950s. Balenciaga was one of the few designers who had hands-on experience of dressmaking techniques, and he sought perfection in every snip and seam. Featuring creative silhouettes, a unique, extra space between the garment and body, and exquisite colors, his designs were so like artworks that Balenciaga became known as "The Master" of *haute couture*. Additionally, since his dresses did not require undergarments to mold the body, they were renowned for comfort. His round-collared suit and slightly fitted, beltless tunic dress of the 1950s became the basis of female garments during the second half of the twentieth century.

In 1954, Gabrielle (Coco) Chanel, who had suspended her work during World War II, made a strong comeback. When women began once again to seek comfort as a respite from the nostalgic fashions of the 1950s, Chanel reintroduced the "Chanel suit," which was a perfected version of her 1920s cardigan ensemble. With their simple structure, functional Chanel suits found worldwide acceptance in the 1960s, and came to represent the style of the modern twentieth century, and this style of suit was later adopted in the international market of *prêt-à-porter* clothing.

Although Parisian *haute couture* was destined to become isolated from the demands of the emerging mass consumer society, it still produced many talented designers in the 1950s and 1960s. People came to appreciate once again the power of traditional *haute couture*, and fashion buyers and journalists from around the world gathered at collections held twice a year in Paris, which again became the fashion capital of the world. The economic infrastructure of fashion in France was much aided by the establishment of a licensing business to approve copyrights of *griffe*, or "brand label" clothing. This started an obsession with brand names that still holds an irresistible appeal to women today. In addition, regulated sales of legally sanctioned clothing patterns known as *toile* and a strong perfume industry helped bolster the Parisian fashion market.

Youth Power

In the 1960s, baby boomers reached their teens, and the era of mass production and mass consumption was in full swing. In 1961, the Soviet Union successfully launched the first manned space flight, and in 1963, President John F. Kennedy was assassinated. The May Student Uprisings in Paris occurred in 1968, and the first landing on the moon was achieved in 1969. In the midst of such explosive drama, the young generation sought its own distinct mode of expression, and the powerful new American culture was an obvious choice. The voice of the young was heard in the lyrics of British bands like The Beatles and their concerns were portrayed in the French cinema movement of *Nouvelle Vague*. Fashion, too, took to presenting fresh and bold emotions.

The young found that displaying their physique was the most effective means of setting themselves apart from the older generation. In 1964, American designer Rudi Gernreich introduced the topless bathing suit, the "monokini," which clearly represented a new concept of the body: a "body consciousness." A dress exposing the legs up to the thighs was tagged the "mini," and proved a simpler and more practical method to express the same concept. Bare legs in women's fashion, which also appeared in the 1920s, developed through various conceptual stages in the 1960s. Marshall McLuhan insisted that clothes were an extension of skin, and Yves Klein expressed his thoughts in his artwork "Anthropometry." London designer Mary Quant also played a hand in bringing the "mini" into the world of fashion and into acceptance as a normal style of the twentieth century. The same can be said of André Courrèges' minidresses, displayed against the powerful background of Parisian *haute couture*.

Before the shock waves created by the mini-skirt had subsided, a women's pants style came into its own in the world of fashion. Although the *garçonne* style of post-World War I had introduced an androgynous look featuring tailored jackets as a form of women's fashion, trousers at that time were meant to be worn only indoors or on the beach. In the United States, jeans, clothing originally designed for manual labor, became casual attire for both men and women in the 1930s. Then, after World War II, trousers found acceptance as women's casual wear. The trend influenced high fashion, and when Courrèges presented a pants-style evening ensemble in Paris in 1964, the taboo on pants for women in *haute couture* was finally broken. Pantsuits became the talk of the town.

Dresses also caused a stir. In his 1964 Space Age Collection, Pierre Cardin unveiled designs for future-oriented dresses shaped in simple geometric patterns and made of inorganic materials. Making his debut in *haute couture* in 1953, Cardin buried the classical elegance of 1950s fashion, but his minimal clothing was more in sync with the soon-to-be thriving *prêt-à-porter*. In 1959, Cardin presented his *prêt-à-porter* line for the first time as a member of the *Chambre Syndicale*, the monitoring body of *haute couture* in Paris. From this position of strength, he was able to pioneer the system of a ready-to-wear business operated by an *haute couture* designer house. Moreover, in 1960, he broke into the field of men's clothing, which up until then had been the closely guarded purlieu of tailors in a system that had remained largely unchanged since the French Revolution. Cardin astutely anticipated the arrival of the "unisex" trend, a powerful shift in sensibility that fed into the hippie movement. By the late 1960s, men wore their hair long and donned brightly colored clothing with lace and frills, earning this period of fashion the apt sobriquet the "Peacock Revolution."

Yves Saint Laurent, a standard-bearer among young designers, was also extremely sensitive to social trends. He became independent from the House of Dior in 1961, and opened a *prêt-à-porter* boutique named Saint Laurent Rive Gauche in 1966, introducing a line of women's tailored pants for city wear. The May Student Uprisings in 1968, which had a profound impact on French social values, also contributed to the spreading popularity of the pants style. In yet another move which fell in step with the times, Saint Laurent created a manifest fusion of fashion and art in two of his dresses, the "Mondrian Look" in 1965 and the "Pop Art Look" in 1966.

New manmade materials opened up various possibilities for minimal fashion in the trendy futuristic and synthetic styles of the 1960s. Although Elsa Schiaparelli had experimented with manmade fibers in clothing from as early as the 1930s, her attempts had been regarded as radical anomalies. In the world of *haute couture*, Paco Rabanne debuted sensationally in 1966 with a dress constructed almost entirely of plastic. It was Rabanne who first systematically moved beyond the idea that only fabric could be used to make garments, and he continued to adopt metal and non-woven materials for clothing.

The reliability of mass-produced manmade fibers supported the development of the ready-to-wear industry. In 1935, Dr. W. H. Carothers invented nylon, the first manmade fiber, at the DuPont Company in the United States. In 1940, the company launched nylon stockings, which quickly became enormously popular. Further manmade fibers for clothing were soon introduced. Imperial Chemical Industries (ICI) put polyester on the market in 1946, and DuPont developed stretchable Lycra in 1958. In the early days, manmade fibers were thought of as an inexhaustible and inexpensive substitute for costly natural materials, but in the mid-twentieth century, synthetic fabrics also began to be appreciated for their various superior functions and their unique textures.

The Rise of *Prêt-à-Porter* (Ready-to-Wear) Clothing

In the 1960s, *haute couture* still controlled the trends of world fashion, but the age of the mass-consumer society was fast approaching. *Prêt-à-porter* arrived to meet the needs of a large market with good quality products. Ready-to-wear clothing had been available since the end of the nineteenth century, but it was considered cheap and poorly made. In the twentieth century, with the advance of mass culture and manmade materials, *prêt-à-porter* gained respect and popularized fashion. In 1973, *prêt-à-porter* designers started showing collections in Paris twice a year, following a similar schedule to *haute couture*. Such collections have been held in Milan and New York since the mid-1970s, and London, Tokyo, and other cities were not slow to follow. The Paris-centered fashion system founded by Charles Frederick Worth at the end of the nineteenth century clearly still plays a crucial role today.

Designers such as Sonia Rykiel and Emmanuelle Khanh introduced *prêt-à-porter* clothing that was stylish as well as suited for everyday life. Another influential designer, Kenzo Takada, made his debut in Paris in 1970. His creations, made of common kimono textiles, appeared on the front cover of *Elle*. He soon became an advocate of *prêt-à-porter*, and he represented a counter-cultural aspect of the era by focusing on daily, relaxed designs and by using Japanese materials in unfamiliar ways.

In the 1970s, as if in a backlash against the futuristic fashions of the 1960s, trends returned to a natural look along the lines of Takada's designs. Hippie and folkloric fashion, including jeans, bloomed. Jeans, in particular, became emblematic of American prosperity, Hollywood movie stars, and rebellious youth. Triggered by the Vietnam War in the late 1960s, people everywhere began to reject the Establishment. Hippies disregarded traditional society and morals, and looked towards foreign cultures and religions for inspiration and enlightenment. Male and female hippies wore their hair long, handcrafted their own folkloric fashions, and favored worn-out jeans. Young people all over the world followed in their footsteps and nearly everyone, it seems, from student demonstrators to folk singers with their antiwar songs, wore T-shirts and jeans. Designers in Paris were not oblivious to this new trend and they presented folklore clothing and torn jeans as items of fashion. Enjoying unprecedented popularity, jeans became recognized as one of the first examples of clothing to cross all boundaries of generation, gender, class, and nation.

In the 1970s, in addition to the naturalistic style of hippies, street fashions added essential elements to the look of the decade. Yves Saint Laurent, while still in the House of Dior in the 1950s, started the then scandalous trend of adopting street styles for fashion when he borrowed the look of Parisian existentialists who gathered in cafes. The trends of mini-skirts and pants also arose from street culture. The hierarchy of the fashion world, which placed *haute couture* at the top of the pyramid, had already begun to collapse. From that time, the street fashions of punks, surfers, skaters, and almost anyone involved in the world of music or sport had a great influence on the look of the late twentieth century.

Power Dressing

By the 1980s, the world had grown more stable where politics and economics were concerned. Consequently, fashion returned to a conservative look. In 1979, Margaret Thatcher became the first female Prime Minister of England, and equality of the sexes as a moral goal gradually gained international attention. Women, suddenly active in the world of professional business and interested in keeping their bodies physically toned, wore a style called "Power Dressing" which simultaneously promoted an image of powerful authority and a soupçon of sexualized femininity. This trend included both conservative elements and a return to "body-conscious" fashion as seen in the 1960s. Azzedine Alaïa led the 1980s body-conscious style by using state-of-the-art stretch materials. Traditional Parisian houses like Chanel and Hermès regained status in the fashion world, meeting the more conservative needs of the time.

By the 1970s, the *prêt-à-porter* industry had developed in many countries. Milan, the center of Italian fashion, distinguished itself by anticipating trends through thorough market research. Giorgio Armani designed clothing for executive men and women, producing sophisticated tailored suits without interfacing or lining, and Gianni Versace drew international attention to Italian fashion in the 1980s with his luxurious yet practical "Real Clothing." Both designers established prestigious Italian fashion brands.

Compared to the clothing of the nineteenth century, which on the whole tended to be voluminous and ornamental, twentieth century apparel appears stripped-down and closer to the body. Indeed in the "body-conscious" era of the 1980s, items that would previously have been considered underwear surfaced as articles of outerwear. Avant-garde designers like the new wave Parisian designer Jean-Paul Gaultier and British Vivienne Westwood transformed traditional lingerie, such as corsets and garter belts, into modern outer garments intended to express the dynamism of the human body. The adoption of traditional clothing as subject matter that is then inverted and presented as a modern creation can be described as post-modern in approach. Trends along these lines continued well into the 1990s.

Japanese Design

Japan gradually adopted Western clothing for daily wear during the Meiji Period (1867–1912), and caught the wave of world fashion after World War II. With the 1970 successful debut of Kenzo Takada in Paris, and supported by postwar economic prosperity, Japanese designers finally found themselves on the catwalks of international fashion.

Issey Miyake held his first show in New York in 1971 and in Paris in 1973. His significant concept, "A Piece of Cloth," highlighted the idea of a flat garment, which is the traditional structure of Japanese clothing. Miyake pointed out that covering the body with a single piece of cloth creates interesting "*ma*" (space) between a body and cloth. Because each person's figure is different, the "*ma*" is unique in each instance, creating an individual form. The concept radically differed from that held by Westerners. By the end of the 1980s, Miyake had designed a line of innovative pleated clothing. The usual process of making pleated clothing is to pleat the cloth first, then construct the article. By reversing this process and pleating the clothing after the cut-and-sew phase, Miyake created new artifacts that organically combine materials, shapes, and functionality. His innovative creations rest on the Japanese textile industry, whose strength is chemical engineering, as well as on the traditional Japanese approach to clothing, which emphasizes the material itself. In 1999, Miyake introduced "A-POC," which proposed an entirely new ethic of future clothing. Combining modern computer technology with traditional knitting methods, he created free-sized garments that arrive as a knit tube. The wearer cuts out the desired clothing shapes from the tube, thereby automatically customizing the ready-made clothing.

In 1982, Rei Kawakubo and Yohji Yamamoto had a startling impact on Western fashion. They showed monochromatic, torn, and non-decorative clothes, bringing shabbiness into fashion to intentionally express a sense of absence rather than existence. Kawakubo, ever unsatisfied with preconceived ideas, has continued to take on new challenges. Yamamoto, on the other hand, more in line with Western principles of clothing, has found his own signature by synthesizing European tailoring and Japanese sensibility. Finally, in the next generation of Japanese designers, Junya Watanabe has produced clothing that makes use of innovative cutting and the unique characteristics of manmade fibers.

Japanese designers have greatly influenced the world's young fashion designers by expressing, consciously or unconsciously, their Japanese aesthetic sense. Part of the reason for their strong impact on world fashion might stem from the suggestion implicit in their work that international clothing can come from a culture other than that of the West.

Diversification of Values

The Wall of Berlin collapsed in 1989, and the Soviet Union was dissolved in 1991. There is no doubt that the late twentieth century witnessed drastic changes in social systems. The fashion system, too, evolved smoothly into a gigantic industry, astonishing the world with remarkable progress through various communication technologies such as TV and the Internet. An infatuation with brands made people acknowledge that fashion is far more than just things, but rather information in and about itself. At the same time, the deterioration of the global environment called into question the material culture of the fashion system. In response, people began to focus on used, recycled, or remade clothes as well as *haute couture* clothing that was not mass-produced. For instance, Belgium-born Martin Margiela, who debuted in 1989 in Paris, recycled his previous works and repeatedly presented the very same items in his shows. His approach expressed an objection to a fashion system that continuously creates new things and discards old ones. His proposal to recycle was widely applauded in the 1990s.

By the end of the twentieth century, in direct opposition to the previous century's finale, clothing had been stripped down practically to the bare body. Instead of then focusing on simplified garments, fashion began to regard the human body itself as the object to "wear." The ancient arts of body decoration – make-up, skin piercings, tattoos – reappeared as the latest fashion trend for men and women at the turn of the twentieth century.

That fashion may seem to repeat certain styles is inevitable because the shape of the human body limits options. However, the reemergence of past styles must each time be considered a completely new expression of the present age, as it arises from an entirely new social context.

The Kyoto Costume Institute (KCI) has attempted to reveal the dominant social circumstances and concerns in history through the study of clothing, which represents culture and the aesthetic aspect of history. A quarter of a century has passed since the KCI launched its collections and began its research on Western clothing. Through clothing, each scene of human history – the luxurious court culture, the awakening of the modern society, the evolution towards a mass-consumer society – appears clearly and tangibly. In the twenty-first century, we are sure that people will continue to express new ethics of beauty through clothing.

Rie Nii, Assistant Curator at The Kyoto Costume Institute

Christian Dior's nostalgic and elegant 1947 collection, which featured a soft rounded shoulder line, thin waist, and wide skirt was quite contrary to the austere style of World War II. This collection, an introduction to the era of peace that was to follow, became known as the "New Look," and gained worldwide success.
Shown here is a dress included in Dior's collection one season after this phenomenal debut, a collection considered to be the next stage in the "New Look" series. This is an extravagant day dress made with dark-colored velvet, against which the leopard skin stands out. The exotic fur blends well with the elegant shape, giving the dress a mysterious harmony.

→ **Christian Dior**
Coat Dress
Label: none
Autumn/Winter 1947

Dark green velvet; cuffs of leopard skin; gold thread, sequin and bead embroidery on bodice and pockets; black suede belt.
Inv. AC10431 2001-1-1AD

← "New Look" by Christian Dior, 1947
Photo: Willy Maywald

Dior's dresses all had a clear line. They were structured with a stiff interlining or boning, as if the hard fabrics and body-shaping undergarments of the past were built into the dresses. The dress on the right has his "Ligne Profilée," presented in 1952. The stiff petticoat creates a shape similar to the *robe à la française* in the eighteenth century.

← **Christian Dior**
Day Dress
Label: Christian Dior PARIS 18027
c.1949

Navy plain-weave wool; curved slit at center-back of skirt, worn with overskirt.
Inv. AC8942 93-31AC

→ **Christian Dior**
Day Dress
Label: Christian Dior PARIS AUTOMNE-HIVER 19522280052751
Autumn/Winter 1952

Grey silk ottoman moiré; nylon tulle petticoat.
Inv. AC391 77-13-8AC

Included in Dior's list of customers were Princess Margaret of England and Evita Perón, the First Lady of Argentina. His elegant style was ideal for people who valued refinement above all.
On the left is embroidery that changes size according to the body line; this emphasizes the thin waist and the wide-spreading skirt, achieving the sort of perfection that only *haute couture* can produce. On the right, the delicate pastel color of this Dior dress brings out the elegant luster of the satin.

← **Christian Dior**
Evening Dress
Label: Christian Dior PARIS MADE IN FRANCE AUTOMNE-HIVER 195575917
Autumn/Winter 1955

Champagne-pink silk satin; with over-layers of tulle embroidered with silver threads and sequins.
Inv. AC7081 92-8-5

→ **Christian Dior**
Evening Dress
Label: Christian Dior PARIS 1902428944
1950s

Double-layered with pearl-pink and white silk satin; ribbon tied at center back.
Inv. AC4226 82-11-1

Roger Vivier, who was known as the couturier of shoes, became independent in 1937 and started making shoes for Dior in 1953. His unique designs fit perfectly with elegant Dior dresses, and it was shoes that he made that were worn during the coronation of Queen Elizabeth II. Many famous people, including Elizabeth II, the Duchess of Windsor, and Elizabeth Taylor were captivated by Vivier shoes.
Shown here are three pumps by Vivier created for Dior. The delicate toes and heels are typical styles of the 1950s.

Above
Roger Vivier / Christian Dior
"Versailles" Pumps
Label: Christian Dior créé par Roger Vivier RITZ
Spring/Summer 1960

White silk and cotton fabric with blue floral print, made by Jouy.
Inv. AC7591 92-22AB

Center
Roger Vivier / Christian Dior
Pumps
Label: Christian Dior Roger Vivier
Late 1950s

Beige silk georgette with gemstones and silver embroidery.
Inv. AC5418 86-31-2AB

Below
Roger Vivier / Christian Dior
Pumps
Label: Christian Dior créé par Roger Vivier RITZ
Late 1950s

Ice-green silk twill with black dot print, ribbon ornamentation.
Inv. AC5419 86-31-3AB

→ Advertisement for shoes by Roger Vivier / Christian Dior
L'Officiel, March 1960

Christian Dior
Souliers créés par
Roger Vivier
VILLANDRY
orme Chantilly en
aravelle marine
129 NF.
VERSAILLES
forme Chantilly en to
de Jouy bleu et bla
129 NF.

This dress, sandals, and bag are all made from the same fabric. *Haute couture maisons* coordinated costumes from head to toe in perfect accordance with the customer's order. This marvelous ensemble epitomizes the elegance of the 1950s.
Shown here is a style where the tight upper body and the bouffant skirt show a clear contrast. Boning is inserted in the bodice. The double-layer silk taffeta, with its tightly woven texture, adds volume to the flounces.

Christian Dior
Evening Dress, Sandals and Handbag
Label: Christian Dior Paris PRINTEMPS-ETE 195679671
Spring/Summer 1956

Turquoise-blue silk taffeta with wave-pattern print; folded flounces on skirt, with silk tulle petticoat.
Inv. AC5489 86-47-2AB, AC5491 86-47-4, AC5492 86-47-5AB

In 1953 Dior formed a licensing department. Daimaru, a Japanese department store immediately applied for a license, and the Daimaru Dior Salon opened that same year. Dior haute couture designs were then produced in Japan. Dior continued to expand the licensing business and strengthened its foundation.
This dress was made with Japanese fabric. This is a specialized design, with a zouave skirt by Yves Saint Laurent, who took over the house in 1957. Christian Dior also often used traditional Japanese silks.

Daimaru Dior Salon
Cocktail Dress
Label: Christian Dior EXCLUSIVITE POUR LE JAPON par DAIMARU
c. 1958

Orange rayon woven with gold and silver Dacron threads, patterned with pine motif; set of bolero and dress with brassiere inside.
Inv. AC7598 92-23-6AB

Dior died suddenly in 1957, and Yves Saint Laurent took over the *maison* at the young age of 21. This was the time of transition from the recovery period after the war to the era of mass-production.
On the right is the first piece Saint Laurent designed after taking over the *maison*. The "trapeze" silhouette had great success. It used the traditional techniques of *haute couture*, but also introduced the new concept of abstract form for the body. This structure looked forward to the coming era of ready-made clothes, which would become standard after the 1960s.

←← **Christian Dior**
Day Dress
Label: Christian Dior PARIS AUTOMNE-HIVER 195790538
Autumn/Winter 1957

Beige wool tweed; cartridge-pleated skirt.
Inv. AC7655 92-43-5AB
Gift of Ms Mona Lutz

← **Yves Saint Laurent / Christian Dior**
"Trapeze" Dress
Label: none
1958

Gray wool tweed; bow-tie at neck.
Inv. AC7657 92-43-7
Gift of Ms Mona Lutz

Cristobal Balenciaga, the master of *haute couture*, was at the pinnacle of fashion in the 1950s. He was one of the few designers who could actually cut and sew, and he created complex forms with his cutting technique. This dress was created in 1948. It reflects the trend of longing for elegance in its classic shape, similar to the bustle style of the nineteenth century. It uses an abundance of fabric, but the dress is surprisingly light. Such was the effect of Balenciaga's refined technique.

← **Cristobal Balenciaga**
Day Dress
(Detail page 521)
Label: BALENCIAGA 10, AVENUE GEORGE V PARIS
Autumn/Winter 1948

Black silk taffeta; fabric shawl-like wrap; belt as part of dress; draped skirt.
Inv. AC6417 89-20-5

Page 520
Eric (Carl Erickson)
Dress by Cristobal Balenciaga
Vogue (British), November 1948

A coat that uses the texture of high-quality velvet to the fullest, with a simple yet highly calculated cut. The rolled collar puts emphasis on the wearer's slender neck, which gives the coat an even more dramatic look.

→ **Cristobal Balenciaga**
Evening Coat
Label: BALENCIAGA 10, AVENUE GEORGE V PARIS
Autumn/Winter 1949

Purple velvet; rolled collar; gathered from front yoke; front opening with wrapped buttons.
Inv. AC6762 90-19-11

Style that hints at the classic and elegant forms of the past is a characteristic of 1950s fashion. This dress is reminiscent of the late-nineteenth-century bustle style. A petticoat with hoops supports the form of the skirt.

Cristobal Balenciaga
Cocktail Dress
Label: BALENCIAGA 10, AVENUE GEORGE V PARIS 52808
1955

Pink silk taffeta; white lace at hem.
Inv. AC5147 85-29-1A

→ **René Gruau**
Dress by Cristobal Balenciaga
Vogue (French), March 1955

Spanish-born Cristobal Balenciaga moved to Paris in 1937, and Paris soon became his center of activity. But elements of the traditional clothing of his homeland are often visible in his work.
On the left, the three-dimensional appliqué with pom-poms looks like a Spanish bullfighter's bolero. On the right, the ruffles are in a style similar to flamenco dresses.

← **Cristobal Balenciaga**
Bolero
Label:BALENCIAGA 10, AVENUE GEORGE V PARIS
1945–1949

Black wool georgette; flower-figured appliqué in the same material; with pom-poms.
Inv. AC4883 84-22-14

→ **Cristobal Balenciaga**
Evening Dress
Label: BALENCIAGA 10, AVENUE GEORGE V PARIS 92556
Autumn/Winter 1961

Black silk with layers of rose patterned lace; lace ruffles from neckline to hem.
Inv. AC140 77-10-4

Balenciaga loved using stiff fabric, to create a beautiful form. One third of Balenciaga creations were made with Abraham's fine fabrics, such as gazar.
On the left is an oblique-line dress where the front hem is short and the back is long. The stiff quality of the gazar is used to its fullest.
On the right is a dress that consists of four parts: a bodice, a skirt, a train, and a strap that crosses at the back. The simple shape of the bodice, the relaxed abdominal area and the train all combine to form a beautiful, three-dimensional silhouette. The taffeta is made by Abraham.

← **Cristobal Balenciaga**
Wedding Dress
Label: none
c. 1967

White gazar; with train.
Inv. AC4889 84-22-20

→ **Cristobal Balenciaga**
Evening Dress
Label: BALENCIAGA 10, AVENUE GEORGE V PARIS 76902
Summer 1961

Yellow and light green silk taffeta chiné woven with floral pattern.
Inv. AC141 77-10-5

These pieces capture the main feature of Balenciaga dresses, the abstract body. The short length, loose waist and trapezoidal form that widens from the shoulder to the hem became popularly known as the "baby doll" dress.
The ensemble on the left is made out of stiff gazar. The dress on the right is made of silk taffeta backed with horsehair to create a perfect shape.

← **Cristobal Balenciaga**
Day Ensemble
Label: BALENCIAGA 10, AVENUE GEORGE V PARIS 28463
c. 1960

Yellow gazar set of coat, top and skirt; stand collar; fly-front closing; yoke at high waist; raglan sleeves.
Inv. AC6996 91-13-1AC

→ **Cristobal Balenciaga**
Cocktail Dress
Label: EISA
Spring/Summer 1959

Blue silk taffeta; fringe at skirt hem.
Inv. AC4879 84-22-10

In 1951 Balenciaga created the "semi-fitted" look, which showed space between the dress and the body. This set the direction of fashion. He then introduced both the tunic dress and the sack dress, which made the body look more abstract. Balenciaga set the standard for the 1960s fashion scene.
The spindle-shaped dress on the left was originally part of a dress and coat ensemble. On the right is a coat with a beautiful shape that is created with the smallest possible number of cuts. Women who wore this model were amazed by the comfort of the coat.

← **Cristobal Balenciaga**
Day Dress
Label: none
Autumn/Winter 1957

Black wool; front opening with wrapped button; front and back bodice cut in one piece; sewn at center back.
Inv. AC6711 90-16-13A

→ **Cristobal Balenciaga**
Coat
Label: BALENCIAGA 10, AVENUE GEORGE V PARIS
1955

Fuchsia silk ottoman woven with striped pattern; cord-wrapped buttons.
Inv. AC5681 87-36-2

The dress on the left has a nostalgic pannier-like line on both sides of the waist. The sharp jets at the top form a strong contrast, and shine like the teeth of a beast.
The dress on the right was made in 1962, a time when Balenciaga was experimenting with new material, plastic. Plastic had been in use since the 1920s, and was in common use in the United States by the 1950s. Well before his time, Balenciaga set about using modern shapes and materials that would later become part of the mainstream.

← **Cristobal Balenciaga**
Evening Dress
Label: BALENCIAGA 10, AVENUE GEORGE V PARIS 89429
Autumn/Winter 1949

Black silk faille; rhinestone, bead and jet embroidery; overskirt of front and back panels.
Inv. AC2072 79-5-2

→ **Cristobal Balenciaga**
Cocktail Dress
Label: none
Autumn/Winter 1962

Black gazar with all-over black plastic paillette embroidery.
Inv. AC7006 91-15-2

Page 536
This is a dress from Saint Laurent's first collection, after he left Dior in 1961. The three-dimensional bead embroidery done by hand shines on top of the simple form. This is a dress from his transitional period, designed at the time when he was shifting from *haute couture* elegance to the sporty pieces of his later period.

Yves Saint Laurent
Dress
Label: none
Spring/Summer 1962

Pale green silk faille top with floral embroidery of beads and sequins; yellow silk faille skirt.
Inv. AC382 77-13-1

Pierre Balmain became independent in 1945, and his main customers were ladies of the wealthy class known as "*Jolies Madames*." Together with Dior, Balmain was one of the designers who revived traditional elegance in Paris in the 1950s. The dress shown here documents that fancy prints were in style.

Pierre Balmain
Evening Dress
Label: PIERRE BALMAIN PARIS 80.030
Spring/Summer 1956

White with red-poppy-patterned silk taffeta chiné; poppy flower pieces appliquéd on bodice; black faille belt.
Inv. AC10365 2000-33

These two dresses show the thin waist and wide skirt typical of the style of the 1950s. Shown on the left is a dress that dates from the last years of Robert Piguet, whose *maison* had opened back in 1933. Piguet's *maison* was known for its excellent technique and the simple beauty of the clothes it produced, as well as for discovering designers such as Dior and Givenchy, who became the main forces of Parisian *haute couture* in the 1950s. On the right is one of Jacques Fath's last works: he passed away suddenly in 1954 at the age of 42. The cotton and polka dots on the classic shape lend exuberance to the dress. The piping serves to emphasize the line of the dress.

Robert Piguet
Evening Dress
Label: ROBERT PIGUET PARIS 18962c.
1950

Blue silk gauze printed with ribbon and dot pattern; halter neck; worn over silk faille underdress and gauze petticoat.
Inv. AC5358 86-15AD

Jacques Fath
Evening Dress
Label: JACQUES FATH PARIS
c.1953

White cotton piqué printed with black polka-dot pattern; black piping ornamentation.
Inv. AC7594 92-23-2

Before World War II, American fashion relied on Parisian *haute couture*, but when the war came, America had to find its own original style. Using simple fabrics like denim and gingham that had been used for laborer's uniforms, Claire McCardell created active and simple clothing for women, and established an original American fashion. The clean-structured clothes that she created were exactly what America, with its well-organized mass-production system, had been waiting for, and ready-to-wear clothes were soon available right across the country.

↖ **Claire McCardell**
Day Dress
Label: claire mccardell clothes by townley
1940s

White, red and green striped cotton satin and cotton broadcloth; cap sleeves; wing collar; self-fabric belt.
Inv. AC9379 96-26-2AB

← **Claire McCardell**
Day Dress
Label: claire mccardell clothes by townley
1940s

Polychrome striped plain-weave cotton; bias-cut bodice; belt of the same material.
Inv. AC9452 97-16-5

→ **Claire McCardell**
Day Dress
Label: claire mccardell clothes by townley
c. 1949

Cherry-red pleated wool jersey; black leather belt with gold buckle.
Inv. AC9275 95-45-2AB

Swimsuit by Claire McCardell
Photo: Louise Dahl-Wolfe
Harper's Bazaar, May 1948

McCardell created simple and fresh American sportswear, and made it popular. In 1942 the diaper-shaped bathing suit, in which a cloth hung from the neck was pulled from the back between the legs, appeared as a new form. Its combination of simplicity and functionality is amazing. This swimsuit on the right has a simple structure, only using shirring at the top and bottom. It was originally worn with a belt at the waist.

→ **Claire McCardell**
Swimsuit
Label: claire mccardell clothes by townley
1950–1954

Navy cotton calico with white pencil stripe; rompers shape.
Inv. AC9222, 95-15AB

Chanel returned to the world of fashion in 1954. Despite the elegance of the 1950s, the Chanel suit, the completed form of the cardigan suit first created in the 1920s, was considered old fashioned and generally ignored; but in fact its clean lines were before its time, and it foreshadowed the ready-to-wear era that was on the way. On the left page is a wool jersey suit; on the right is one of wool tweed. This high-quality fabric is surprisingly light, and on the inside hem a chain is sewn on as weight.

← **Gabrielle Chanel**
Day Ensemble
Label: CHANEL
Late 1950s

Navy wool jersey jacket and skirt; white wool braid; wrapped buttons at cuffs.
Inv. AC4812 84-10-2AB
Gift of Fashion Institute of Technology, SUNY

→ **Gabrielle Chanel**
Day Ensemble
Label: none
c. 1966

Pink, yellow and purple plaid wool tweed; jacket and skirt; gold buttons; lining and blouse in quilted plaid silk twill.
Inv. AC383 77-13-2AC

→→ **Gabrielle Chanel**
Day Ensemble
Label: CHANEL
c. 1969

Pink, yellow and blue plaid wool tweed; jacket and skirt; gold buttons; lining and blouse in quilted plaid silk twill; detachable cuffs in the same fabric.
Inv. AC4811 84-10-1AG

A homage to Chanel done by Yohji Yamamoto, who created the *boro*, "ragged" or "beggar" look in the 1980s. The suit is well made, but the sleeves and the skirt hem are left unsewn and the yarn is hanging out.

← **Yohji Yamamoto**
Suits, hats and shoes
Label: Yohji Yamamoto
Spring/Summer 1997

Left: Black, gray and white silk tweed with black rayon trim; jacket, skirt, hat and shoes; black silk satin blouse with bow

Right: Black and white silk tweed with gold sequin embroidery, jacket, skirt, hat and shoes; satin crepe blouse
Inv. AC9423 97-5-1AF, Inv. AC9424 97-5-2AF

Gabrielle Chanel died in 1971 at the age of 87, but the brand went on.
These are works by Karl Lagerfeld, who has been head of design at Chanel since 1983. The classic Chanel style remains, but modern elements are added, such as the skirt cut off above the knee and a prominent bold label. Lagerfeld is famous for his uncanny ability to spot the latest trends; and his position is backed by the stable, long-established "Chanel style".

→ **Karl Lagerfeld / Chanel**
Ensemble and Coat Suit
Label: CHANEL
Autumn/Winter 2000

Left: Beige coat of alpaca and wool tweed; synthetic sweater; pants of logo-printed silk crepe and silk muslin; logo-printed tights.

Right: White wool tweed with black braid ornament; scarf, necklace, camellia; logo-printed tights.
Inv. AC10412 2000-47-2AG,
AC10413 2000-47-1AG

Mini skirts appeared in the 1960s, when fashion started to be controlled by the younger generation. The word "mini" came from "minimum", which in fashion indicated skirts that showed the thighs. André Courrèges, who debuted in 1961, created the mini in 1965. With the respected position of *haute couture*, the mini skirt came to be accepted by society. A few years before that, in 1963, he introduced a pants ensemble for evening wear, and tried to revitalize the old-fashioned image of *haute couture*. Women were already wearing trousers for leisure wear, but after their acceptance by leading *maisons*, they became far more common.

← Dresses by André Courrèges
Photo: Guégan
L'Officiel, September 1967

→ **André Courrèges**
Pantsuit
Label: COURRÈGES PARIS
Autumn/Winter 1969

White cotton twill vest and pants; gold buttons; patch pockets.
Inv. AC5713 87-46-2AB

↓ **André Courrèges**
Dress
Label: COURRÈGES PARIS
Autumn/Winter 1967

White cotton satin layered with silk organdy with light green floral embroidery; silk organdy at waist.
Inv. AC9101 94-7-3

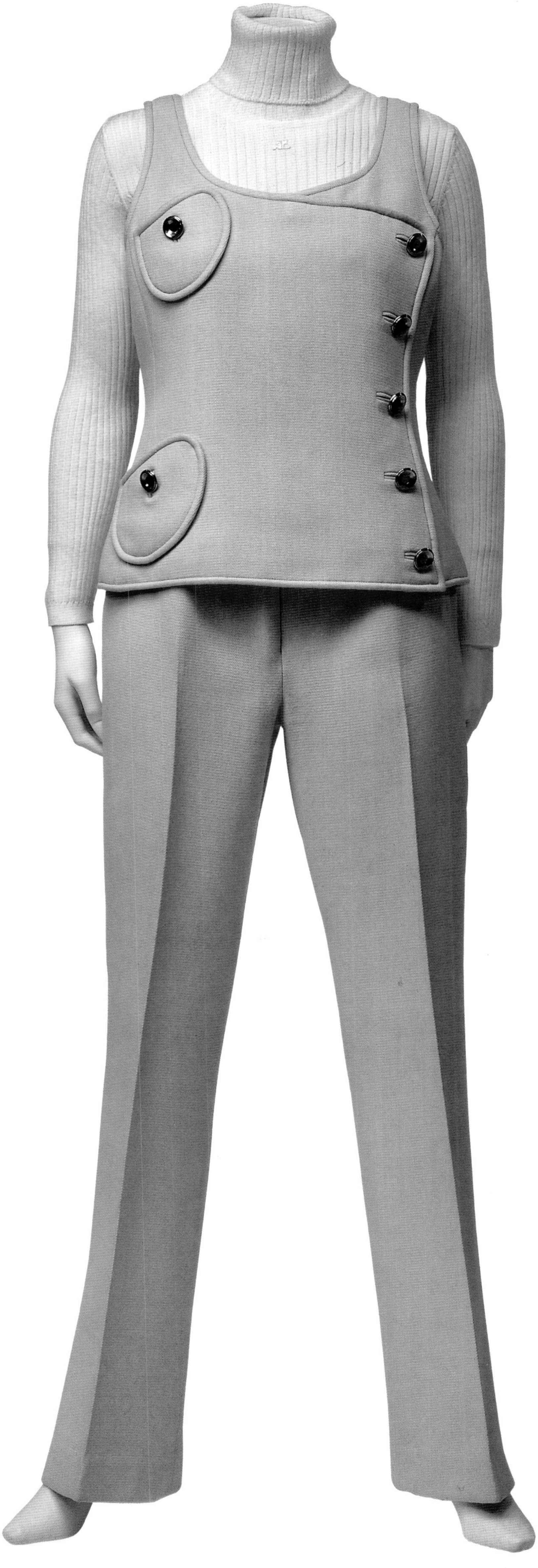

In the 1960s, young designers such as Courrèges presented the clear and simple A-line silhouettes. They also used synthetic fabrics and tried to show futuristic, innovative designs.

← **André Courrèges**
Dress
Label: Courrèges Paris 60351
c. 1967

Black cotton and wool with white ornamentation in the same fabric; plastic zipper at center front.
Inv. AC9102 94-7-4

→ **André Courrèges**
Coat Dress
Label: Courrèges Paris 104110
c. 1970

Orange vinyl; stand collar; matching belt; white dot-button at center-front; Courrèges logo on left breast.
Inv. AC10336 2000-23-1AB

With the May Student Uprisings in Paris in 1968, people's values changed dramatically, and keeping up with this, Saint Laurent created a new look based on pants, which up until then had been considered taboo to wear out in public.
On the right is a safari look based on the theme "African," which was presented in the Spring and Summer collection of 1968. Saint Laurent transformed the functional hunting suit into town wear for women. On the left is a city suit intended to play the same role as a suit for men.

Left
Yves Saint Laurent
"City Pants" Pantsuit
Label: none
Autumn/Winter 1967

Charcoal-gray wool jersey jacket with belt and trousers; patch pockets with flap.
Inv. AC6600 90-11-1AC
Gift of Ms Shoko Hisada

Right
Yves Saint Laurent
Safari Suit
Label: SAINT LAURENT rive gauche PARIS
Spring/Summer 1968

Khaki cotton gabardine jacket with front-lacing, patch pocket with flap, and pants.
Inv. AC9753 98-47AC

→ Verushka in Yves Saint Laurent's Safari Suit; Photo: Franco Rubartelli, 1968

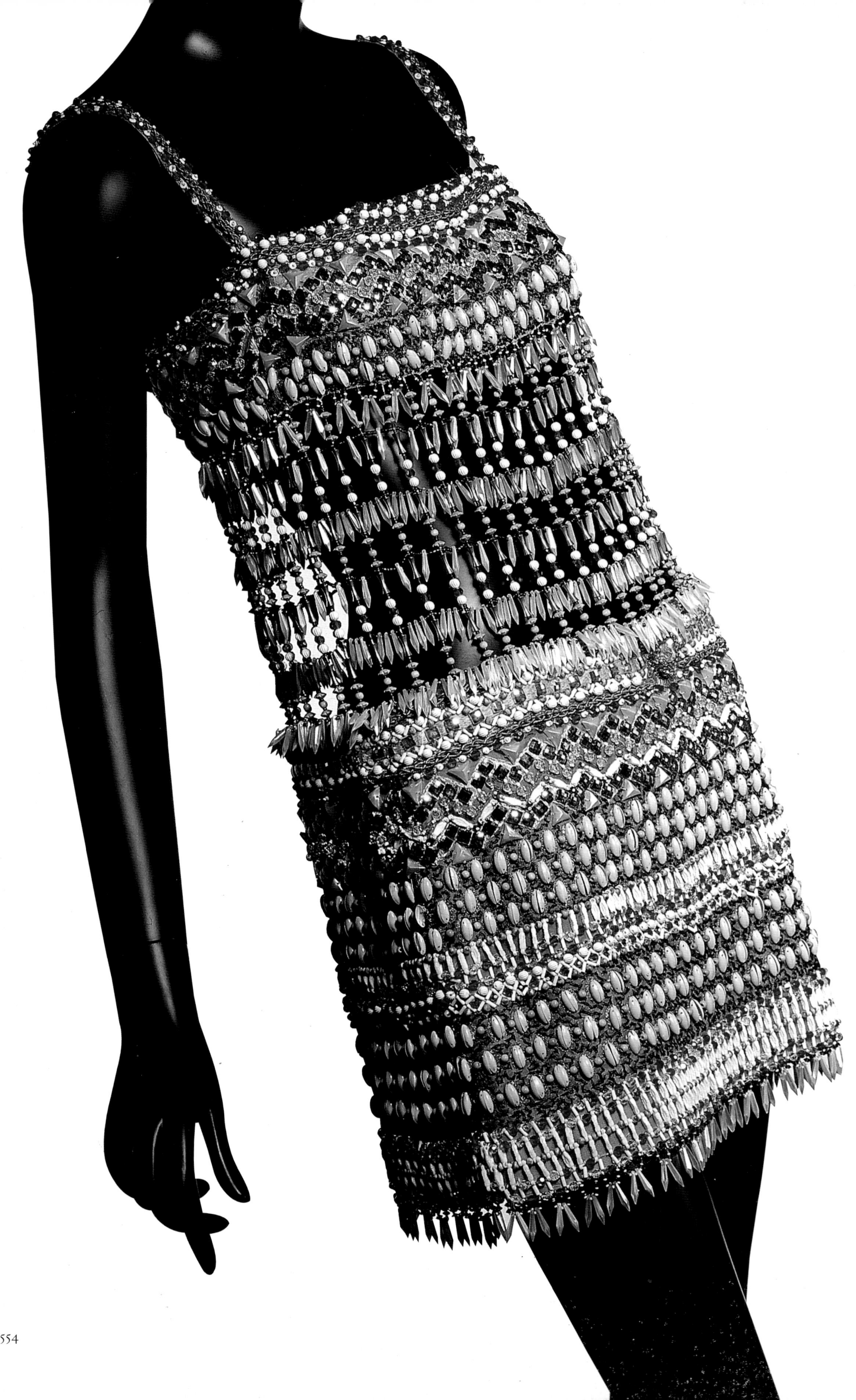

Yves Saint Laurent
Dress
Label: YVES SAINT LAURENT PARIS
Spring/Summer 1967

Beige silk organdy base embroidered with metallic threads, beads, wooden beads and rhinestones; mesh-like beading without backing around waist.
Inv. AC9464 97-21-2

An "African Look" mini dress decorated with seashells and animal-tooth-shaped beads. This exotic and wild mini dress revolutionized the staid image of haute couture. Saint Laurent broke through the urban modernist style of the 1960s, and was one of the first to create the ethnic "back to nature" style that became the trend in the 1970s.

Yves Saint Laurent
Dress
Label: YVES SAINT LAURENT PARIS 015494
Spring/Summer 1967

Black, pink, yellow, red and green printed silk twill with psychedelic pattern; wooden and glass-bead embroidery at yoke.
Inv. AC7078 92-8-2

In the 1950s, Vivier created impressive shoes to harmonize with the classic and elegant style then in vogue; in the 1960s, new, futuristic designs were in demand. He quickly read the trend, and created, as shown here, a casual shoe with a wide toe and thick heels. The use of patent leather and mirrors corresponded to the artificial texture of clothes in the 1960s.

Above
Roger Vivier
Pumps
Label: Roger Vivier PARIS
1960–1965

White silk faille; mirror-work on heel.
Inv. AC6280 89-2AB

Below
Roger Vivier
Pumps
Label: Roger Vivier PARIS
c. 1965

Black patent leather with buckle.
Inv. AC5651 87-28-3AB

→ "Mondrian Look" by Yves Saint Laurent
Photo: Willy Rizzo
Marie Claire (French), September 1, 1965

PIET MONDRIAN 28

In 1965, Saint Laurent created the "Mondrian Look", and the "Pop Art Look" was presented the following year. Art became a fashion motif. With the simple forms of the 1960s, images of paintings could be applied directly to the dress. From then on, fashion took inspiration from the art styles that were popular at the time, such as Op Art and psychedelic designs, and fashion designs developed in another direction.
Shown here is a dress created by Saint Laurent. It was inspired by Piet Mondrian, the father of neoplasticism, and was called the "Mondrian Look." It brought a new elegance to haute couture.

← **Piet Mondrian**
Composition with Red, Yellow and Blue,
1928
Wilhelm-Hack-Museum, Ludwigshafen on the Rhine

Yves Saint Laurent
"Mondrian" Dress
Label: YVES SAINT LAURENT PARIS
Autumn/Winter 1965

White, red and black wool jersey.
Inv. AC5626 87-18-1
Gift of Mr Yves Saint Laurent

Although the 1960s was the era of mass-production, the delicate handwork of *haute couture* was still highly esteemed. The intricate embroidery and perfect sewing seen on these examples demonstrate well the technical skill required.

← **Pierre Cardin**
Dress
Label: Pierre Cardin PARIS
Autumn/Winter 1966

A-line mini dress; oblique wavy pattern with embroidery of gold and silver sequins and paillettes.
Inv. AC10091 99-14-4A

→ **Yves Saint Laurent**
Jacket and Dress
Label: YVES SAINT LAURENT PARIS
Spring/Summer 1966

Jacket with navy, white and silver border sequin embroidery on navy silk base. Dress: v-neck silver top and navy skirt of sequin embroidery.
Inv. AC5499 86-47-12AB

Pages 564/565
Designs by Pierre Cardin, Spring/Summer 1967
L'Officiel, June 1967

Pierre Cardin introduced the space-oriented, futuristic style in 1966. His geometric, simply designed garments were novel but also functional and in sync with the newly established *prêt-à-porter* market of the 1960s. The two examples on the left were most likely made for American licensing. After the appearance of *prêt-à-porter* in the 1960s, the licensing business was the financial backbone that supported the *haute couture maisons*. On the right is a suit from 1966. The bias cut and precise sewing makes the shape stand out, its mini length giving it a fresh look.

←← **Pierre Cardin**
Jumper
Label: Pierre CARDIN PARIS NEW YORK
c. 1970

Navy wool jersey with red vinyl strap.
Inv. AC10089 99-14-2

← **Pierre Cardin**
Dress
Label: Pierre CARDIN PARIS NEW YORK
c. 1968

Black wool jersey mini dress with white vinyl panel ornamentation.
Inv. AC5714 87-46-3

→ **Pierre Cardin**
Suit
Label: Pierre Cardin PARIS
Autumn/Winter 1966

Beige and black plaid wool tweed; jacket and mini skirt; large turtleneck; camel wool jersey sleeveless top.
Inv. 10090 99-40-3AD

The modern men's suit, which came into being after the French Revolution, had a set look that had remained practically unchanged for 150 years. In 1960, Cardin foresaw the "unisex" trend, and suggested a fashionable line of men's clothing. On the left he used zippers, which was one step toward removing the differences in style between the sexes. The ties are in ethnic-style ikat and batik prints, which were a trend in the 1970s.

← **Pierre Cardin**
Vest, Knickerbockers and Sweater
Label: (vest) PIERRE CARDIN BOUTIQUE PARIS, (sweater) LES TRICOTS DE PIERRE CARDIN PARIS
c. 1966

Dark red wool flannel vest with rolled collar, zipper and patent-leather belt and knickerbockers; white wool sweater.
Inv. AC10389 2000-42-9AD
Gift of Mr Richard Weller

→ **Neckties**
Label: Pierre Cardin PARIS
1965–1974

Polychrome silk, wool etc.
Inv. AC10386, 10392, 10401-3
Gift of Mr Richard Weller

In 1966 Paco Rabanne made his *haute couture* debut. He overturned the common belief that clothes had to use thread and fabric, and shocked many with his use of new materials like plastic as fabric.
The two examples shown here are early works. The inorganic, metal "fabric" makes a striking contrast against the skin. In the 1960s, the metallic glimmer of silver was the center of attention in a variety of fields, such as art and films.

← **Paco Rabanne**
Dress
Label: none
c. 1967

Mini dress made of aluminum plates and brass wire.
Inv. AC9472 97-23-3

→ **Paco Rabanne**
Top and Skirt
Label: paco rabanne paris
Spring/Summer 1967

Set of bare-midriff top and hip-hugger mini skirt made of aluminum disks linked by metal wire.
Inv. AC10212 99-38-1AB

↓ **Paco Rabanne**
Dress
Label: none
Spring/Summer 1969

Mini-dress of chrome-plated plastic and steel disks linked by stainless steel rings.
Inv. AC6755 90-19-4

→ **Paco Rabanne**
Top
Label: none
c. 1969

Pink and white plastic disks and white beads linked by stainless steel rings.
Inv. AC6753 90-19-2

Op Art was cutting-edge in the 1960s, and Victor Vasarely and Bridget Riley were key figures in the movement. Op Art's optical illusions were also used as an effect in fashion. In the 1960s, fashion resonated with Op and Pop Art. On page 576 is a piece by 20471120, a young Japanese designer team. Op Art made a big comeback in the 1990s.

Victor Vasarely
Vega 200 (detail), 1968
Private collection

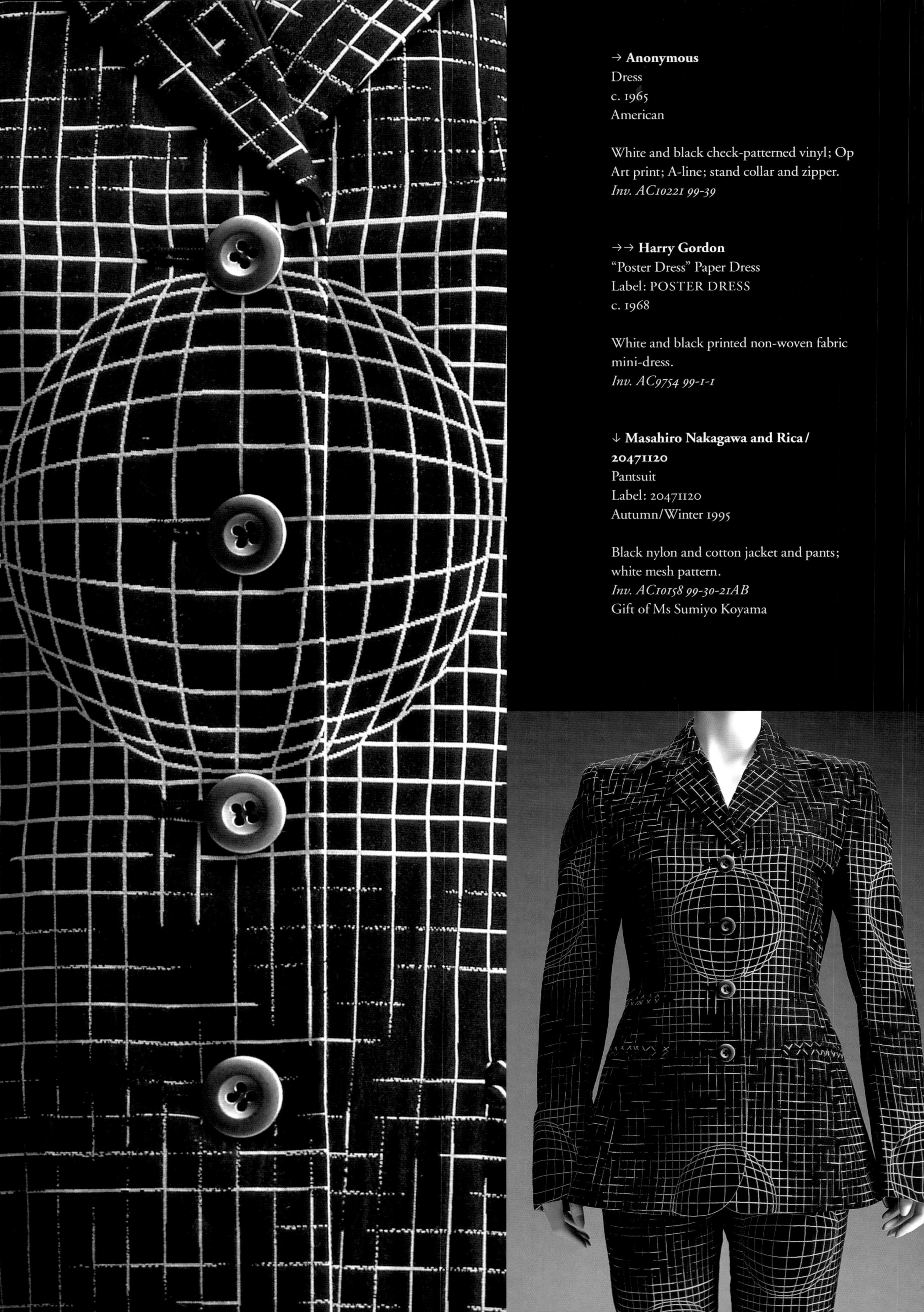

→ **Anonymous**
Dress
c. 1965
American

White and black check-patterned vinyl; Op Art print; A-line; stand collar and zipper.
Inv. AC10221 99-39

→→ **Harry Gordon**
"Poster Dress" Paper Dress
Label: POSTER DRESS
c. 1968

White and black printed non-woven fabric mini-dress.
Inv. AC9754 99-1-1

↓ **Masahiro Nakagawa and Rica / 20471120**
Pantsuit
Label: 20471120
Autumn/Winter 1995

Black nylon and cotton jacket and pants; white mesh pattern.
Inv. AC10158 99-30-21AB
Gift of Ms Sumiyo Koyama

SOUP
SOUP
Campbell's
Campbell's
SOUP
SOUP
Campbell's
Campbell's

In 1962, when Andy Warhol had his first exhibition, *32 Soup Cans* was one of the paintings that was revealed to the world. Pop Art, which was art made with imagery of the mass-production era that could be found anywhere, grabbed the attention of the masses.
The paper dress shown here is a dress that ties in well with Pop Art, symbolizing the 1960s culture of consumption. Warhol himself made the "banana dress" and the "fragile dress" in 1966.

→ **Anonymous**
"Souper Dress" Paper Dress
Label: Souper Dress
c. 1966
American

"Campbell's Soup" can-motif printed non-woven mini dress with black bias tape.
Inv. AC9561 98-14-2

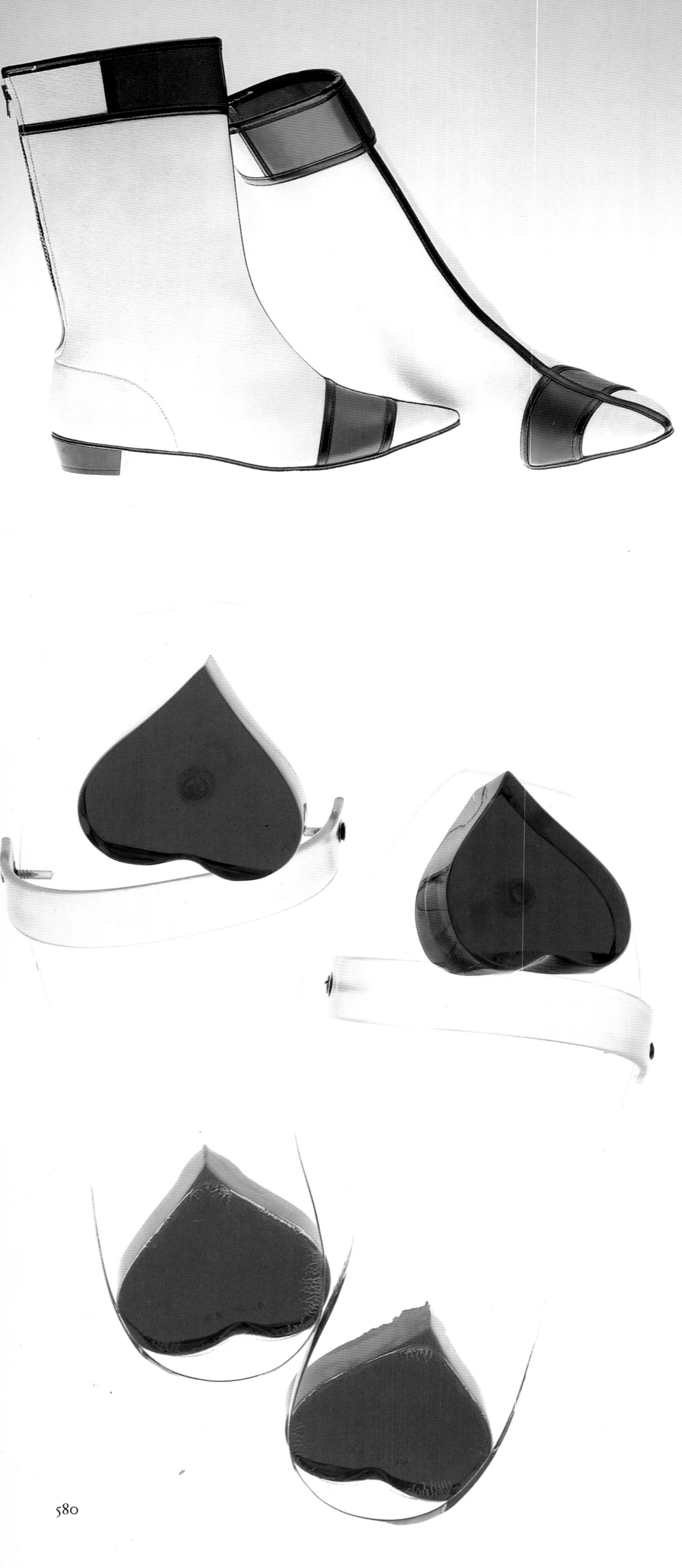

← **Hi Brows**
Boots
Label: Hi BROWS
1965–1969

White, black, red and blue fake leather sewn together in "Mondrian" pattern; with zipper.
Inv. AC9103 94-70-5AB

↙ **Anonymous**
Sandals
1960s

Clear and red plastic with heart-shaped decoration and heel; vinyl strap.
Inv. AC9106 94-70-8AB

→ **Beth Levine / Herbert Levine**
"Barefoot in the Grass" Sandals
Label: none
c. 1968

Astroturf; clear vinyl; rubber sole.
Inv. AC9104 94-7-6AB

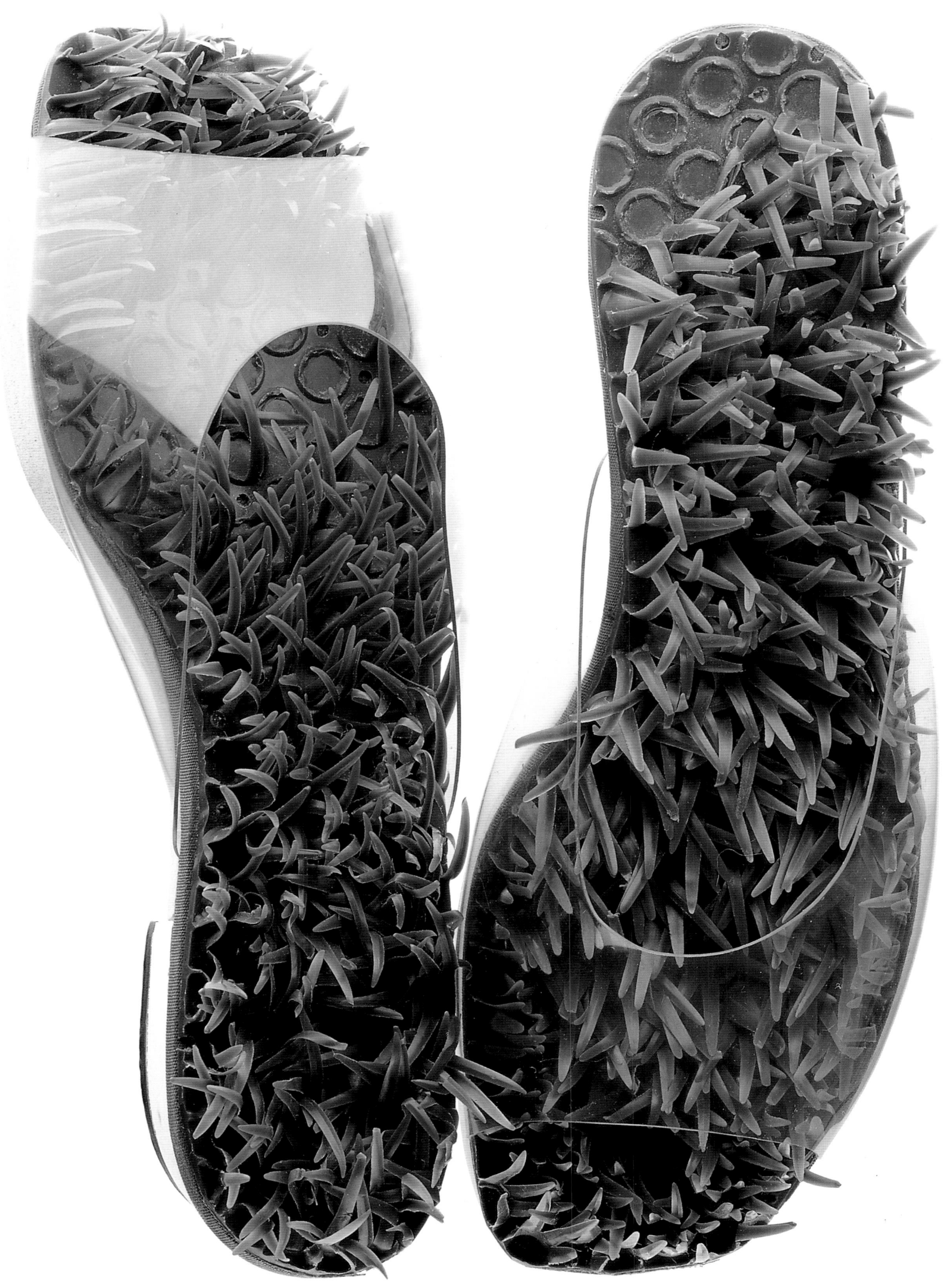

Emilio Pucci began in Florence around 1950. By creating sporty outfits with brilliant print fabrics based on traditional Italian designs, Pucci took the American market by storm. In the 1960s, Pucci fashion spread around the world with bold color combinations similar to the psychedelic design popular at the time. Light, thin silk fabric was used for these outfits, which became essential resort wear for the jet set.

Emilio Pucci
Cape
Label: EMILIO PUCCI FLORENCE-ITALY
1965–1969

Pink silk georgette hooded cape; printed with mask motif.
Inv. AC6821 90-26-1

IT'S NOT THE C-COLD I MIND, IT'S THE TOPLESS B-BATHING SUIT!
BEER

Harvey Kurtzman, Will Elder, Jack Davis and Frank Frazetta
Satirical illustration of "mono-kini" from comic "Little Annie Fanny", 1965

Rudi Gernreich, who was active in America, created the topless swimsuit in 1964, and in 1965 made the thin skin-colored nylon brassiere known as the "No Bra." These sprang the new concept of "body-consciousness" on the unsuspecting world.
On the left is the "mono-kini", the topless bathing suit that caused a scandal. On the right is a bathing suit with crossing black straps. This showed the novel idea that the skin itself could become a beautiful garment.

→ **Rudi Gernreich**
Topless Swimsuit
Label: RUDI GERNREICH DESIGN FOR HARMON KNITWEAR
1964

Black and taupe striped wool jersey; strap-only top.
Inv. AC10127 99-27

→→ **Rudi Gernreich**
Swimsuit
Label: RUDI GERNREICH DESIGN FOR HARMON KNITWEAR
1971

Black and taupe wool jersey with black strap.
Inv. AC9560 98-14-1

Pages 588/589
Kenzo Takada debuted in Paris in 1970 as a designer in the fast-growing Paris *prêt-à-porter* scene. A dress designed by Takada made with simple ordinary kimono fabric was chosen as the cover of *Elle* magazine, and he became an overnight sensation in the fashion world. Takada's designs had a simple and relaxed style, combined with the esoteric image of Japan, which matched the spirit of the times that followed May 1968.
The kimono-sleeve sweaters are meant to be worn over a long-sleeved shirt, styled with jeans and hot pants of the day.

Kenzo Takada
Sweaters
Label: JAP PARIS TOKYO
1970

Left: white, pink, red and purple wool knit; rib-knit at neck, hem and sleeves.

Right: white wool knit; red anchor knitted mark; navy rib-knit at neck, hem and sleeves.
Inv. AC9255 95-63-3, AC4897 84-26-1

In the 1970s, *prêt-à- porter* presented clothes which were well suited to normal daily life, while also being highly fashionable. *Haute couture* was no longer the source of new trends, and *prêt-à- porter* took its place. Many new designers appeared on the scene. Daniel Hechter opened a boutique in 1962, and was famous for sporty casual wear. Sonia Rykiel started in 1962, creating knit outfits that emphasized the slender female body. Rykiel transformed the sweater and cardigan, which had been plain casual wear for daytime, into the fashion of the time.

← **Daniel Hechter**
Coat
Label: daniel hechter paris
c.1970

Yellow, red, navy and light green plaid wool twill; large patch pockets.
Inv. AC7777 93-22-1
Gift of Ms Yoshiko Okamura

→ **Sonia Rykiel**
Sweater
Label: SONIA RYKIEL
c. 1971

Dark green knit woven with girl motif at front; rib-knit around sleeves and hem.
Inv. AC7778 93-22-2
Gift of Ms Yoshiko Okamura

→→ **Sonia Rykiel**
Blouse and Vest
Label: (blouse) SONIA RYKIEL
1974

Red cotton gauze blouse with fruit print; black and red knit jacquard vest, black mohair around sleeves and neck, rib-knit at hem.
Inv. AC9350 96-20-9, AC4898 84-26-2

In the late 1960s, protest against the Vietnam War started to spread. Hippies abandoned the values of modern society, and empathized with non-Western cultures and religions. Both men and women grew their hair long and wore a hand-made type of fashion which became popular with younger generations around the world.
Designers in Paris did not fail to pick up on these street fashions, and the trends made their way into Paris designs as folkloric fashion and patchwork-designed jeans.

Page 593, Left
Emmanuelle Khanh
Smock
Label: Emmanuelle Khanh diffusion Froisa Paris
Spring/Summer 1971

White cotton gauze with polychrome scenic cotton embroidery near square neck; floral and butterfly-motif embroidery.
Inv. AC7781 93-22-5
Gift of Ms. Yoshiko Okamura

Levi's
Jeans
Label: Levi's
c.1971

Deep- and light-color blue denim patchwork bell-bottoms.
Inv. AC9758 99-1-5

Page 593, Right above
Left: **Thea Porter**
Dress
Label: thea porter london
c. 1970

Yellow ground with red stripe Indian cotton; orange cotton with mirror work at front; blue velvet ribbon.
Inv. AC9749 98-43-10

Right: **Barbara Hulanicki / BIBA**
Dress
Label: BIBA
Early 1970s

Beige-pink wool; floral print; large square neck; matching belt.
Inv. AC10414 2000-48-1

Page 593, Right below
Left: **Giorgio Sant'Angelo**
Tunic and Pants
Label: SANT'ANGELO
c.1970

Red tricot tunic with purple and orange turtleneck and cuffs, long tie with fringe; red polyester tricot pants.
Inv. AC9731 98-38-1, AC9742 98-43-3

Right: **Stephen Burrows**
Tunic and Pants
Label: stephen burrows
Early 1970s

Green tricot bodice and light yellow sleeves; red stitching at hem and cuff.
Inv. AC9740 98-43-1AB

↓ Singer Joan Baez and actress Vanessa Redgrave at a demonstration against the Vietnam War, 1965.

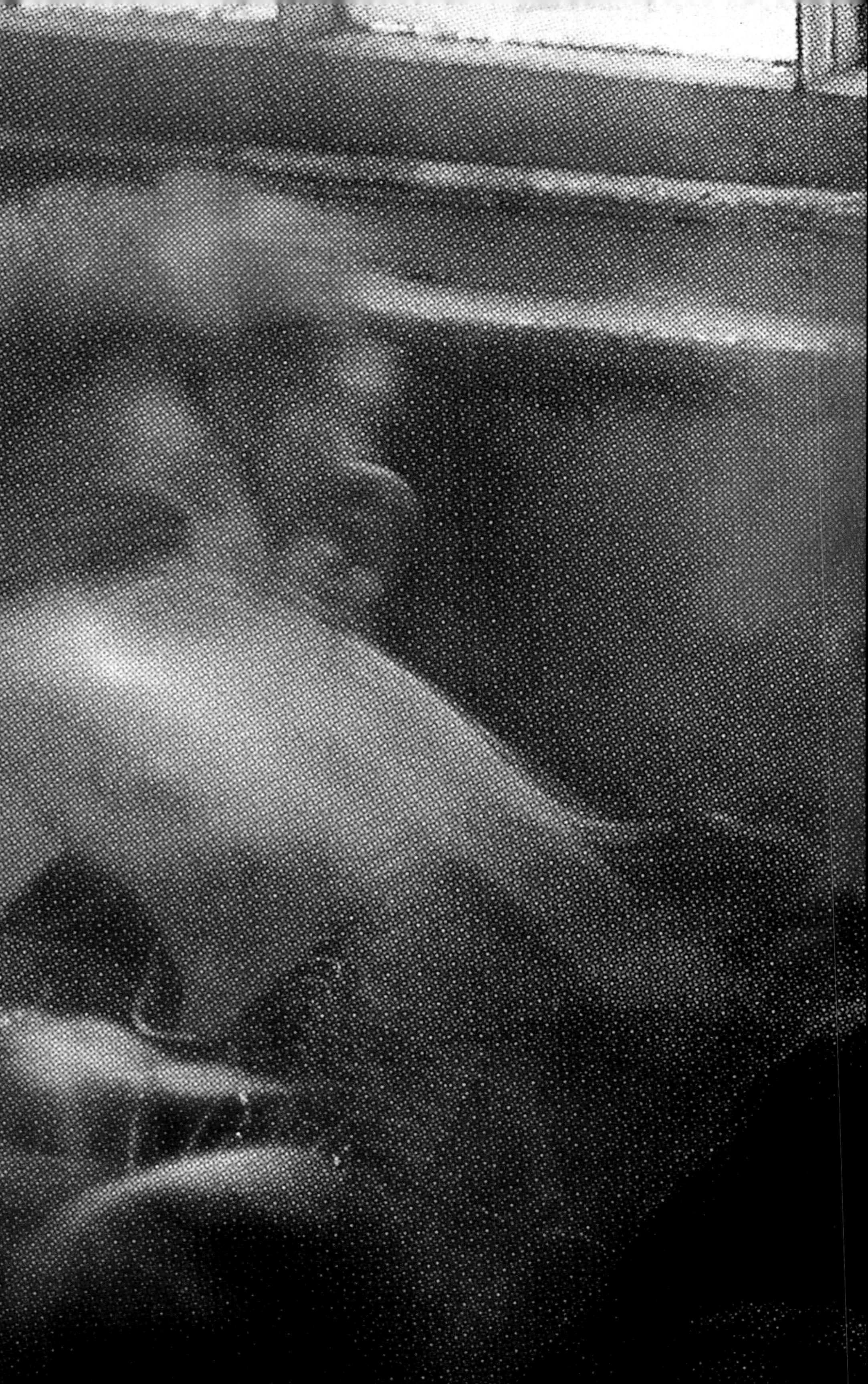

In 1976 Malcolm McLaren launched the punk group the Sex Pistols. The Sex Pistols shouted out explicit lyrics that mocked a class-divided society, and wore fashions such as bondage styles and torn clothes pinned together with safety pins, available from "Seditionaries", the boutique owned by McLaren and Vivienne Westwood. Their combination of music and fashion gained passionate followers among the young generation. Westwood never forgot the surrealist spirit of the punk style era.

Page 596
Vivienne Westwood and Malcolm McLaren / Seditionaries
Shirt
Label: SEDS 430 King's Rd., Chelsea tel: 3510764
c. 1977

White cotton gauze with photo print of female breasts; strap; Velcro; metal.
Inv. AC10367 2000-34-2

Page 597
Vivienne Westwood
Mule
Label: Vivienne Westwood MADE IN ENGLAND
Spring/Summer 2000

Beige leather with foot-shaped toe.
Inv. AC10267 2000-5-1AB

Punks at a King's Cross pub, London, 1987
Photo: Gavin Watson

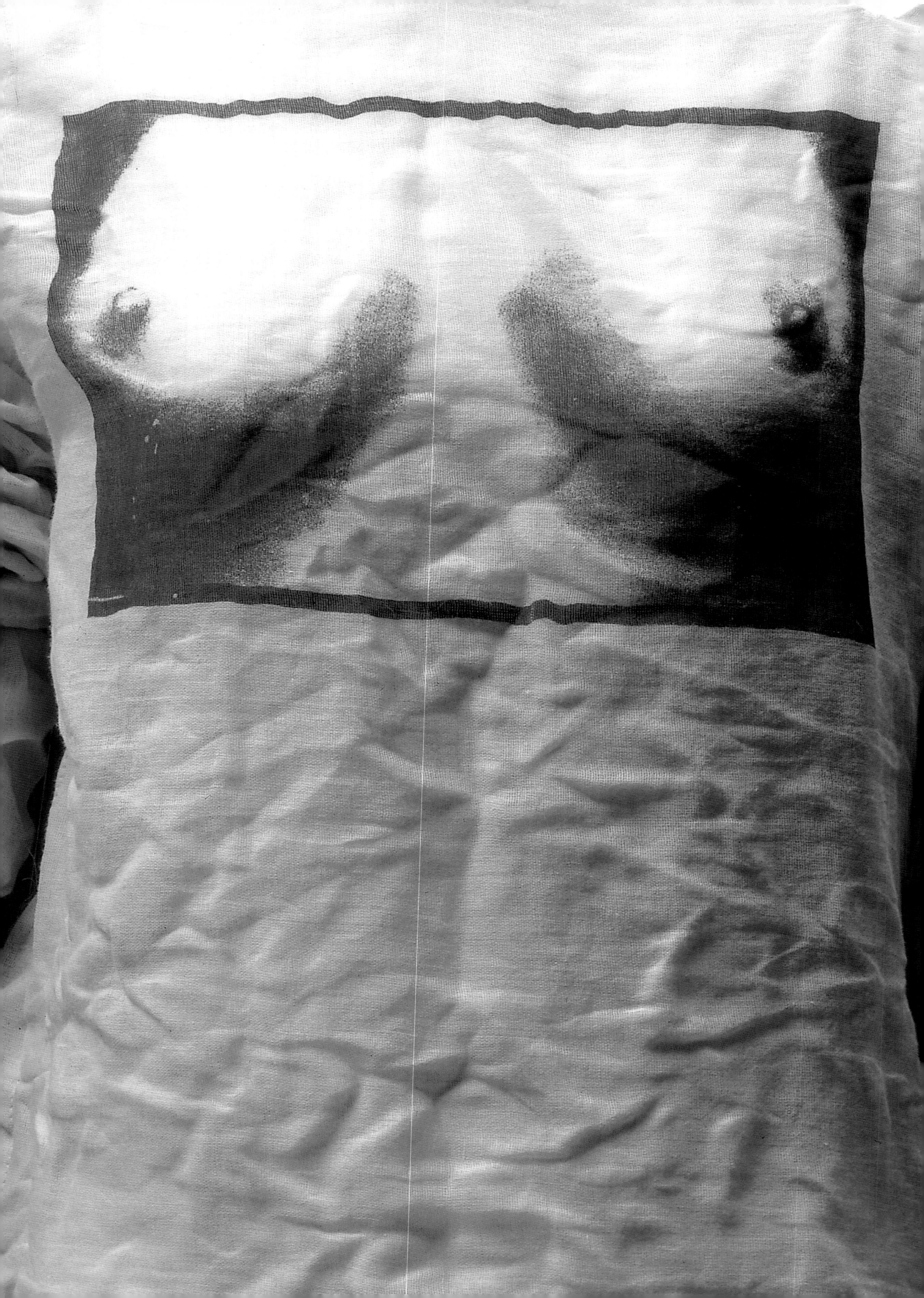

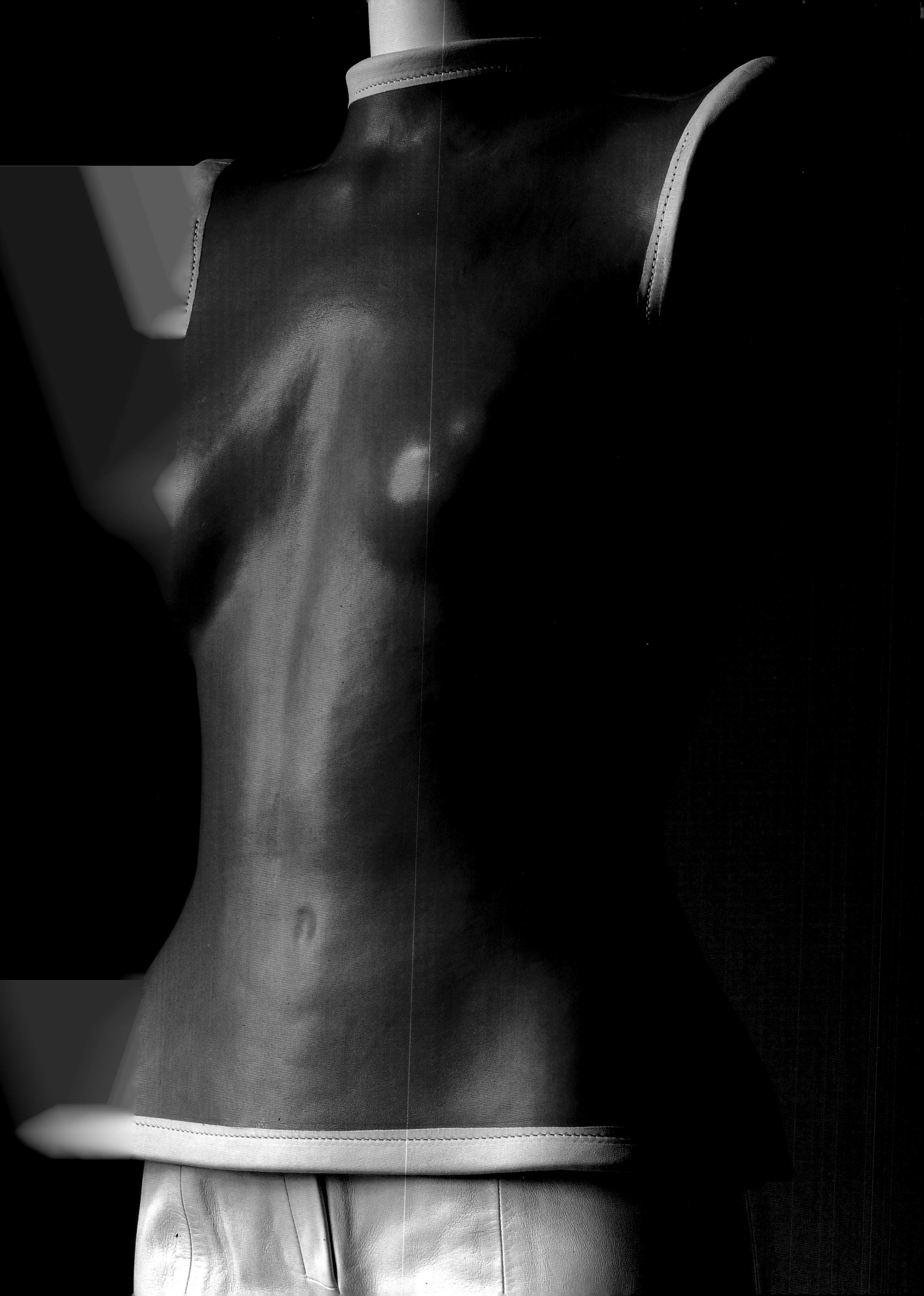

In the two bodices shown here, McQueen pressed leather and Miyake converted plastic into a realistic second skin. Their new way of looking at the human body as the basis of clothing is very apparent here.

← **Alexander McQueen / Givenchy**
Bodice and Pants
Label: GIVENCHY COUTURE
Autumn/Winter 1999

Red pressed-leather bodice; white leather pants.
Inv. AC10105 99-17AB

↓ **Issey Miyake**
Bodice
Label: none
Autumn/Winter 1980

Red plastic bodice; embossed inside.
Inv. AC5643 87-25A
Gift of Miyake Design Studio

Pages 600/601
In 1979 the first female Prime Minister of England was elected, and male and female equality was more apparent than ever. Women moved out into society, and began to display their well-toned bodies proudly, and the body-conscious movement that originated in the 1960s began to rise again. Alaïa, who used the stretch-knit fabrics that were increasingly popular at the time, shaped the functional body-conscious style of the 1980s.

Page 600
Azzedine Alaïa
Dress
Label: ALAÏA PARIS
1987

Green wool jersey.
Inv. AC5809 88-24

Page 601
Azzedine Alaïa
Dress
Label: ALAÏA PARIS
c. 1987

Black rayon, nylon and lycra mixed; crocheted seams.
Inv. AC9746 98-43-7

These two examples both show Western culture's ways of creating a style that solves the problem of fitting the body for the ideal shape. One way of forming the ideal shape is stretch fabric; the other is the traditional *haute couture* style.

On the left is a suit by Galliano, from London. He became the designer for Dior in 1996, and takes his inspiration from historical and ethnic garments to create the modern styles of today.

On the right is a dress made by Alaïa. Lycra, created by DuPont in 1958, developed through the years to gain a high-quality elasticity.

← **John Galliano / Christian Dior**
Suit and Choker
Label: Christian Dior HAUTE COUTURE AH97 PARIS 29374
Autumn/Winter 1997

Set of jacket and skirt of gray wool tweed; pad at jacket hem; train with long skirt; choker of 35 rings of two-toned silver.
Inv. AC9559 98-13AC

→ **Azzedine Alaïa**
Dress
Label: ALAÏA PARIS
1985–1989

Navy rayon lycra; large v-cut at back; seam line and pleats at hem.
Inv. AC9744 98-43-5

Gaultier debuted in 1976. He loved parody, and in the 1980s took what had traditionally been undergarments, such as the corset and girdle, and transformed them into active outerwear for women, obliterating the negative image of underwear. The transformation of underwear into outerwear is a major phenomenon of the late twentieth century, originating in the body-conscious movement of the 1980s that emphasized the beauty of a fit, healthy body.

Jean-Paul Gaultier
Dress
Label: Jean-Paul GAULTIER pour GIBO
Spring/Summer 1987

Red silk satin, nylon and lycra mixed; transparent elastic nylon section from side to back.
Inv. AC5640 87-24-3

→ Gaultier's dress from Spring/Summer 1987

Gaultier used new types of fabrics, and tried to create a style that was functional enough to fit with everyday life, while retaining an original, vivid look.
On the left is a pair of pants, and on the right is a skirt and gloves that use elastic fabric and fit tightly to the skin. The top is made of bonded fabric that makes the body look three-dimensional.

→ **Jean-Paul Gaultier**
Jacket, Brassiere and Pants
Label: Jean-Paul GAULTIER pour GIBO
Spring/Summer 1987

Black rayon jacket; mixed synthetic and silk brassiere, same material used for center of pants; transparent panels at sides of pants.
Inv. AC5642 87-24-5AC

→→ **Jean-Paul Gaultier**
Top, Skirt and Gloves
Label: Jean-Paul GAULTIER Pour EQUATOR
Autumn/Winter 1987

Black bonded polyester knit top; bronze color elastic polyester skirt and gloves.
Inv. AC5722 87-51-3AB, AC5723 87-51-3CD

Pages 608/609
The artificial glow in the fabric has been taken out of the elastic material, so that it looks almost like real skin. The human-body-patterned moiré was printed to give a blurry visual effect.

Jean-Paul Gaultier
Dress
Label: Jean-Paul GAULTIER MAILLE
Spring/Summer 1996

Blue nylon net printed with navy and beige moiré pattern of human body.
Inv. AC9309 96-5-1

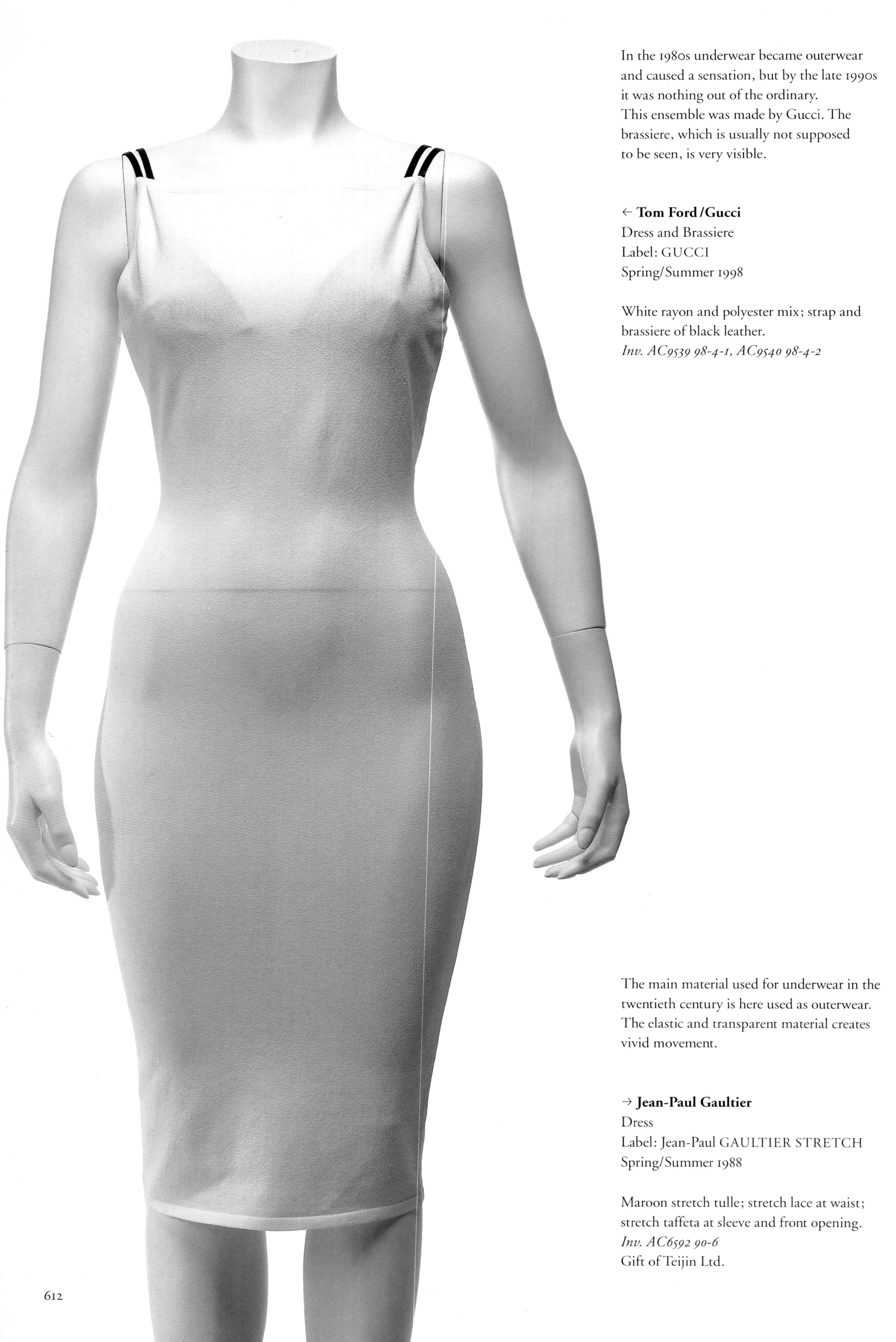

In the 1980s underwear became outerwear and caused a sensation, but by the late 1990s it was nothing out of the ordinary. This ensemble was made by Gucci. The brassiere, which is usually not supposed to be seen, is very visible.

← **Tom Ford / Gucci**
Dress and Brassiere
Label: GUCCI
Spring/Summer 1998

White rayon and polyester mix; strap and brassiere of black leather.
Inv. AC9539 98-4-1, AC9540 98-4-2

The main material used for underwear in the twentieth century is here used as outerwear. The elastic and transparent material creates vivid movement.

→ **Jean-Paul Gaultier**
Dress
Label: Jean-Paul GAULTIER STRETCH
Spring/Summer 1988

Maroon stretch tulle; stretch lace at waist; stretch taffeta at sleeve and front opening.
Inv. AC6592 90-6
Gift of Teijin Ltd.

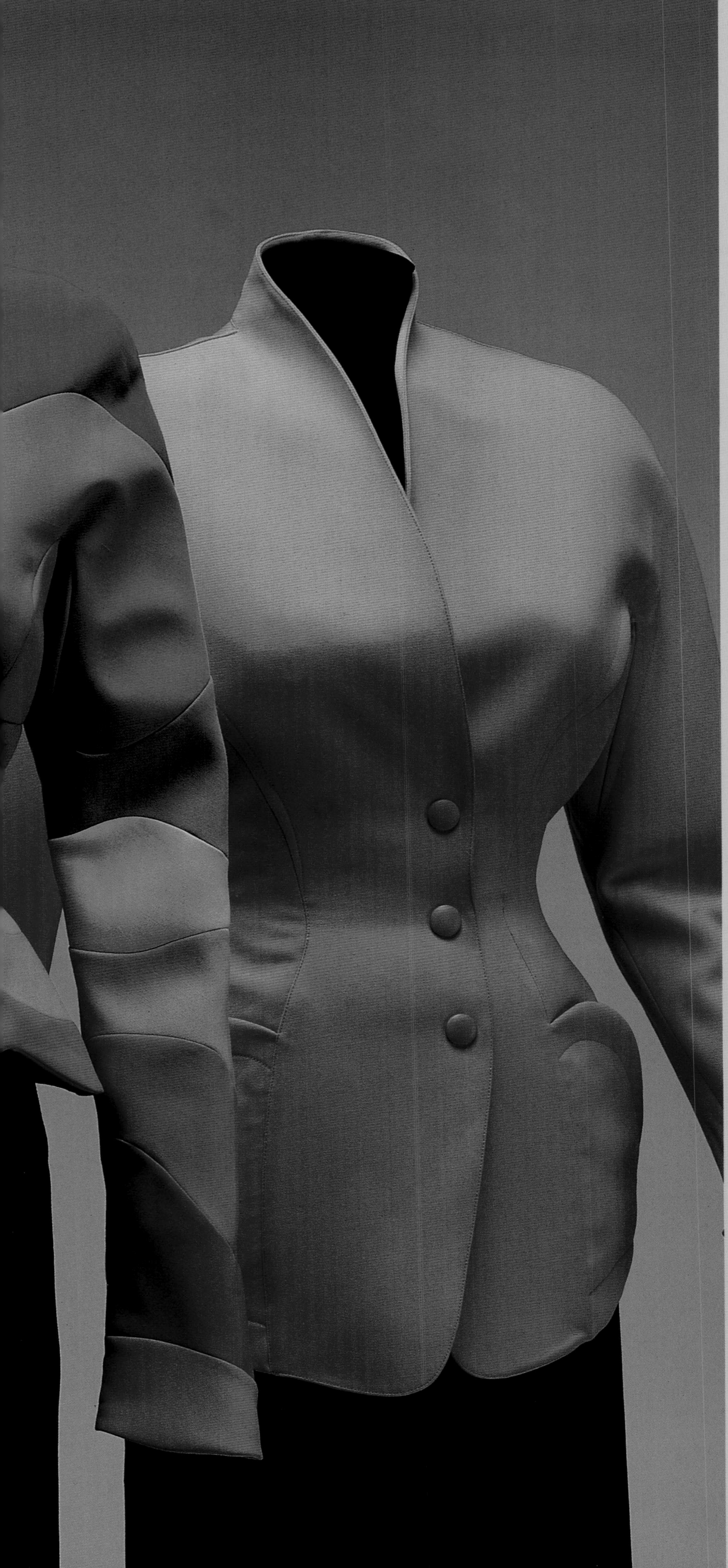

Thierry Mugler debuted in 1973, and is one of the major forces in "power dressing." The sexy and powerful designs help define the perfect image of a woman. The thick shoulder padding typical of the 1980s gives a sharp, downward triangular silhouette.

Left
Thierry Mugler
Jacket
Label: Thierry Mugler PARIS
Autumn/Winter 1988

Yellow polyester-triacetate mix; zigzag cutting at hem; slanted sleeve cuffs.
Inv. AC10151 99-30-14A
Gift of Ms Sumiyo Koyama

Center
Thierry Mugler
Jacket
Label: Thierry Mugler PARIS
Spring/Summer 1990

Eight-colored wool gabardine patchwork; five colored snaps at front; oblique cut at right hem.
Inv. AC10155 99-30-18
Gift of Ms Sumiyo Koyama

Right
Thierry Mugler
Jacket
Label: Thierry Mugler PARIS
Late 1980s

Salmon-pink wool gabardine; high neck.
Inv. AC10153 99-30-16
Gift of Ms Sumiyo Koyama

More women started working, and following in the footsteps of men, they wore subtle-colored tailored suits.
For working women in Milan, Giorgio Armani created soft-lined tailored suits without stiff structures; in Paris, Claude Montana and Anne-Marie Beretta created suits with strong and simple shapes.

Giorgio Armani
Pantsuit
Label: GIORGIO ARMANI
1985–1989

Jacket of red and gray striped, double-faced wool, bias-cut; pants of gray wool gabardine.
Inv. AC10191 99-36-2AC

Giorgio Armani
Pantsuit
Label: GIORGIO ARMANI
1985–1989

Set of jacket and pants of navy and white striped wool twill.
Inv. AC10192 99-36-3AB

Anne-Marie Beretta
Suit
Label: ANNE MARIE BERETTA PARIS
c. 1983

Pin-stripe wool flannel jacket and skirt; patch pockets; slit at skirt-front.
Inv. AC10346 2000-29-1AB

Claude Montana
Suit
Label: claude montana
c. 1990

Pin-stripe wool flannel jacket and skirt with zipper.
Inv. AC10194 99-36-5AB

Romeo Gigli debuted in Milan in 1983. He eliminated the thick shoulder padding of that time, and created a silhouette with soft rounded shoulder lines.
The cocoon silhouette was another feature of his works. This full-bodied coat looks light because of its lacy knit fabric.

Romeo Gigli
Coat
Label: ROMEO GIGLI
Spring/Summer 1991

Black raffia lacy knit coat with hood.
Inv. AC10196 99-36-7

→ **Christian Lacroix**
Bolero and Dress
Label: CHRISTIAN LACROIX prêt-a-porter
c. 1990

Bolero of purple silk satin jacquard woven with black floral pattern; silk taffeta frill; dress of purple silk printed with angel, animal and plant pattern.
Inv. AC9605 98-16-43AB
Gift of Ms Mari Yoshimura

↘ **Vivienne Westwood**
Top and Skirt
Label: none
Spring/Summer 1986

Pink cotton jersey top with dot print; gray rayon satin skirt with three hoops inside; frilled hem; draw strings.
Inv. AC5486 86-46-1, AC5487 86-46-2

In 1980, Kumagai opened a shoe boutique. By using the painting style of artists such as Dalí and Pollock, he came up with a never-before-imagined style of shoes.
In the "Shoes to eat" series, using Japanese plastic food sample production methods, he put hyperreal images of beef, red-bean rice and sundaes on shoes. In the past Elsa Schiaparelli had made a hat shaped like a pair of pumps; now Kumagai decorated the toes with food and surprised the fashion scene.

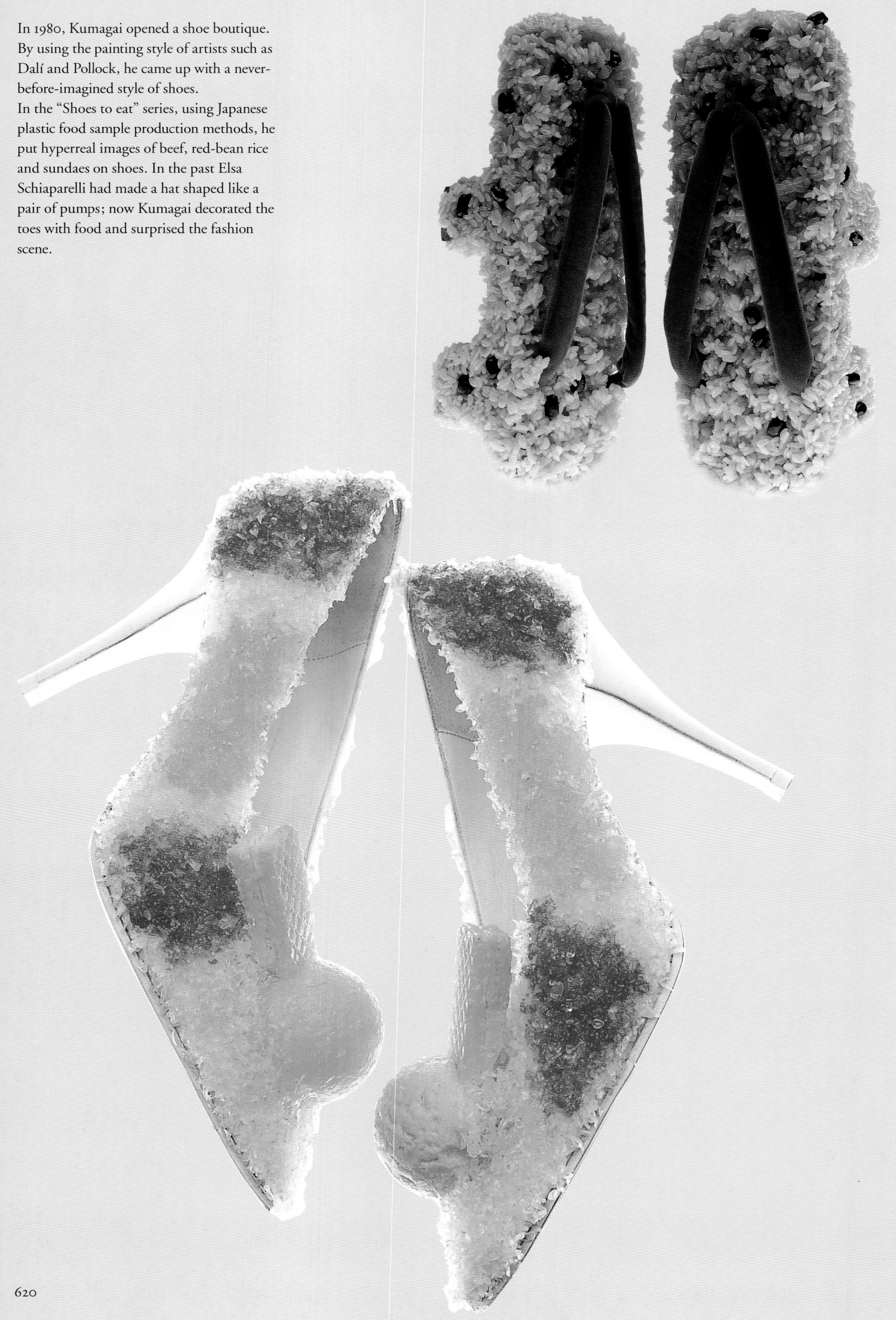

Tokio Kumagai
Taberu Kutsu ("Eating Shoes")
Label: TOKIO KUMAGAÏ PARIS
c. 1984

Resin
Inv. AC7560 92-13-471AB, AC7561 92-13-472AB, AC7558 92-13-469AB, AC7559 92-13-470
Gift of Mr Tokio Kumagai

TOKIO KUMAGAÏ
PARIS
MADE IN ITALY

This design was inspired by the sculpture *Le Baiser* (1908), created by Constantin Brancusi, a Romanian sculptor known for abstract forms. The left is a profile of a man, the right is a profile of a woman.

← **Tokio Kumagai**
Pumps
Label: TOKIO KUMAGAÏ PARIS
c. 1984

Black back-skin leather with elastic tape, ribbon, ring and leather appliqué.
Inv. AC5528 87-70-2AB
Gift of Mr Tokio Kumagai

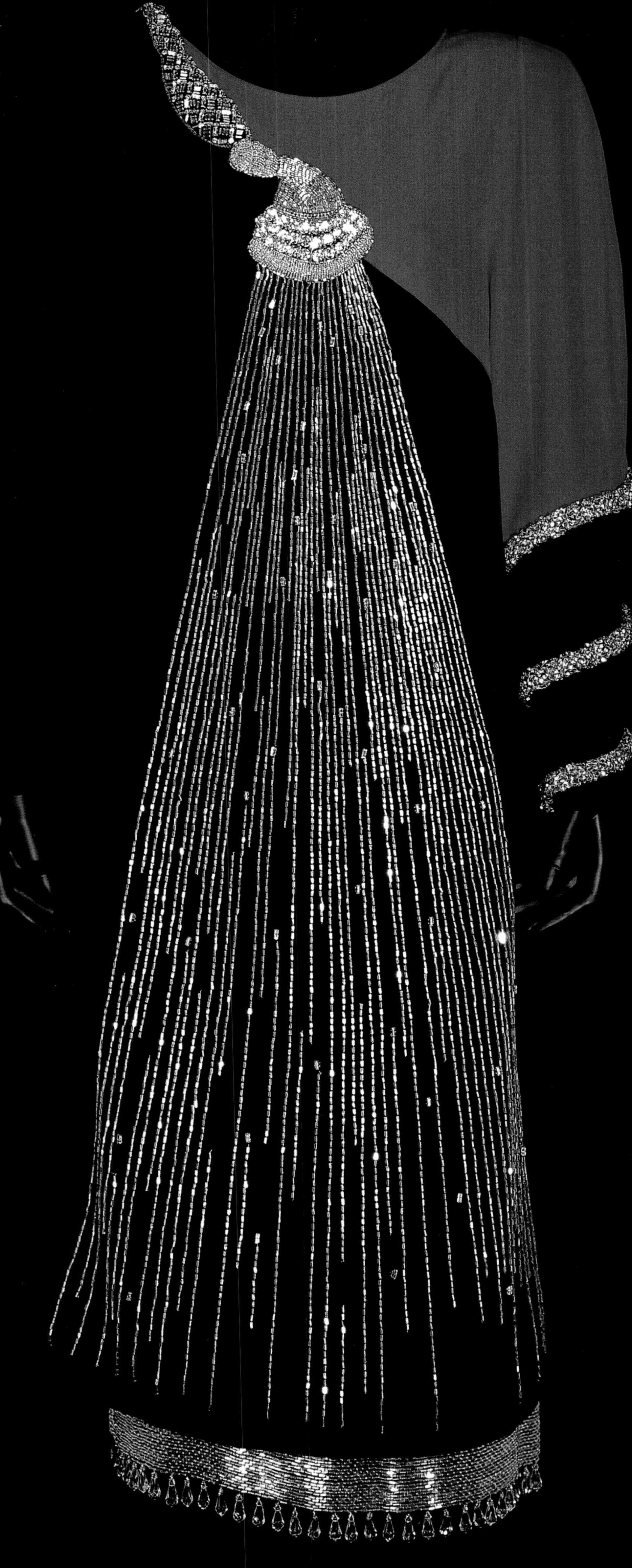

The shower-hose embroidery on the bodice leads to the back, and curls around the left sleeve, in a design with surrealistic taste. Made by Lagerfeld, who was the Chloé designer from 1963 to 1984.

→ **Karl Lagerfeld / Chloé**
Dress and Skirt
Label: Chloé
Autumn/Winter 1983

Dress of red and black acetate-back satin embroidered with shower motif in beads and rhinestones; skirt of black crêpe de chine, bead embroidery at hem.
Inv. AC5309 86-60-13AB

In October, 1982, Kawakubo and Yamamoto held their second Paris *prêt-à-porter* show. The style that debuted that year was colorless, rag-like, and full of holes, which promoted shabby clothing. Their collection created a new vocabulary in fashion: the "*boro* look", "beggar look", and the "ragged look". The designs expressed a Japanese concept of beauty, the beauty of conscious destitution.

Their collection shook up the concept of Western-style clothing, and threw the Parisian fashion world into controversy. The world was shocked, because Japanese designers had proved that there was a possibility that clothes accepted worldwide could come from cultures other than that of Western Europe.

← **Rei Kawakubo / Comme des Garçons**
Blouse and Dress
Label: COMME des GARÇONS
Spring/Summer 1983

Off-white cotton jersey blouse with cotton ribbon appliqué; washed white patchwork dress of sheeting and rayon satin.
Inv. AC7801 93-24-9AB
Gift of Comme des Garçons Co., Ltd.

→ **Yohji Yamamoto**
Jacket, Dress and Pants
Label: Yohji Yamamoto
Spring/Summer 1983

White cotton cut-work jacket, dress and pants.
Inv. AC7755 93-15B,E, AC8984 93-42-8
Jacket and Pants: Gift of Mr Hiroshi Tanaka; Dress: Gift of Ms Sumiyo Koyama

Ever since her debut, Rei Kawakubo has never relied on the standardized concepts of fashion when creating her own designs. Her designs are always noble and beautiful. This sweater looks complex, but it is basically structured by one straight-line panel. There is an abundance of space inside, and when the sleeve is open to the side, it is shaped like a Japanese kimono.

Rei Kawakubo / Comme des Garçons
Sweater and Skirt
Label: tricot COMME des GARÇONS (sweater), COMME des GARÇONS (skirt)
Autumn/Winter 1983

Off-white wool garter-stitch knit sweater, rib-knit at hem; off-white wool jersey skirt.
Inv. AC7842 93-24-5AB
Gift of Comme des Garçons Co., Ltd.

Sweater and skirt by Rei Kawakubo
Photo: Peter Lindbergh, 1983

Two of Kawakubo's early designs that go completely against the Western aim to contour the body.
On the left the top is double-layered but the bottom is a single layer. Some parts of the underarm are not sewn to the body. The unique cut gives the piece an irregular shape that changes according to the body's movements or the wind.
On the right, elastic is sewn in all directions onto this comfortably shaped form, creating an asymmetrical silhouette. The fabric is reminiscent of the *ai-zome* (indigo dyed) fabric that was used for ordinary clothing for the Japanese, and gives a nostalgic and friendly presence to the dress.

← **Rei Kawakubo / Comme des Garçons**
Dress
Label: COMME des GARÇONS
Spring/Summer 1984

White plain-weave cotton one-piece dress with cutwork, shirring.
Inv. AC7909 93-24-117
Gift of Comme des Garçons Co., Ltd.

→ **Rei Kawakubo / Comme des Garçons**
Dress
Label: COMME des GARÇONS
Autumn/Winter 1984

Navy acetate like *ai-zome* (indigo-dyed japanese fabric), stencil-like print with chrysanthemum pattern.
Inv. AC7048 91-27-5
Gift of Comme des Garçons Co., Ltd.

The two examples on the right are asymmetrically designed pantsuits; Yamamoto mixed the Japanese concept of asymmetry with the symmetrical clothes design of the West.

← **Yohji Yamamoto**
Jacket, Vest and Skirt
Label: Yohji Yamamoto
Autumn/Winter 1990

Jacket of moss-green feather-stuffed nylon; sleeve detachable by zipper; skirt of moss-green cotton-padded polyester with quilting; brown leather vest.
Inv. AC6884 90-44-1, AC6885 90-44-2, AC6886 90-44-3AC

→ **Yohji Yamamoto**
Pantsuit
Label: Yohji Yamamoto
Autumn/Winter 1984

Black wool challis jacket and pants with white wool challis lining; asymmetrical shape of pants with bigger left leg.
Inv. AC8975 93-41-3AB
Gift of Ms Sumiyo Koyama

→→ **Yohji Yamamoto**
Pantsuit
Label: Yohji Yamamoto
Autumn/Winter 1986

Gray-beige wool gabardine jacket and pants; brown leather patch on jacket; similar panel on pants.
Inv. AC9706 98-28-1AB

Sakyū ("dune") Mode, designs by Takeo Kikuchi from his catalogue Autumn/Winter 1983; Photo: Shoji Ueda

In 1971 Miyake debuted in New York with his body tights collection. He printed Japanese-style tattoo-like images of Jimi Hendrix and Janis Joplin onto skin-colored elastic material.
Twenty years later, Miyake introduced the "Tattoo Body." The texture almost looks as though a real tattoo were engraved on the body. The combination of the elasticity of the synthetic textile and the decorative function of the tattoo, an art practiced since ancient times, created something that can be considered a new type of skin. In the fashion show, the dress on the left was worn over the body stocking.

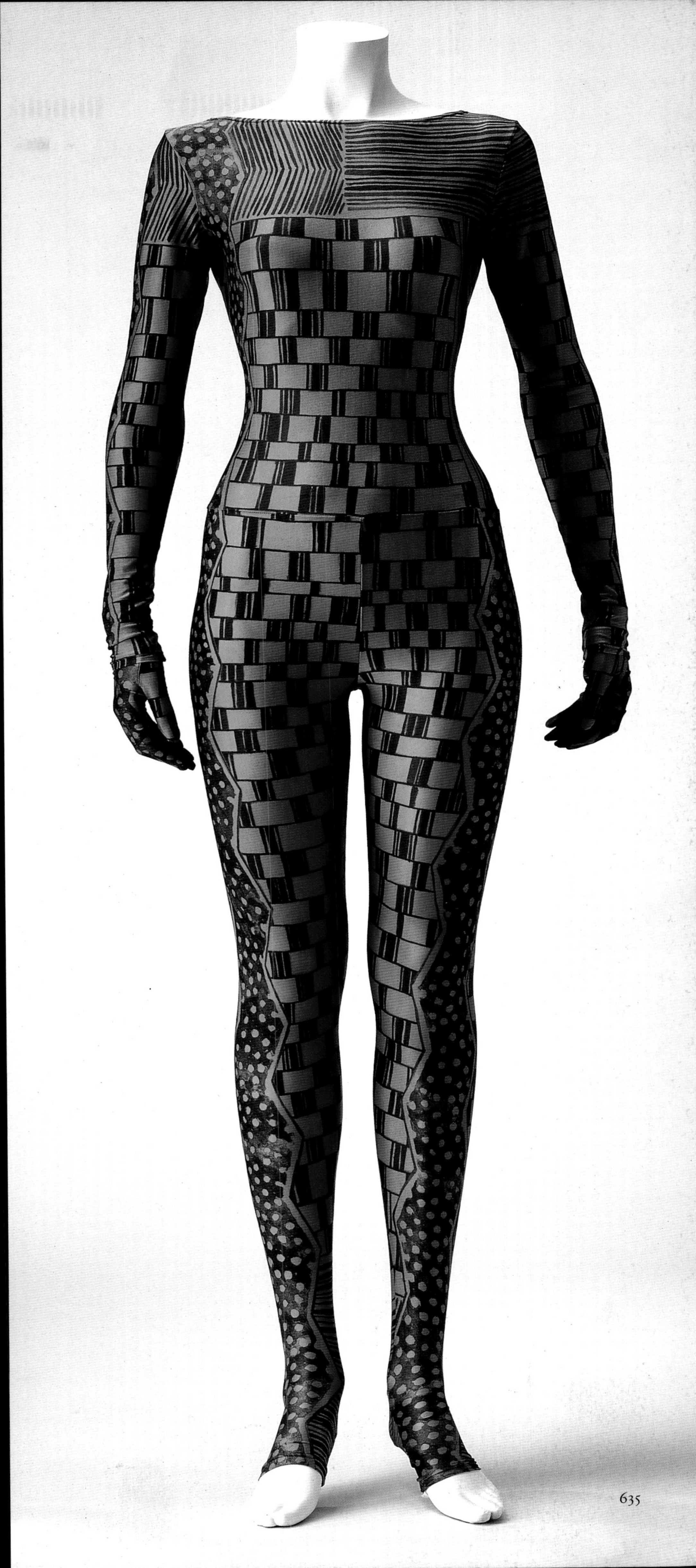

← **Issey Miyake**
Dress
Label: none
Autumn/Winter 1989

Brown pleated polyester organdy.
Inv. AC6595 90-7-3

→ **Issey Miyake**
"Tattoo Body" Body Stocking
Label: none
Autumn/Winter 1989

Brown polyester tricot printed with tattoo-like pattern.
Inv. AC6776 90-21-1, AC6777 90-21-2AB
Gift of Miyake Design Studio

In 1976 Miyake presented the flat "a piece of cloth" design, which is in many ways the basic concept behind Japanese clothes. In the late 1980s, Miyake developed this concept in his pleated ensembles. He made the pieces contrary to the standard style, sewing the outfit first, then putting the pleats on afterwards. By the use of all the characteristics of polyester, the shape and the function combined organically and gave birth to a new type of clothing.
Shown here is a coat created by this innovative technique, with a form that looks like a stage costume for a traditional Japanese *No* dance.

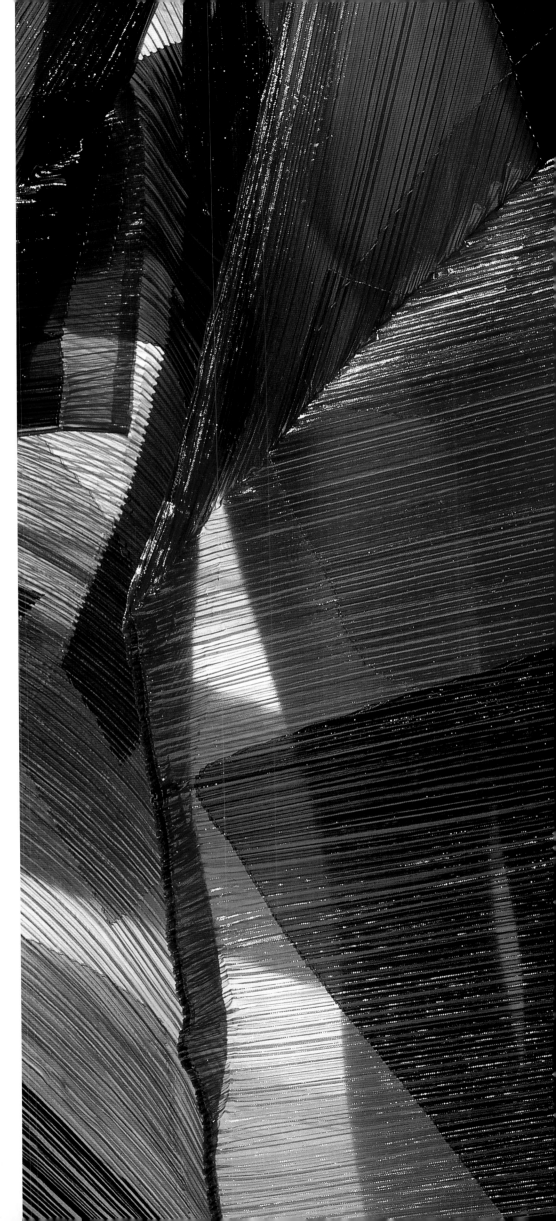

Issey Miyake
Coat
Label: ISSEY MIYAKE
Spring/Summer1995

Clear-pink pleated polyester monofilament appliquéd with red, blue and green pieces.
Inv. AC9214 95-10-2

The pleated designs developed into a more comfortable series known as "Pleats Please." From 1996, the Pleats Please series involved collaborations with other artists on designs known as the "Pleats Please Issey Miyake Guest Artist Series."
Shown below is the first of the artist series, created with Japanese artist Yasumasa Morimura. Morimura's art, inspired by *La Source* by Ingres (1856, Musée d'Orsay, Paris), created a trick effect on the pleats.

The second guest for the "Pleats Please Issey Miyake Guest Artist Series" was photographer Nobuyoshi Araki (pages 640/641). Araki is well known for the eroticism of his photography, which is sometimes extreme. On the left is *Iro-shōjo*, and on the right is the "Araki" print. The contrast between the clean and crisp shape and pop coloring of the Pleats Please and the image of ennui in Araki's photographs gives the series an interesting twist.

→ **Issey Miyake**
Dress: "Pleats Please Issey Miyake Guest Artist Series No.1: Yasumasa Morimura on Pleats Please"
Label: PLEATS PLEASE
Autumn/Winter 1996

Orange pleated polyester one-piece dress with print.
Inv. AC9359 96-22-2
Gift of Miyake Design Studio

Yasumasa Morimura
Portrait (La Source1,2,3), 1986–1990

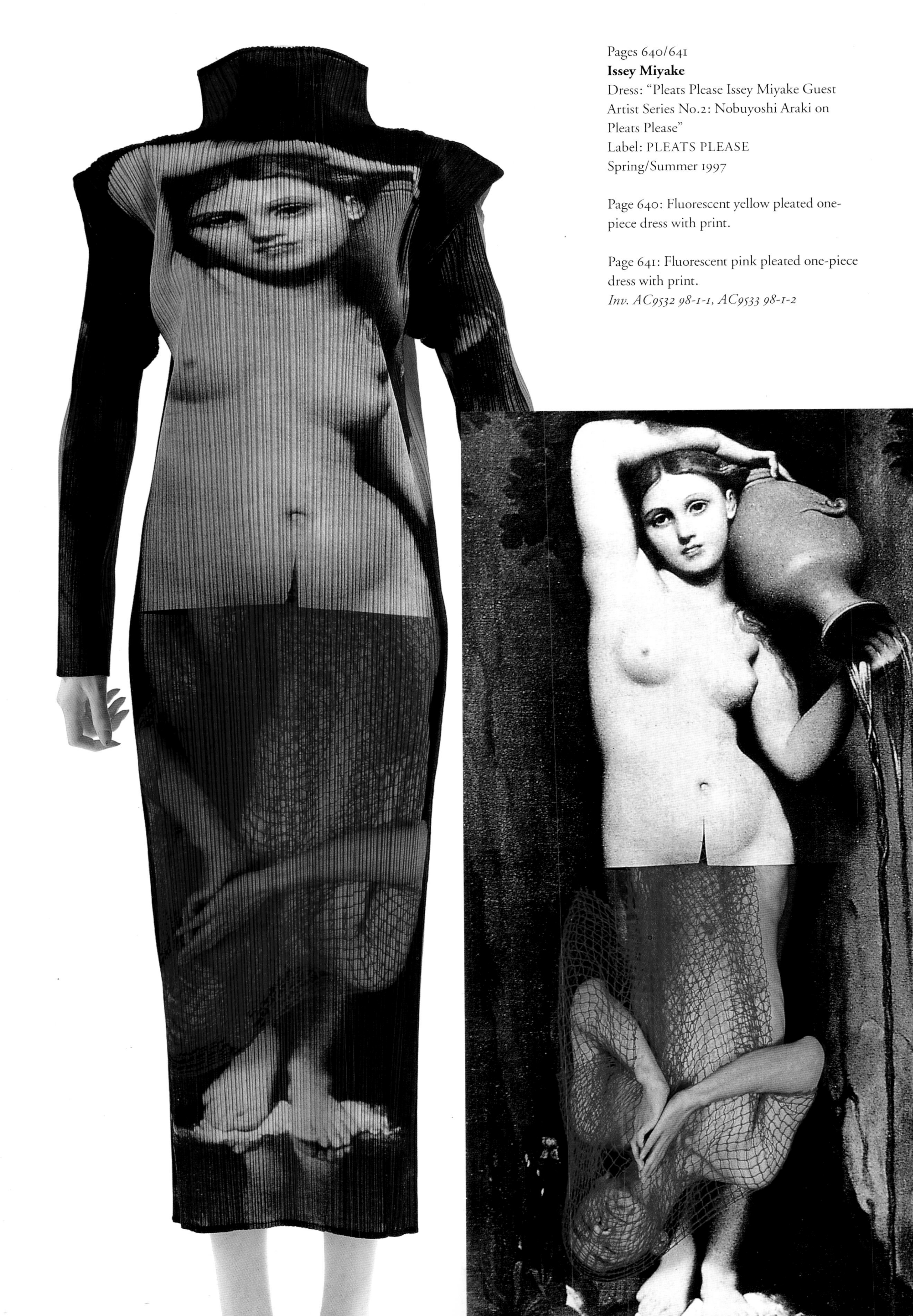

Pages 640/641
Issey Miyake
Dress: "Pleats Please Issey Miyake Guest Artist Series No.2: Nobuyoshi Araki on Pleats Please"
Label: PLEATS PLEASE
Spring/Summer 1997

Page 640: Fluorescent yellow pleated one-piece dress with print.

Page 641: Fluorescent pink pleated one-piece dress with print.
Inv. AC9532 98-1-1, AC9533 98-1-2

In 1998, Miyake became interested in tubular knits, and started research on how to apply the functional features of knits. Miyake's determination led to the mixture of knitting and contemporary innovative technology, which culminated in the birth of "A-POC."
As shown here, the top is a cylindrically knitted piece. A long knit cylinder is folded at the shoulders, pulled down to the waist, and covers over the arms. The design that locks the arm stands out, because it goes against all the functional features of a knit, such as lightness, resistance to wrinkles, and adaptability to any shape.

Issey Miyake
Dress
Label: ISSEY MIYAKE
Spring/Summer 1998

→ Beige woolly nylon knit one-piece dress; cotton and silk mix skirt.

→→ Beige-pink woolly nylon knit one-piece dress; cotton and silk mix underdress.
Inv. AC9552 98-12-2, AC9553 98-12-3

High-tech fabric combined with a shape that resembles the crinoline style. The common belief that chemical means artificial is overturned, and the piece makes a soft and warm impression.
On the right is an outfit that resembles the bustle, which was a nineteenth-century undergarment that put emphasis on the back. Kawakubo is trying to express the dissonance between the body and the form of the outfit.

← **Rei Kawakubo / Comme des Garçons**
Wedding Dress
Label: COMME des GARÇONS
Autumn/Winter 1990

White non-woven fabric one-piece dress with ribbon around hem; petticoat in the same material.
Inv. AC6778 90-22AB
Gift of Comme des Garçons Co., Ltd.

→ **Rei Kawakubo / Comme des Garçons**
Sweater and Skirt
Label: COMME des GARÇONS NOIR
Autumn/Winter 1995

Baby-pink acrylic knit sweater; matching long skirt with embroidery; bustle-like tube sewn to back of skirt; tulle petticoat.
Inv. AC9273 95-44-2AC

COMME des GARCONS scena

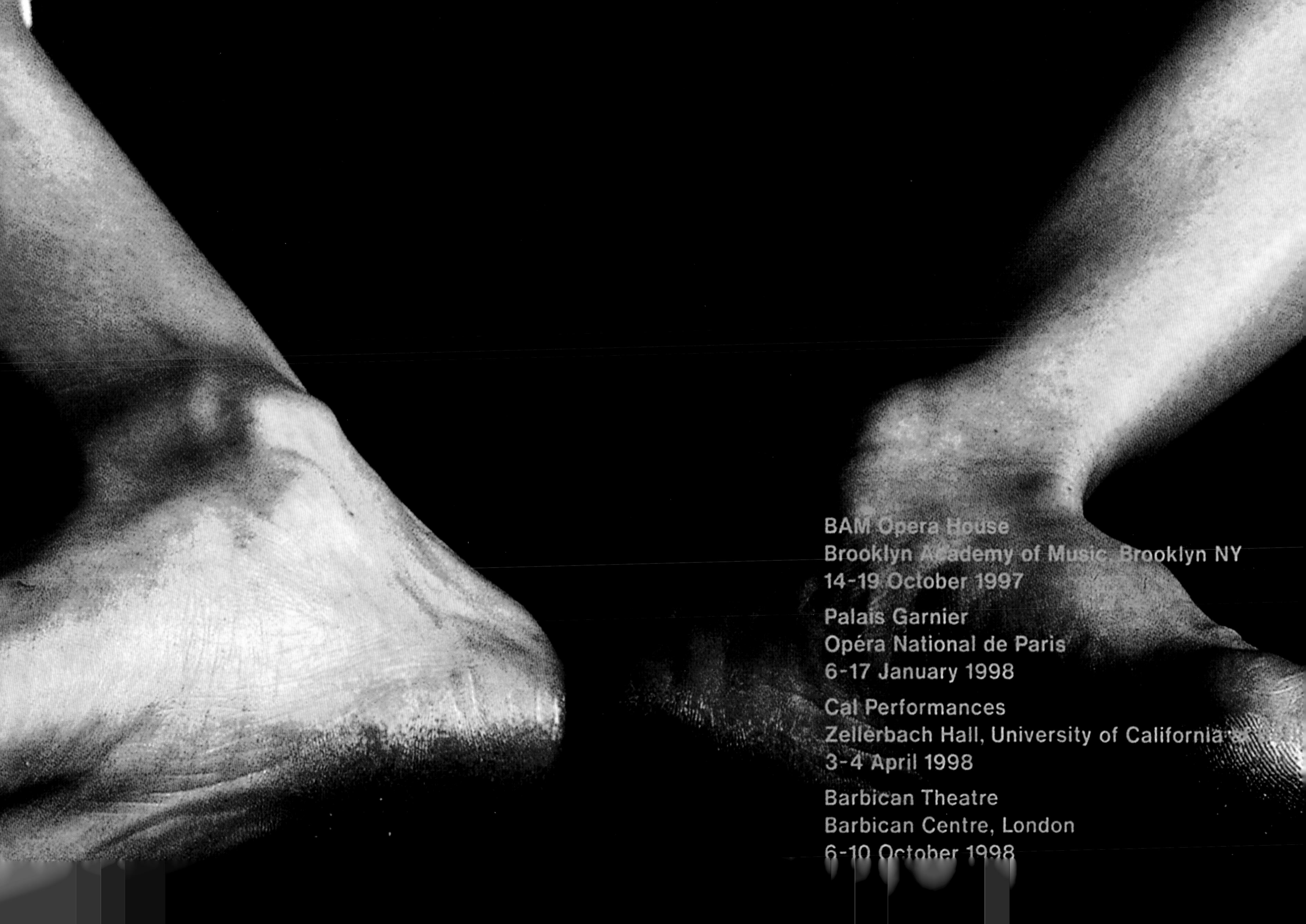
BAM Opera House
Brooklyn Academy of Music, Brooklyn NY
14-19 October 1997
Palais Garnier
Opéra National de Paris
6-17 January 1998
Cal Performances
Zellerbach Hall, University of California
3-4 April 1998
Barbican Theatre
Barbican Centre, London
6-10 October 1998

"Not what has been seen before, not what has been repeated; instead, new discoveries that look towards the future, that are liberated and lively." This was the message written by Comme des Garcons in the spring of 1997.
Shown here are outfits with down pads sewn inside, creating irregular mounds on the surface of the clothes. The shape of the body is deformed by the clothes, and this shook up the standardized concept people have of their bodies. Twentieth-century fashion discovered the body; however, the clothes seemed to conform to the shape of the body. Kawakubo tried to free the clothes from their enslavement to the body, and discovered this new shape.

← **Rei Kawakubo / Comme des Garçons**
Dress
Label: COMME des GARÇONS
Spring/Summer 1997

White stretch nylon-urethane fabric with light blue gingham check print; down pad.
Inv. AC9412 96-32-8A

→ **Rei Kawakubo / Comme des Garçons**
Dress
Label: COMME des GARÇONS
Spring/Summer 1997

Orange stretch nylon-urethane fabric; down pad; underdress of stretch polyester and polyurethane mix fabric.
Inv. AC9413 96-32-9AB

Pages 646/647
Poster for "Scenario" by Merce Cunningham Dance Company, 1997. Rei Kawakubo did the costumes and art design.
Photo: Timothy Greenfield-Sanders

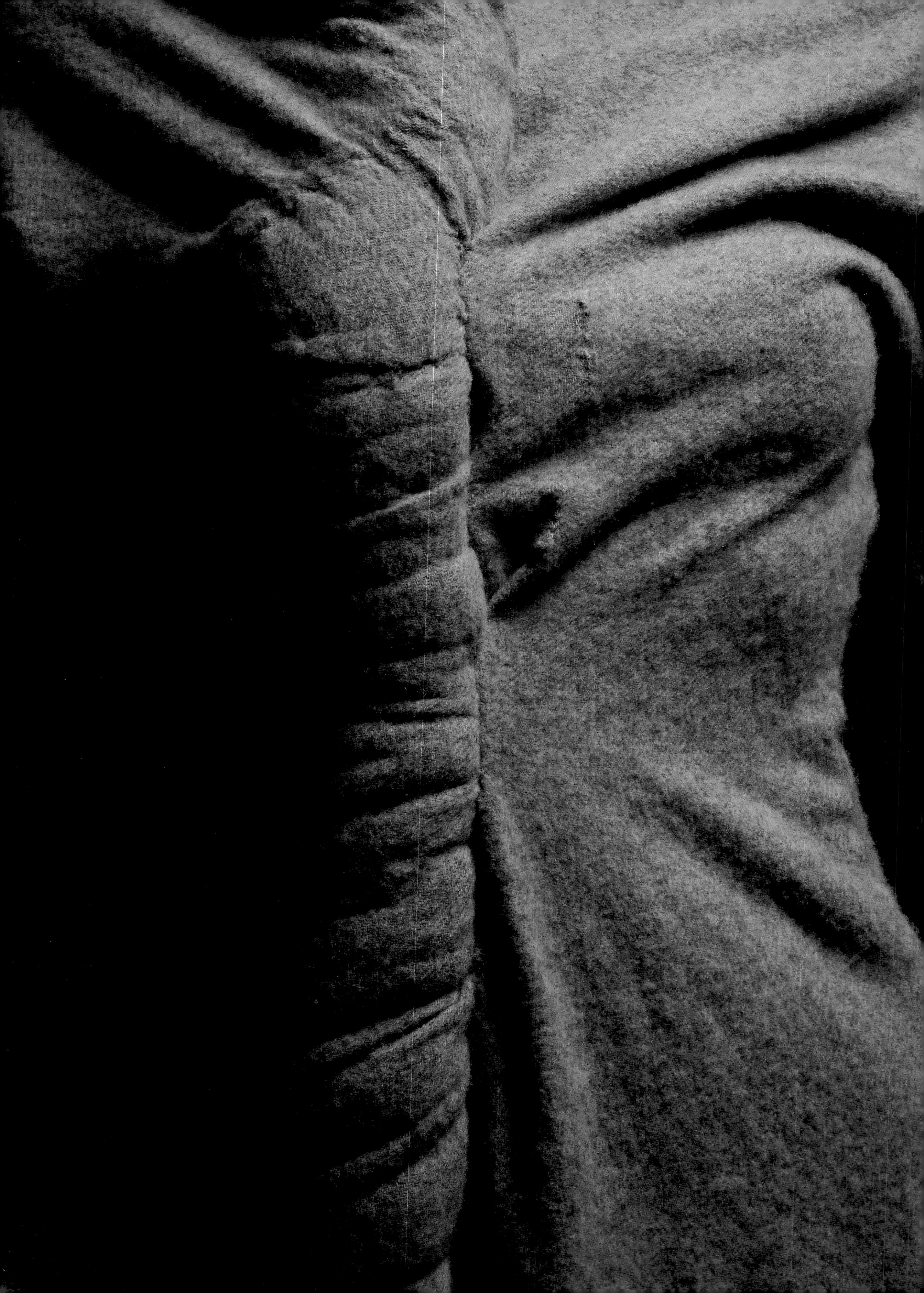

In the fall/winter collection of 1994, Kawakubo exhibited a new idea: a dress that looked as if it had been worn for years, created by washing a dress to give it as shrunk effect. Shown here is a dress where the loose part of garment was twisted, bundled up and sewn together into monstrous lumps, before a shrunk effect was given to the fabric. The fabric is worn, the yarn has come loose, and the result is a dress with an air of unsettling tension.

Rei Kawakubo / Comme des Garçons
Dress
Label: COMME des GARÇONS NOIR
Autumn/Winter 1994

Gray wool-nylon with shrunk effect; fabric twisted in tube shape at front.
Inv. AC9121 94-13-1

This dress looks like a wide cylinder of accordion pleats. The form of the body has completely disappeared.

← **Rei Kawakubo / Comme des Garçons**
Dress
Label: COMME des GARÇONS
Spring/Summer 1998

Off-white cotton lawn base; nine layers of identical fabric are pleated and sewn together as bodice and skirt; the top layer has a print and vinyl coating.
Inv. AC9537 98-3-2A

Interlining is usually only used as an inner material for clothes, but in this case the structure of the outfit features on the outside.

→ **Rei Kawakubo / Comme des Garçons**
Blouse, Skirt and Leggings
Label: COMME des GARÇONS
Autumn/Winter 1998

White cotton broad blouse, beige wool interlining cloth at back-yoke; vest and part of skirt of interlining cloth; navy wool pleated skirt; wool jersey leggings.
Inv. AC 9686 98-18-2AC

Dresses made of paper were worn in Japan during the Kamakura period (1192–1333), and during the Edo period (1603–1867) expensive paper dresses were considered extremely stylish.

This paper dress would probably fit nicely into Japanese tradition. Japanese stencil paper designers created the cut pattern known as *goshoguruma* and *momiji*. Kawakubo thought that this cut pattern, used during production, looked like lace, but thought it a shame that after its use as a stencil the pattern never came out in the open. The use of paper as material for a dress, and the idea of using the cutout pattern itself as the main feature of the dress demonstrate Kawakubo's original point of view where fabrics are concerned.

Rei Kawakubo / Comme des Garçons
Dresses
Label: COMME des GARÇONS NOIR
Spring/Summer 1992

Polyester-rayon-paper with cutwork. Japanese pattern of *goshoguruma* on left, *momiji* on right.
Inv. AC8931 93-25-2AB, AC8930 93-25-1AC
Gift of Comme des Garçons Co., Ltd.

A shape structured in rectangular form. When the wool jersey bow is tied by crossing it at the back, the sides swell a little, and a unique form takes shape. Yamamoto re-examined the relationship between the kimono and the kimono belt, and applied it to the modern wardrobe.

← **Yohji Yamamoto**
Dress
Label: Yohji Yamamoto
Spring/Summer 1995

Black and white silk/rayon jersey and red and gold synthetic brocade of chrysanthemum crest pattern.
Inv. AC9166 94-34

In these pieces created by Kawakubo, although the form is a typical Western European style, the fabric was designed by a Japanese *yuzen* kimono painter. The hem's decoration resembles the *fuki* in kimonos.

→ **Rei Kawakubo / Comme des Garçons**
Dresses
Label: COMME des GARÇONS NOIR
Autumn/Winter 1991

Left: White silk taffeta one-piece dress with hand-painting of pine tree; gold lamé wadded hem.

Right: Black silk taffeta with hand-painting of flying cranes; red wadded hem.
Inv. AC8916 93-23-1124 Gift of COMME des GARÇONS Co., Ltd., AC7076 92-7-4AB

The Japanese designer Yamamoto, known worldwide for his original insight into fashion, has paid the greatest respect to Western-style clothing. After more than 10 years of participating in the Paris collections, in fall/winter 1994 Yamamoto presented various elements of the kimono in their modern-day essence. This set the standard for the so-called "Neo-Japonism" movement.

← **Yohji Yamamoto**
Dress
Label: Yohji Yamamoto
Autumn/Winter 1993

Black wool serge one-piece dress with stitchin-g in white string.
Inv. AC8941 93-30A

→ **Yohji Yamamoto**
Coat Dress
Label: Yohji Yamamoto
Spring/Summer 1995

Light green silk crepe de chine one-piece dress; straight-cut; *shibori* dyeing.
Inv. AC9157 94-30-1

The image of Japan continues to remain inspirational to the designers of the world. In the 1960s Gernreich expressed the kimono through knits. He showed a wide-ranging interest in Japan, and used samurai, sumo, and elementary school uniforms as motifs. In the 1990s, Galliano used transparent fabrics, the micro-mini, and a garter belt to create a sexy geisha girl for modern times. High-quality tailoring techniques can be seen.

← **Rudi Gernreich**
"Kabuki" Dress
Label: Rudi Gernreich Design for Harmon Knitwear
Autumn 1963

White and black wool jacquard knit; check pattern; kimono-like v-neck; sash and sash-band in the same material.
Inv. AC9186 95-3

→ **John Galliano**
Ensembles
Label: John Galliano
Autumn/Winter 1994

Left: Pink silk organdy one-piece dress and sash with floral embroidery.

Right: Black wool one-piece dress and sash covered by lace with floral embroidery.
Inv. AC9115 94-12-1, AC9116 94-12-2, AC9118 94-12-5, AC9119 94-12-6

In the spring of 1994, the Kyoto Costume Institute held the "Japonism in Fashion" exhibition in Kyoto. This looked historically at the influence Japan has had on fashion. In 1996 the exhibit went on to be held in Paris and Tokyo, and in 1998 it went to the United States. Possibly as a result of this exhibition, fashion at the end of the twentieth century saw a worldwide wave of Japonism.

↓ **Consuelo Castiglioni / Marni**
Blouse and Skirt
Label: MARNI
Spring/Summer 2000

Lavender silk georgette blouse with printed frill; skirt of silk and cupra mix fabric with chrysanthemum print and sequin embroidery.
Inv. AC10322 2000-21AB

↘ **Hiroshige Maki / Gomme**
Ensembles
Label: gomme
Spring/Summer 1997

Left: Black polyester jacket with "G"-letter print like family crest; belt of leather strap; black jumpsuit with floral print; vinyl cording.
Inv. AC9383 96-28-2AB

Right: dark brown polyester tunic with "G"-letter print like a family crest; asymmetrical draping; polyester pants.
Inv. AC9385 96-28-4AB
Gift of Maki Hiroshige Atelier Co., Ltd.

→ **Masaki Matsushima**
Dress
Label: MASAKĬ MATSUSHĬMA
Spring/Summer 1997

Left: Black cotton with white scale motif printed on reverse side; one-piece dress.

Right: Black cotton with printed white scale motif; one-piece dress. The right dress was worn over the left dress at his collection.
Inv. AC9469 97-22-2AB
Gift of Masaki Matsushima International Co., Ltd.

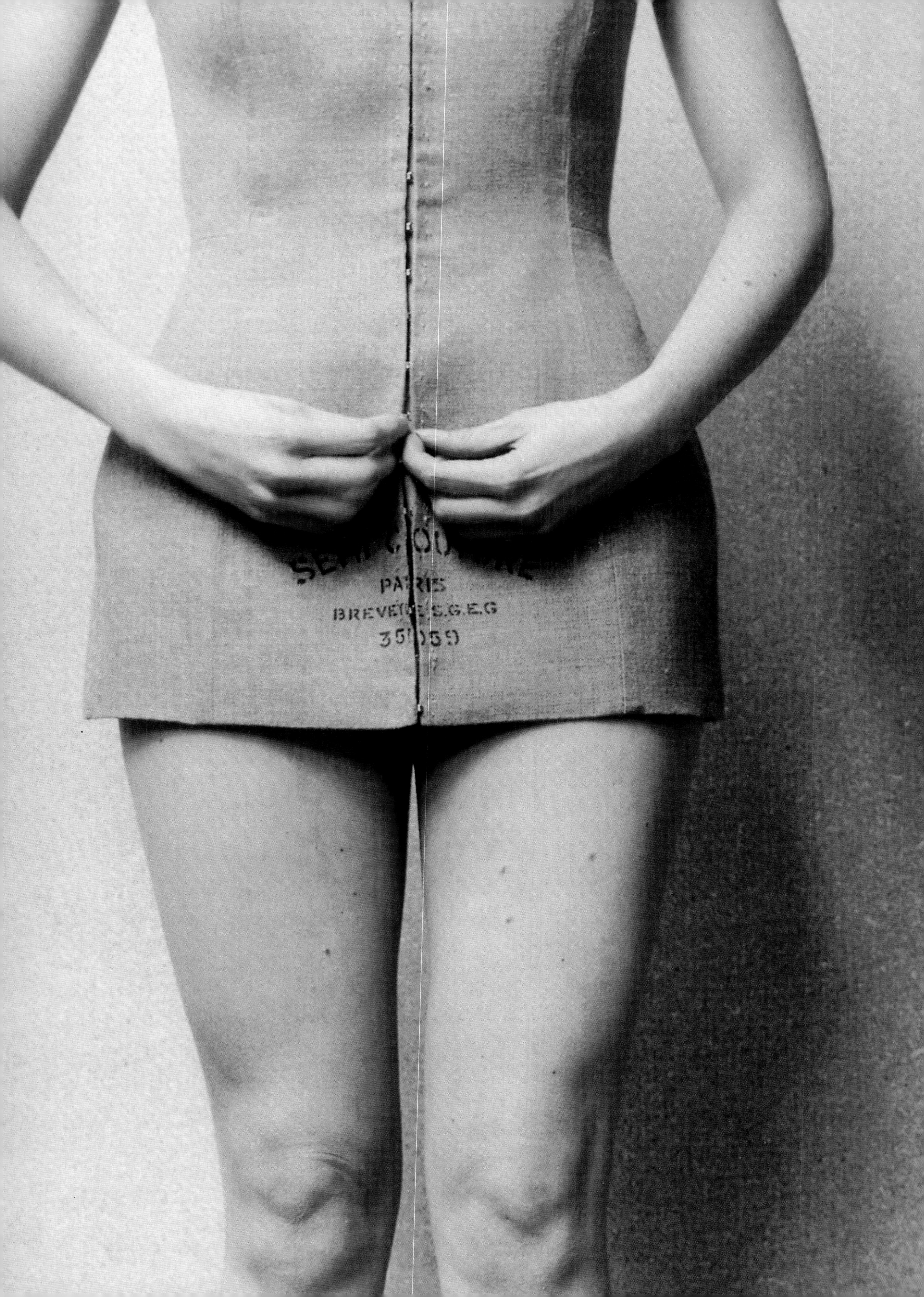
PARIS

The torso dress-form that was used in *haute couture*, created by Stockman, came into production at the end of the nineteenth century, and became indispensable to the mass-production system that developed in the twentieth century. Although each human body is different, the body is classified into one of several sizes when made into a torso form, and is forced to be a standardized body no matter what. In this Margiela jacket, which takes the shape of a Stockman form, the harsh reality is made apparent: in modern fashion, the individual body of each human being is almost completely ignored.

Martin Margiela
Jacket
Label: (white cotton tape)
Spring/Summer 1997

Beige linen used for dress-form; print of "42" at neck, "SEMI COUTURE PARIS BREVETE. S. G. E. G 35059" at hem.
Inv. AC9427 97-7A

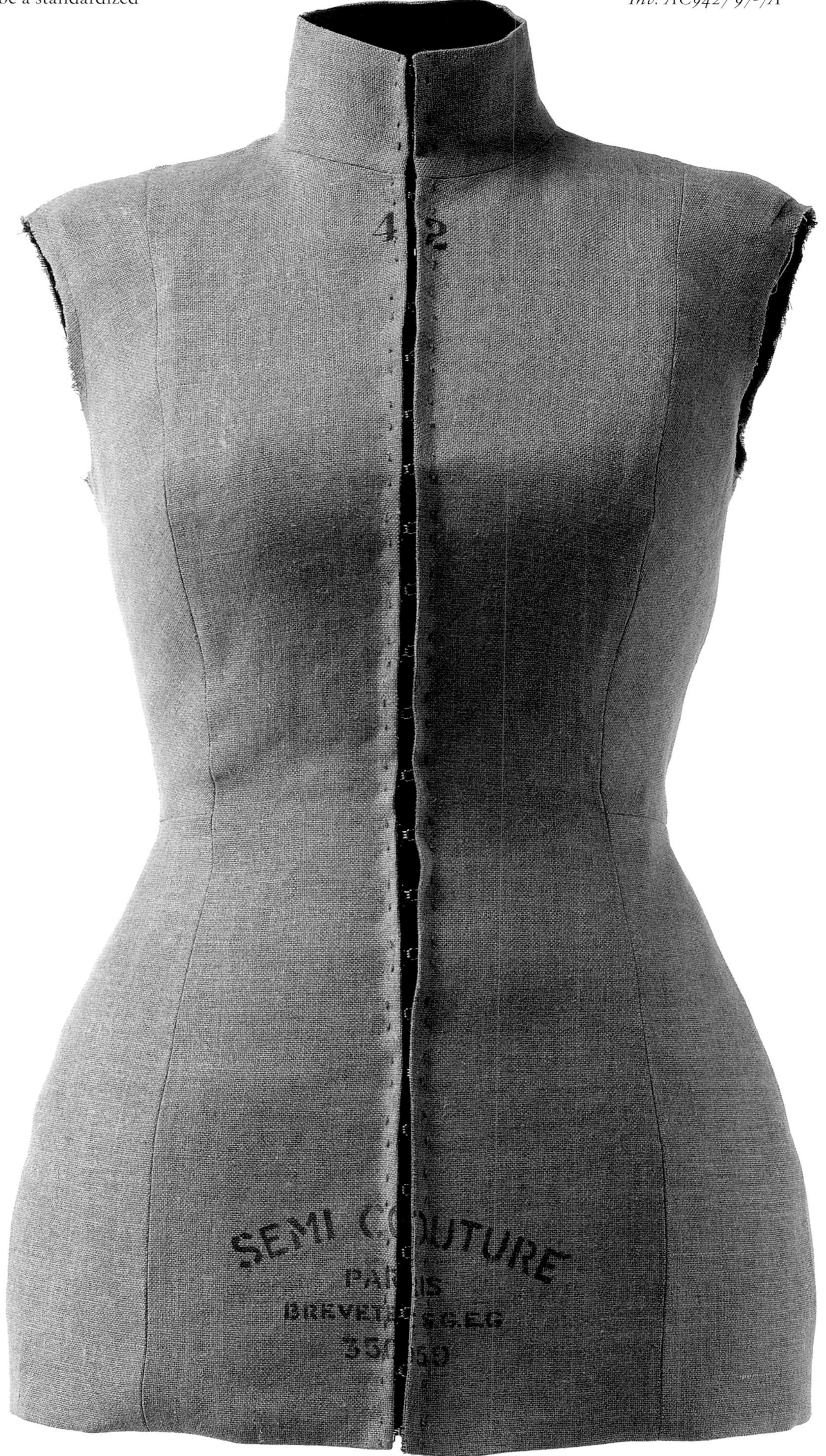

← Jacket by Martin Margiela; Photo: Anders Edström

The Japanese idea of flat-surfaced clothes has had a strong effect on Western fashion, especially in the 1920s and 1980s. Margiela, who embraces the Japanese mentality of Kawakubo and others, presented a show together with Rei Kawakubo in the spring/summer of 1998. The pieces presented included the item shown here. The armholes were moved to the front, and pressed after the sewing process. While hung on a hanger it looks flat, but when it is worn a dimensional shoulder line appears.

← **Martin Margiela**
Jacket
Label: (white cotton tape)
Spring/Summer 1998

Beige polyester; armholes placed forward; pressed after sewing.
Inv. AC9543 98-6-2

The photographic-print style became popular in the 1960s, but with the development of technology a higher quality print was achieved in the 1990s. Seen here is a pattern of the stitches of a knit photographically printed onto tricot, a knit fabric. The slight difference one senses between the photographic print and the actual fabric creates a provocative dissonance between the feel of the texture of the knit, and the feel of the texture of the knit that exists in one's memory.

→ **Martin Margiela**
Cardigan, Pullover, Dress and Belt
Label: (white cotton tape)
Spring/Summer 1996

Brown rayon tricot cardigan; nylon mesh pullover; acetate dress; photo-printing on tops; vinyl belt.
Inv. AC9311 96-6AD

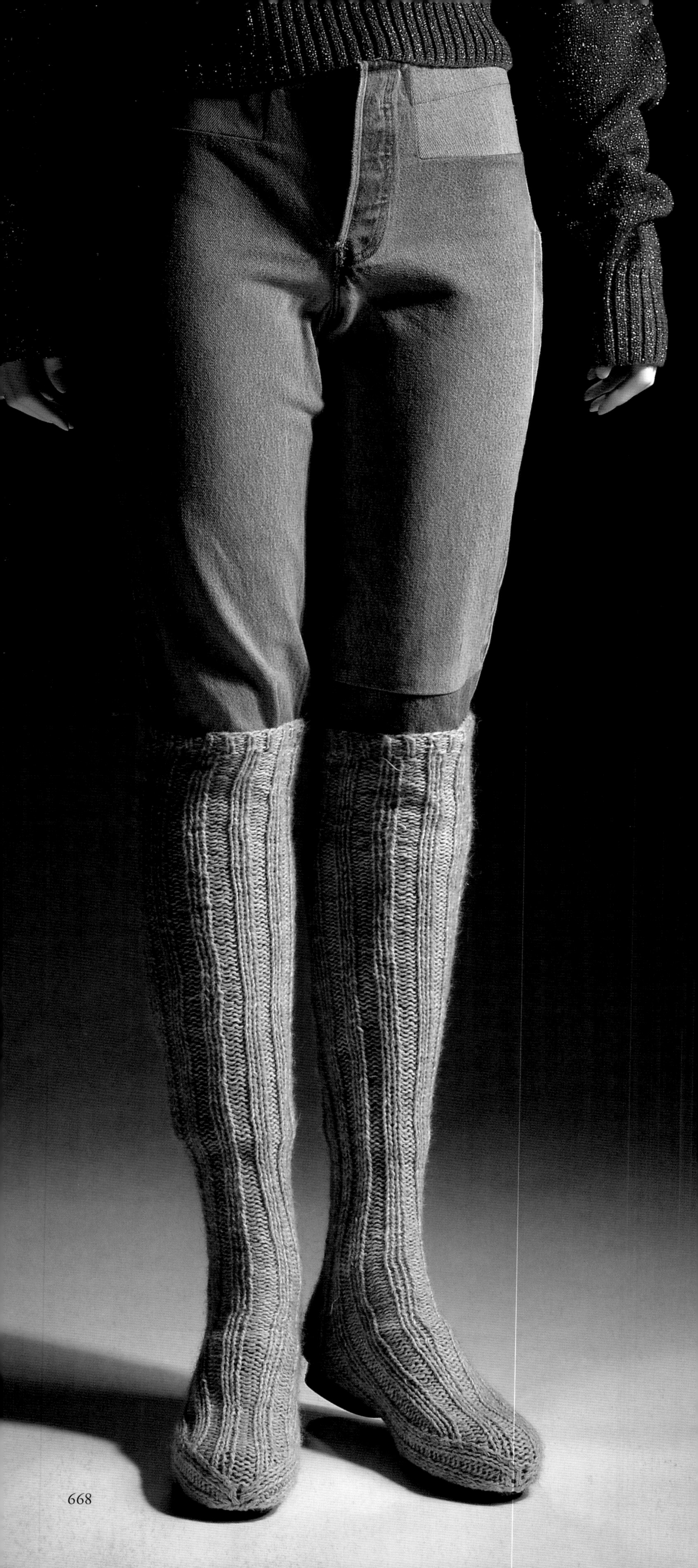

Fashion designers continue to search for varied shapes in fashionable clothing. At the end of the twentieth century, the development of new technologies allowed new shaping methods to be attempted.
On the left, the shape of the dress is determined by the inserted wire. The spiral-shaped wire leads the fabric to create a unique and lively form.
On the right is a skirt that forms a wavy shape, created out of a synthetic fabric with plastic woven into it.

← **Junya Watanabe**
Dress and Skirt
Label: JUNYA WATANABE COMME des GARÇONS
Autumn/Winter 1998

White cotton shirt-dress; skirt of green wool serge, wired inside.
Inv. AC9689 98-18-5AB

→ **Yohji Yamamoto**
Dress
Label: Yohji Yamamoto
Spring/Summer 1999

White polyester printed with gray stripes; quilted.
Inv. AC9739 98-42-3AB
Gift of Yohji Yamamoto Inc.

This dress is shaped neither by darts nor by cutting, but is given its shape through the primitive method of twisting or rolling the cloth.

→ **Yohji Yamamoto**
Dress
Label: Yohji Yamamoto
Spring/Summer 1998

White silk and wool mix satin; twisted fabrics continued to shoulder straps.
Inv. AC9690 98-19A

Designs by Yohji Yamamoto
Spring/Summer 1998
Photo: Peter Lindbergh
Vogue (Italian), January 1998

After his Paris debut with asymmetrical clothes using hanging fabric, Yamamoto returned to a more traditional Western dressmaking style in the mid-1980s. The felt dress on the right has a close resemblance to a nostalgic form based on historical costumes. Through its exaggeration of the back and hips, this dress is trying to create a new recognition of the human body.

Yohji Yamamoto
Dress
Label: Yohji Yamamoto
Autumn/Winter 1996

Black and white felt; black knit under skirt.
Inv. AC9328 96-13-2AB

Wooden parts and hinges, materials normally far removed from clothing, were used in this piece. It seems as if it is trying to escape from the human body, which will always remain the same. This outfit resembles the costume for the role of the manager in *Parade*, a ballet performed by the Ballets Russes in 1917. Pablo Picasso designed the costumes.

Yohji Yamamoto
Vest and Skirt
Label: Yohji Yamamoto
Autumn/Winter 1991

Set of wooden vest and skirt; black wool pieces; jointed with hinges.
Inv. AC9723 98-37-1AL
Gift of Yohji Yamamoto Inc.

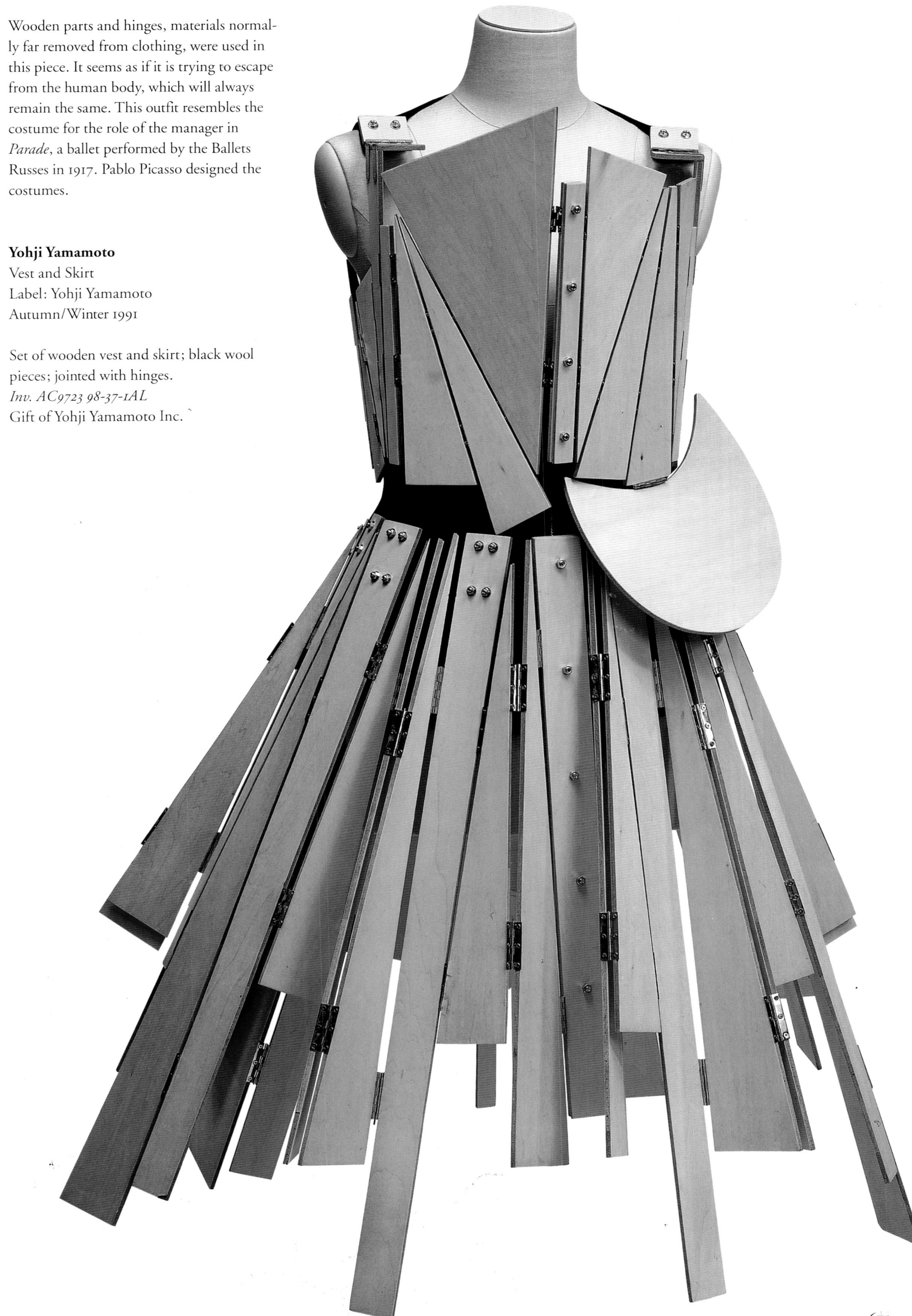

Hussein Chalayan debuted in London in 1994. He looked at the body and clothes from a technological point of view, and has created outfits with an innovative and assured approach. When wearing this corset, the wooden bodice binds to the skin, and it feels as if the metal bolts have been screwed into the body.

Hussein Chalayan
Corset
Label: (curved mark) P' Ben 95
Autumn/Winter 1995

Four wooden pieces; front, back and two sides, joined by metal bolts.
Inv. AC9268 95-42

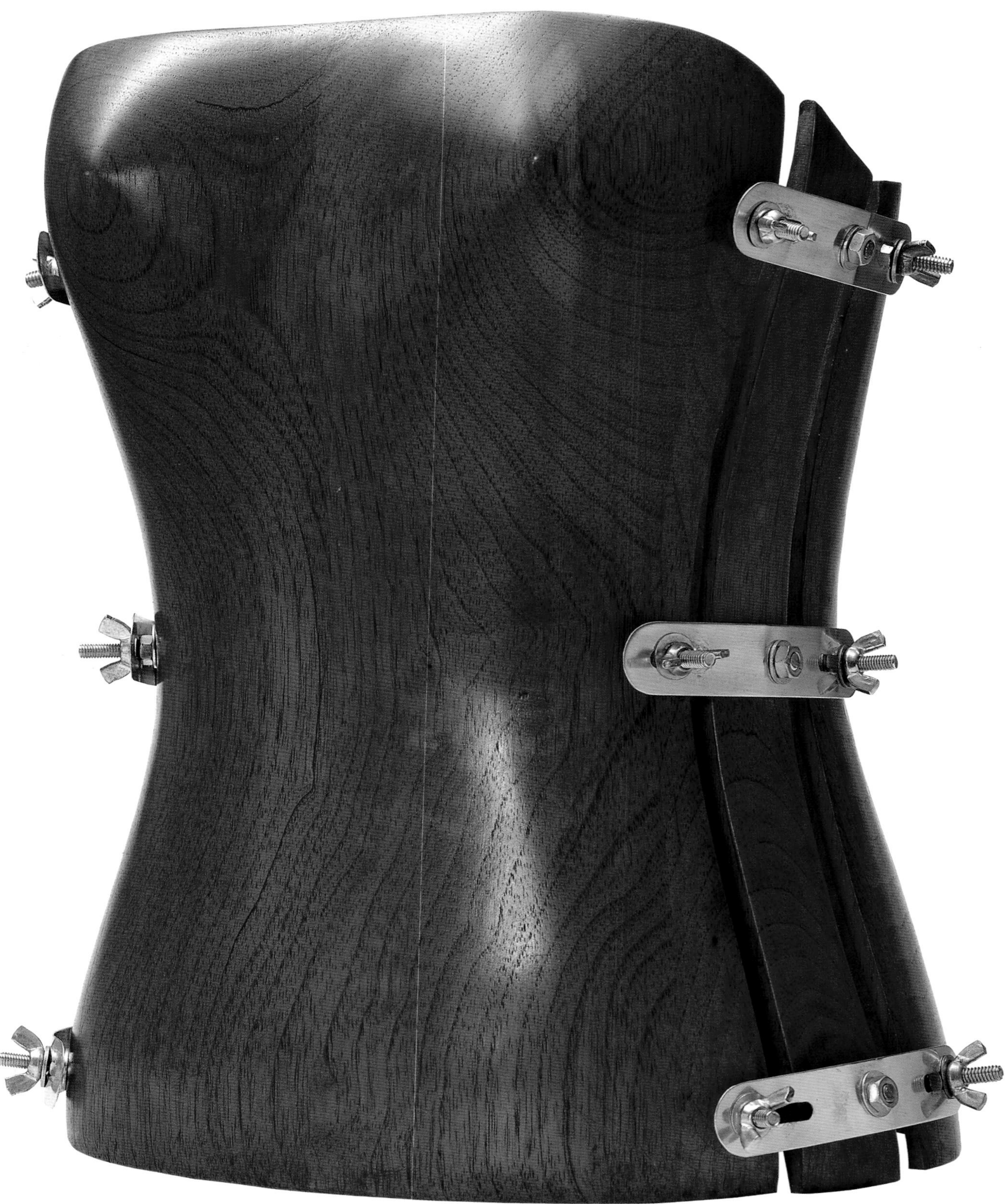

At the end of the twentieth century, a variety of expressions that explored the essence of the skin appeared on the fashion scene. Maurizio Galante made his debut in Milan in 1987 and in Paris in 1991, and is known for presenting a modern style infused with a feeling of warmth and the strength of human life.

On the left is a dress with organdy tubes, which, every time they swing, look like the tentacles of aquatic organisms. This image stimulates the viewer's senses. The pullover on the right uses *shibori*, Japanese twisted and dyed silk fabric, which gives it a feel new to the touch.

← **Maurizio Galante**
Dress
Label: MAURIZIO GALANTE CIRCOLARE
Spring/Summer 1992

Pale green silk organdy dress with fabric tubes in the same material all over.
Inv. AC7616 92-30

→ **Maurizio Galante**
Pullover
Label: MAURIZIO GALANTE
Autumn/Winter 1994

Green *Arimatsu shibori.*
Inv. AC9155 94-28AB
Gift of Mr. Maurizio Galante

The *shibori*, Japanese twisted silk fabric used as an elastic fabric, molds freely and dimensionally to the body through the bias cut.

← **Fukuko Ando**
Dress
Label: Fukuko Ando
1996

Dark green synthetic one-piece dress with *shibori* effect; patchworked red chiffon; scallop stitching.
Inv. AC9404 96-31-2

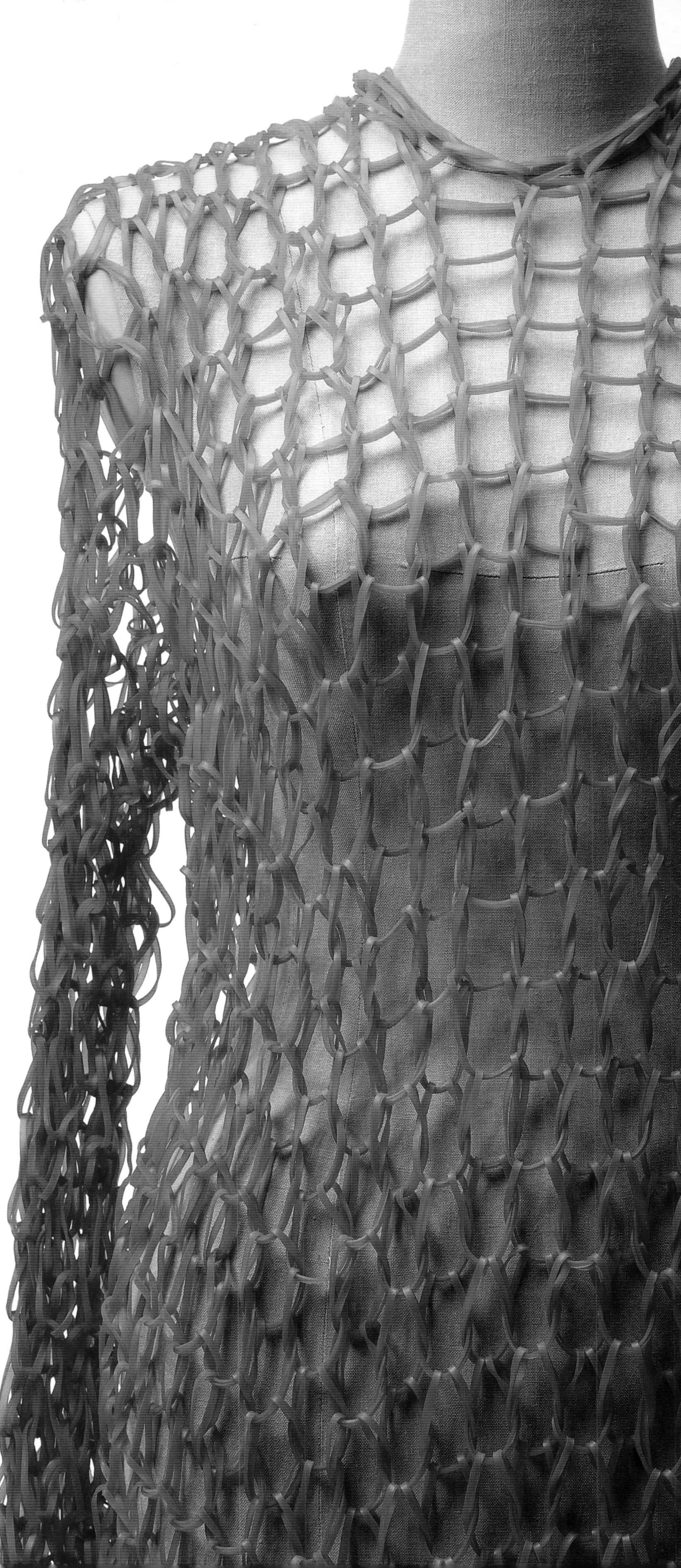

Rubber, which was used for this dress and makes it look like stretched skin, is also the name of Maki's brand, "Gomme" ("rubber" in French). "Gomme" took its name to express the concept of garments covering the body like rubber.

→ **Hiroshige Maki / Gomme**
Dress
Label: none
Autumn/Winter 1993

One-piece dress made of jointed rubber bands.
Inv. AC9388 96-28-7
Gift of Maki Hiroshige Atelier Co., Ltd.

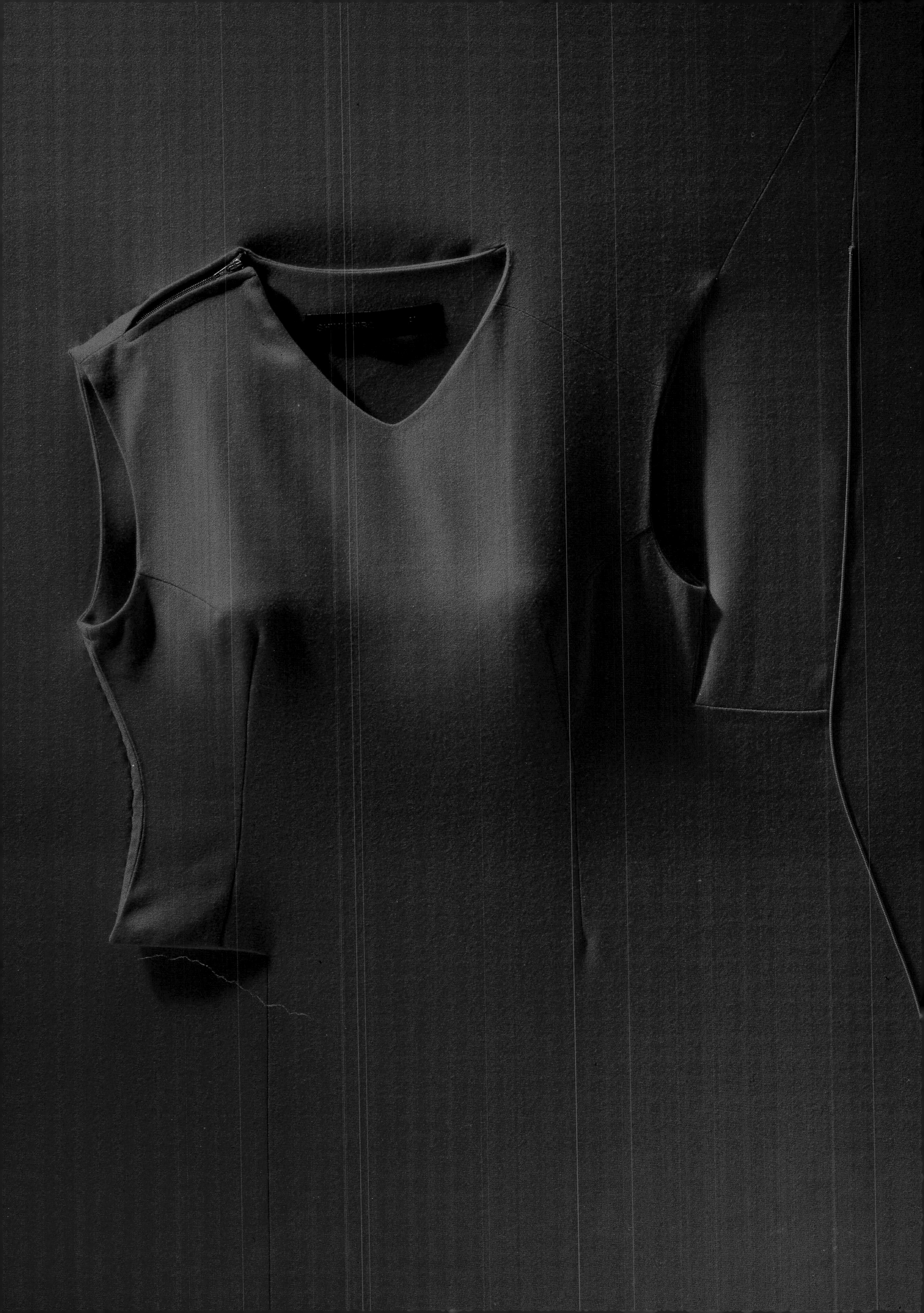

Pages 682/683
At first this looks like a painting, but it is in fact clothing. To wear it, the head and arms go through first, and the fabric covers the front and back. As the loose fabric is rolled inside and zipped up, the flat piece of fabric transforms into a three-dimensional dress.
Arakawa created a new structure for clothing by combining the rolling, folding, wrapping, and zipping techniques for working with fabric.

Page 682
Clothes by Shinichiro Arakawa; Spring/Summer 1998; Photo: Taishi Hirokawa
ZOLA, February 1998

Page 683
Shinichiro Arakawa
Dress
Label: SHINICHIRO ARAKAWA
Autumn/Winter 1999

Red wool twill dress screwed to a panel; rectangular fabric that shapes into a dress by fastening with a zipper.
Inv. AC9773 99-9-2

Fashion in the twentieth century moved in the direction of taking off clothes. At the end of the century clothes became as simple as possible, and instead of wearing clothes, it became fashionable to "wear" the body itself. Cosmetic make-up, piercing and tattoos, all of which are direct forms of decorating the body and have existed since primitive times, became the cutting-edge of fashion at the turn of the century. Takahashi painted body tattoos in places where the skin was not covered by the dress. Clothes had turned into skin, and the border between the skin and clothes was becoming ambiguous.

Jun Takahashi / Undercover
Ensemble
Label: under cover JUN TAKAHASHI
Autumn/Winter 2000

Set of jacket, sweater, skirt, pants, scarf, belt, bag, gloves, stockings and wig; six kinds of material including wool, mohair, fake leather; plaid pattern by paint, print, sequin and bead embroidery.
Inv. AC10377 2000-41-1AN

→→ Clothes by Jun Takahashi; Autumn/Winter 1997; Photo: Taishi Hirokawa
ZOLA, November 1997

世界のコイン
アクセサリー
新宿松竹

In the 1990s, synthetic materials such as paper and non-woven fabric appeared in fashion collections worldwide, looking back to the 1960s.
Prada, which has participated in the Milan collections since 1988, uses 1960s fashion as its base, but also applies the spirit of the 1990s to create a more urban and sensible functional style.
On the right are ensembles by Watanabe, who debuted in Paris in 1994 and is skillful at innovative cutting and the use of synthetic fibers. His adoption of the 1990s taste for bright colors and synthetic fibers, combined with original techniques such as folding and cutting, gave birth to these futuristic outfits.

← **Prada**
Top and Skirt
Label: PRADA
Autumn/Winter 1998

Top of white silk chiffon and organdy, clear plastic panels inside; pleated skirt of non-woven fabric appliquéd with plastic panels.
Inv. AC9714 98-31AB

→ **Junya Watanabe**
Blouse, Tunic and Pants
All-in-one, Tunic and Pants
Label: JUNYA WATANABE COMME des GARÇONS
Spring/Summer 1996

Left: Blouse, Tunic and Pants
Vermilion nylon blouse; pink tunic of non-woven cloth; nylon pants.
Inv. AC9299 96-10-3AB, AC9300 96-10-4B

Right: All-in-one, Tunic and Pants
Blue nylon all-in-one; orange nylon tunic; black nylon pants.
Inv. AC9278 95-47-1AB, AC9279 95-47-2

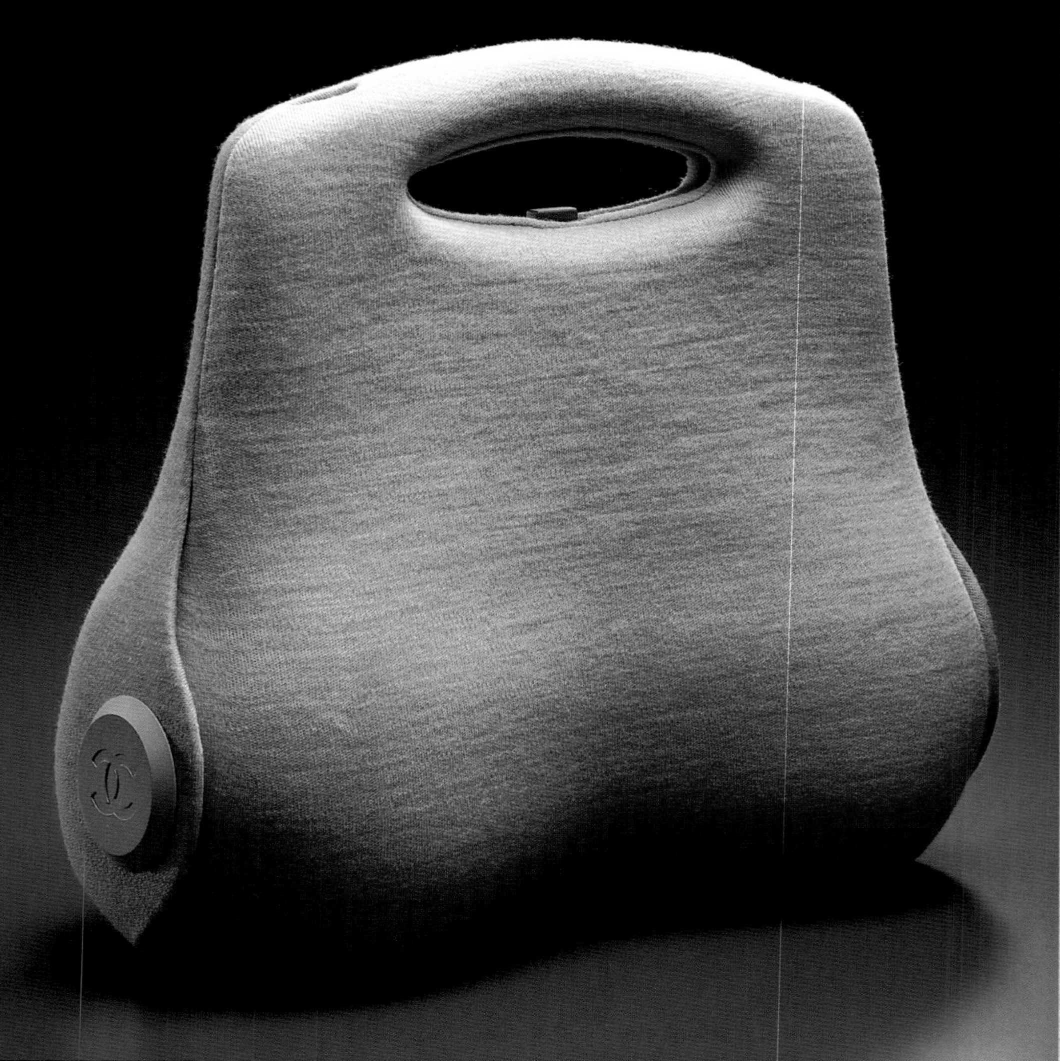

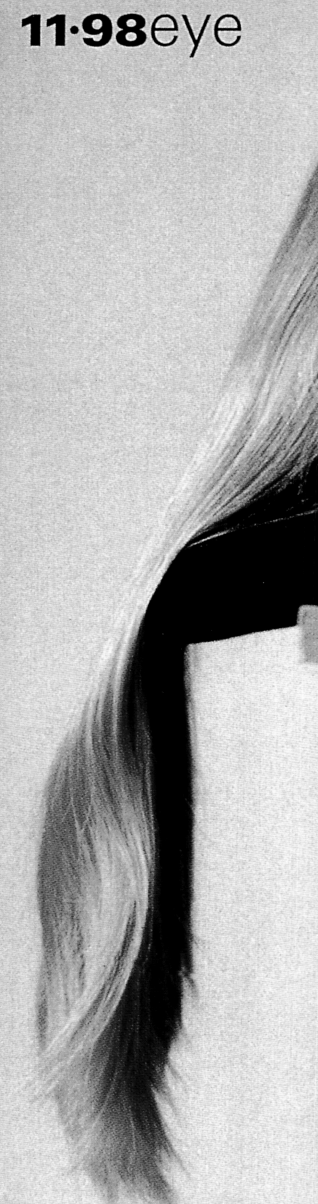

11·98eye

The shape looks either like a breast or a woman's hip. It was created through the most up-to-date technology of inserting polyester into an aluminum frame. The name "2005" comes from the fact that it was "2"years before the twenty-first century; the international dial code "00" was then added, and finally at the end was added the symbolic number of Chanel, "5."

Karl Lagerfeld / Chanel
"2005" Bag
Label: '99-'00 AW
Autumn/Winter 1999

Orange wool jersey; Chanel logo mark.
Inv. AC10111 99-22A

→ Bag by Chanel
Photo: Nathalie Fowler
i-D, November 1998

At the end of the twentieth century, shoe design was finally freed from rigid frameworks. Prada's diffusion brand, Miu Miu, uses the rubber soles that are usually used in sneakers for heeled sandals. The driving shoe-like non-slip tread is functional as well as acting as a decoration.

↓ **Miu Miu**
Sandals
Label: MIU MIU MADE IN ITALY
Autumn/Winter 1999

Green suede with rubber sole.
Inv. AC10373 2000-39AD

Jil Sander, from Germany, debuted in Paris in 1976, and has presented her collections in Milan since 1982. Sander has created essential and high-quality styles for two decades now. This round-silhouette dress made by darts and cutting has an inorganic look.

→ **Jil Sander**
Dress
Label: JIL SANDER
Spring/Summer 1999

Gold polyester jacquard.
Inv. AC9761 99-3

In spring/summer 2000, Watanabe used Japan's leading hi-tech fabric: the super-light, water-resistant microfiber. A wearer of this dress can even run through the city in the rain.
On the right is an outfit made with many layers of ultra-light synthetic fabric. The skirt, which spreads out like a beehive, can be folded flat.

← **Junya Watanabe**
Dress
Label: JUNYA WATANABE COMME des GARÇONS
Spring/Summer 2000

Polyester printed with orange, gray and brown plaid pattern; sewn with tucked clear film all over; matching hood.
Inv. AC10284 2000-6-15

→ **Junya Watanabe**
Jacket and skirt
Label: JUNYA WATANABE COMME des GARÇONS
Autumn/Winter 2000

Red polyester jacket; yellow polyester skirt.
Inv. AC10362 2000-31-9AC

Pages 694/695
Coat by Martin Margiela
Photo: Yoshie Tominaga (FEMME)
Fashion editor: Hiroaki Kamiyama
Hair-make: Katsuya Kamo (mod's hair)
Ryuko Tsushin, November 1999

The nightmare of the earth's atmosphere in danger became a reality at the end of the twentieth century. As a result, clothes whose function was to protect the body came back into the spotlight once again.
Tsumura presented a nylon coat called "Final Home." It has more than forty pockets, suggesting that it could be used as a survival jacket for urban life. For example, if pieces of newspaper are put in these pockets, the coat can become a warm and mobile "home from homes."
Margiela used bed blankets filled with down as fabric for a coat. By putting the cover over it, it can be worn even in rainy weather, and is guaranteed to be warm and lightweight.

← **Kosuke Tsumura**
"Final Home" Coat
Label: FINAL HOME
1994

Nylon, zipper
Inv. AC9420 97-2
Gift of Mr Kosuke Tsumura

→ **Martin Margiela**
Coat
Label: (white cotton tape)
Autumn/Winter 1999

White cotton plain-weave filled with down; brown cotton piping at edge; rectangular shape when unfolded; detachable sleeves.
Inv. AC10188 99-35-1A,CD

Designers and Fashion Houses

Alaïa, Azzedine (b. 1940)
Born in Tunisia. After studying sculpture he worked at the houses of Dior and Guy Laroche in Paris, before going on to start his own label. His work drew much attention in the 1980s, thanks to his radical riveting of leather and jersey, and his use of many zippers. He experimented with the many stretch materials that were developing rapidly at that time, and presented streamlined dresses, mini skirts, and bodysuits in quick succession. With the revival of body-consciousness in the 1980s, he set trends by presenting dresses that fit as tightly as if stuck directly to women's bodies.

Albouy (1938–1964)
A hat shop in Paris famous for decorative baroque-style hats. In 1941, during the German occupation, Albouy made small, beautiful veiled hats out of recycled newspaper. The most famous Albouy work was the *mollusque* ("invertebrate"), and was made without any interlining.

Ando, Fukuko (b. 1964)
Born in Japan, Ando moved to France in 1991. She has been a freelance clothing creator since 1995. Making use of tie-dye techniques and strings made of small slips of cloth, she makes and promotes "clothing that is neither haute couture nor *prêt-à-porter*."

Arakawa, Shinichiro (b. 1966)
Born in Japan. He moved to France in 1989 and showed his first collection in Paris in Spring/Summer 1994. Since Autumn/Winter 1995, he has participated in the Tokyo Collection. His collections often have themes that subvert existing concepts. His approach to the creation of clothing is to regard clothes in the same way as painting or sculpture.

Armani, Giorgio (b. 1934)
Born in Italy. He established his company in 1975, and produced soft tailored suits, using soft materials and interlining, putting his long experience of tailoring men's clothing to good use. His well-tailored suits became very popular worldwide, especially in the U.S., and were a response to the increasing importance of women in society. His works were regarded as the business suits for male and female intellectuals who achieved success, and he dominated fashion circles in the 1980s. Industrializing his delicate cutting and high-standard sewing techniques, he produced epoch-making ready-made clothes.

Babani (1895–1940)
Vitaldi Babani, born in the Middle East, opened his shop in 1895 in Paris. Babani imported and sold artworks and crafts, interior decorations, embroideries, and silks. Around 1904, he sold kimono-style gowns made of Japanese fabric, which became highly renowned. In the 1910s and 1920s he dealt in the works of Fortuny and the fabrics of Liberty & Co., and produced items that bore their influence. He is said to have had embroidery factories in Constantinople (now Istanbul) and Kyoto.

Balenciaga, Cristobal (1895–1972)
Born in Spain. In 1919, he opened his first shop in San Sebastian. Due to the Civil War in Spain, he moved to Paris and set up house there in 1937. After World War II, he presented dresses with abstract-shaped silhouettes, which his masterful cutting and sewing techniques

allowed him to create. He constantly created new shapes, and started to simplify forms in fashion and to focus on materials, well before the 1960s when such concepts became more widespread. His tunic dress, sack dress, baby doll, etc. became the bases of contemporary wear and set in motion the movement toward *prêt-à-porter*. His unique designs and high-level skill worked in perfect harmony and elevated haute couture to the realm of art. He is one of the designers most representative of the twentieth century.

Balmain, Pierre (1914–1982)
Born in France. After training at Molyneux and Lelong, he opened his house in 1945. During the era of material shortages that followed the war, the small-waisted dresses with long, bell-shaped skirts that he presented seemed to prefigure Dior's "New Look" of 1947. Balmain's work was a search for the beauty of elegant, classical figures. Together with Balenciaga and Dior, he was one of the "Big Three" in the heyday of haute couture in the 1950s. *Jolie Madame*, a perfume he presented in 1957, perfectly symbolized his design themes.

Beer (1905–?)
A Parisian house opened by German-born designer Gustav Beer in Paris in 1905. Based on his own concept of fashion, "conservative elegance for conservative customers," he created luxuriously elegant clothes. The clothes were not particularly innovative, but were gorgeously elaborate in all their details and were highly appreciated. One of his most successful promotion activities was to visit big hotels during the tourist season and sell his collections to tourists from abroad.

Beretta, Anne-Marie (b. 1938)
Born in France, she established her own label in 1974. Her works feature moderate colors and simple but constructive and dynamic forms. She took the initiative in *prêt-à-porter* of the 1980s as a new, unique type of designer.

Biba (1964)
A boutique opened in London by the Polish-born designer Barbara Hulanicki (b. 1936), and a symbol of 1960s London fashion. Young people rebelling against authority enthusiastically welcomed Biba's inexpensive, loose-fitting fashion as an alternative to the mainstream elegant style. Biba closed in 1975. In the 1990s, a new syndicate revived the Biba label.

Bruyère (1928)
A house opened in Paris by Marie-Louise Bruyère in 1928. After studying under Callot Sœurs and Lanvin, she became independent. Bruyère presented collections of haute couture until the 1950s, after which they turned to *prêt-à-porter*.

Bulloz (dates unknown)
A house in Paris. Its details are unknown. It was situated at 140, Avenue des Champs-Elysées, Paris, and appeared in *Vogue* several times in the 1910s.

Burrows, Stephen (b. 1943)
Born in the US, he opened his boutique in 1968. He is famous for his unique sense of color, design composition, and above all his *avant-garde* style. He was the first black fashion designer to achieve widespread recognition.

Callot Sœurs (1895–1937)
A Parisian house created by four sisters, Marie, Marthe, Régine, and Joséphine Callot, who were born in France into a Russian family. They started a lingerie and lace shop in 1888 and opened their haute couture *maison* in 1895. As chief designer, the eldest sister, Marie (Mme Gerber), produced beautiful garments with delicate handwork like lace and embroidery. The work of the Callot sisters featured special materials such as antique lace, velvet, and silk from China. They often created works with orientalist themes, in many of which a Japanese influence can be discerned.

Cardin, Pierre (b. 1922)
A Frenchman born in Italy. At the age of 17, he started training in a tailor's shop. He worked for Paquin and Schiaparelli from 1945. At the house of Dior he took part in the creation of the "New Look" that was presented in 1947 and which became so influential. He opened his own house in Paris in 1950. He became dissatisfied with the extravagance and troublesome procedures of haute couture and turned to *prêt-à-porter* in advance of other designers. In the 1960s, he proposed front-opening clothes, closed with zippers to eliminate the sexual differences implied by the direction of lapped closures. In 1964, his innovative, futuristic Space Age Collection won widespread recognition and resulted in increased popularity for his label. He was a pioneer of the licensing industry, and today the name Cardin can be seen worldwide in various different fields. In 1992, he was the first designer to be given a *fauteuil* in the French Academy of Beaux-Arts.

Chalayan, Hussein (b. 1970)
Born in Cyprus, he debuted in London in Autumn/Winter 1994. Since then he has created clothes based on abstract themes of his own invention. He always challenges ready-made concepts in fashion, making restricting outfits for example that ignore the usual relationship between body and clothes.

Chanel, Gabrielle (1883–1971)
Born in Saumur, France and nicknamed "Coco." She started designing millinery in 1909, and in 1913 opened her house at Rue Cambon. In 1916, she presented innovative, functional suits made out of jersey, a cheap material which at the time was normally used for underwear. She firmly established a new active and functional concept of elegance, adapting elements from men's wear. Chanel, who herself was slim and had her hair cut short in a boyish style, greatly influenced fashion circles as a *garçonne*, the new image of an active woman after World War I. After closing her house during World War II, she returned to fashion circles at the age of 71. The "Chanel suit," which was a big hit worldwide in the 1960s, reestablished Chanel's reputation and is now regarded as an icon of 20th-century women's clothing. After her death in 1971, Karl Lagerfeld came to the house as the chief designer and another global Chanel boom took place.

Chloé (1952)
A house established in 1952. At the height of haute couture's prosperity, Chloé pioneered a new *prêt-à-porter* shop. From 1963 to the Spring/Summer Collection in 1984, and from the Spring/Summer Col-

lection in 1993 to the Fall/Winter Collection in 1997, the German designer Karl Lagerfeld (b. 1938) was in charge. Stella McCartney took over as its designer until Spring/Summer 2002. Phoebe Philo is in charge today.

Courrèges, André (b. 1923)
Born in France. After working at the house of Balenciaga, he opened his own house in 1961. Around 1964, he presented the miniskirts worn in the streets in an haute couture collection. The miniskirts that he presented in 1965 showed healthy bare knees and became immensely popular throughout the world. Also in 1963, he designed an evening ensemble with pants, which at the time were taboo in haute couture circles. He seized the wave of body-consciousness which arose in the 1960s, and continuously produced many innovative designs. In the mid-1960s, like Pierre Cardin, he took a "cosmic" look as his theme and designed eye-catching futuristic clothes. In the late 1960s he dealt in *prêt-à-porter* and mass-produced easy-to-wear clothes.

Creed (1710–?)
An exclusive London shop for men's and women's riding habits famous even before the French Revolution. In 1854, they opened a branch in Paris, and the shop was highly renowned for its tailored suits and beautifully sewn women's riding wear. Clients included the British royal family, the Empress Eugénie, and Réjane, a famous actress. The shop was forced to close down during World War II, but after the war, Charles Creed VII (1909–1966) reopened the shop in London. Their elegant and sophisticated classic-style suits regained a reputation there.

Czeschka, Carl Otto (1878–1960)
Born in Vienna. He studied at the Akademie der bildenden Künste, and started his teaching career at schools of industrial arts in Vienna and Hamburg. In the fall of 1905, he joined the Wiener Werkstätte, and continued to participate in it even after moving to Hamburg. He produced furniture, sculpture, lacquer work, textiles and jewelry for the studio.

Delaunay, Sonia (1884–1979)
Born in Ukraine. After studying painting in Saint Petersburg she moved to Paris in 1905. She married a painter, Robert Delaunay, and the couple pursued geometric, rhythmic and abstract expressions strongly influenced by cubism. She came to realize that anything used in daily life could become an artistic work. She attempted to unify art and fashion by reproducing abstract paintings with vivid colors on textiles and tailoring them into clothes of innovative design.

Dior, Christian (1905–1957)
Born in France. He worked as an art dealer, and then trained at Piguet and Lelong. In 1946 he opened his own Paris house, supported by the "Cotton King" Boussac. His 1947 work, with its widely flaring skirt and nostalgic silhouette, was a worldwide sensational and quickly accepted as the "New Look." He revitalized haute couture in Paris, which was losing its prestige due to the war. In the ten years before his death at the age of 52, he consecutively produced the "tulip," "H," "A," "Y" and other lines, and led the contemporary trend of fashion in the 1950s. After Dior's death, Yves Saint Laurent, Marc Bohan, Gianfranco Ferré and other designers successively designed for the house. John Galliano has been in charge of Dior design since 1997.

Doucet, Jacques (1853–1929)
Born in Paris. He developed his family's lingerie shop into a haute couture house. He made elegant dresses with a profusion of lace and other decorations. He was strongly supported by royal families all over the world and by female celebrities in Paris society like Réjane and Sarah Bernhardt. He dealt delicately in fine, light colors and silk materials, and used fur like a light fabric. His style was a model of the elaborate femininity of the *Belle Epoque*. He was well known as a patron of fashion illustrators and as a collector of rococo art, and his discovery of the talent of the young Paul Poiret is legendary. After the death of Doucet, the house was united with Doeuillet, and the house that resulted, Doucet-Doeuillet, lasted until the 1930s.

Dubois (dates unknown)
Details unknown. A French house that sold dresses and coats in the second half of the nineteenth century at 29, Avenue de Wagram, Paris.

Dunand, Jean (1877–1942)
Born in Switzerland. His forte was lacquer work. He was a representative sculptor and decorative artist of the Art Deco movement in France. His first efforts were decorations made of brass, but he then learned a traditional lacquer technique from Japanese industrial artists, and this led him to lacquer on metallic objects. He painted the colors peculiar to Japanese lacquer on geometrical patterns, uniting Art Deco motifs with Eastern coloring. He is renowned for his meticulous, complex works like. his decorative technique of mixing small chips of eggshells in lacquer.

Mrs. Evans (dates unknown)
Details unknown. In the 1880s, her house was at 52 & 53 Sloane Street, London.

Fath, Jacques (1912–1954)
Born in France, he opened his house in 1937. His house grew to a considerable size after World War II. In 1948, it tied up with Joseph Halpert Inc., a large American manufacturer of ready-made clothes, and was one of the first to move into *prêt-à-porter.* Fath became especially famous in the United States. He specialized in making clothes with soft lines and structured shapes. The house closed in 1957.

Flögl, Mathilde (1893–1950)
Born in Austria, Flögl studied at the Akademie der bildenden Künste and became a member of the Wiener Werkstätte. From 1916 to 1931 she was an independent creator of woodcraft, ceramics, cloisonné ware, glass decoration, accessories, clothing, textiles, wallpaper, etc.

Ford, Tom (b. 1961)
Born in Texas, Tom studied at the Parsons School of Design, New York. He joined Italian house Gucci in 1990 and became its creative director in 1994. Gucci's switch to sexy modern style was largely thanks to his re-mixing of various elements of the 1960s and the 1970s. Since 2001, he has also designed for the *prêt-à-porter* lines of Yves Saint Laurent.

Fortuny, Mariano (1871–1949)
Born in Spain. Fortuny was active in various fields, including painting and the design of clothes, stage sets, and lighting. In 1889, he moved to Venice, and in the

following decade he started creating textiles and clothes on which motifs of the Middle Ages, the Renaissance and the Orient were stenciled in gold and silver. His works are thought to be one of the leitmotifs of Proust's *Remembrance of Things Past*. Around 1907 he began to make the "Delphos", a dress in the style of the ancient Greeks lapping delicately pleated Japanese and Chinese silk cloth. The pleats hanging from the shoulders smoothly covered the whole body in a remarkably sensual manner, and the result was the creation of a brand-new form. The body-conscious forms that Fortuny invented prefigured 20th century fashion trends, and continue to exert their influence even now.

Galante, Maurizio (b. 1963)
Born in Italy. In 1987, he made his debut in Milan. He first presented his collection in Paris in Fall/Winter 1991, and in Fall/Winter 1993, he joined the haute couture circuit. His work seeks simple forms, while simultaneously exploring new fabric expressions through the use of special materials.

Gallenga, Maria Monaci (1880–1944)
Born in Italy. She started producing dresses in 1914, and opened her ateliers in Rome and Florence in the early 1920s. She moved to Paris in 1927. She was committed to the Pre-Raphaelites, and continuously made "medievalist" dresses with stencil prints influenced by Fortuny. In 1925, her stencil prints received a gold prize at the Exposition des Arts Décoratifs. She retired in 1938.

Galliano, John (b. 1960)
An Englishman, born in Gibraltar. In 1984, his graduation collection at St. Martin's School of Art, London, attracted a great deal of attention. He moved to Paris for the Fall/Winter season of 1990. He was a designer for Givenchy in 1996, and then moved to Dior in 1997. He turns historical costume and ethnic wear into *avant-garde* street fashion. He is also known for the dramatic stage direction of his spectacular shows.

Gaultier, Jean-Paul (b. 1952)
Born in Paris. After working at Cardin and Patou, he presented his first *prêt-à-porter* collection in Paris in 1976. Since then he has presented fashion with a clear social message. At the Spring/Summer Collection in 1983, he recreated underwear as outerwear with the corset, which historically was a typical woman's undergarment. The underwear-fashion that he went on to produce is now established firmly as functional, liberated women's clothing. At the Spring/Summer Collection in 1985, he presented androgynous fashion, blurring the boundaries of sexual differences in clothing. With his free imagination, he reconfigured historical clothes and non-Western costume into astonishingly fresh styles. He launched his haute couture collection at the Spring/Summer Collection in 1997. He elegantly unites street and traditional fashion with the very best techniques and materials.

Gernreich, Rudi (1922–1985)
Born in Austria. A former dancer and costume designer, he started his career as a fashion designer in New York in 1948, before branching out on his own in 1958. After the highly constructed fashion of the 1950s, he led the trend toward a more youthful and body-liberating fashion. Beginning in the 1960s, he produced works emphasizing the body itself. In 1964, the "Monokini," his topless bathing suit, caused a scandal, and in the following years he continued to present works that strongly represented his new concept of the body, like 1965's "no-bra bras". In the 1970s, he produced unisex fashions that eliminated sexual differences. He attempted to liberate the body by his own unique approach, ignoring conventional concepts.

Gigli, Romeo (b. 1950)
Born in Italy. He presented his first collection at the Spring/Summer Milan Collection in 1983. His early works, which softly wrapped women's bodies with his distinctive deep colors, were in opposition to the strong image of contemporary Milan fashion, which at the time had its emphasis on large padded shoulders. In Fall/Winter in 1989 Gigli started presenting collections in Paris, where he produced brightly-colored, decorative works. His work is consistently influenced by ethnic styles.

Givenchy (1952)
A house opened in 1952 by French-born designer Hubert de Givenchy (b. 1927). Female celebrities all over the world such as Audrey Hepburn loved his refined and elegant style. Givenchy is one of the most representative *maisons* of the golden age of haute couture. After Givenchy's retirement in 1995, John Galliano took over as the label's designer, before being succeeded by Alexander McQueen. From Spring/Summer 2002, Julien MacDonald will be in charge of design for Givenchy.

Grès, Alix (1899–1993)
Born in Paris, and usually known simply as Madame Grès. After giving up her dream to become a sculptor, she opened her house, Alix, in 1934. She closed it during World War II (1939), but reopened again in 1942 under her husband's pseudonym "Grès". She was renowned for delicate dresses with beautiful drapes of wide silk jersey. She pursued the perfectly molded beauty of ancient Greek sculptures with their superbly beautiful drapery.

Gucci (1921)
Italian leather fashion house. In 1921, Guccio Gucci opened a saddlery in Florence, and by the 1950s, the shop had developed into one of the most representative of all Italian labels. Business slumped after the 1970s, but in 1994, Tom Ford, an American designer, became the company's creative director and supervised all Gucci designs. The traditional Gucci label was elegantly reborn as an avant-garde and exclusive brand.

Hechter, Daniel (b. 1938)
Born in France, he opened his first boutique in 1962. In 1966, working with Scott, an American paper manufacturer, he presented a paper dress made out of non-woven fabric, which drew widespread attention as an avant-garde work. He is renowned for his use of vivid colors and his refined and practical style inspired by sportswear and work clothes. He led the *prêt-à-porter* wave in the late 1960's and early 1970s.

Iida Takashimaya (1831)
A Japanese store. In 1831, Shinshichi Iida I started a shop selling used clothes and cotton in Karasuma, Kyoto. The shop later began to deal in fabrics for kimono. They opened their Tokyo quarters and

Yokohama branch for export in 1900, and set up a joint-stock corporation in 1918. In 1922, they started to manage in the style of a modern department store from their new store in Osaka. They took the initiative in the invention of commodities for foreigners, and enthusiastically presented their goods at various world exhibitions. They also sold silk fabric designed for Western clothes or gowns in kimono style for foreign tourists at their shops in Japan. In 1899, they set up an office in Lyons, and founded Takashimaya Iida Inc., an independent company that grew out of their export section. Takashimaya is still one of the most representative department stores in Japan today.

Jenny (1909–1940)
A Parisian house opened by Jeanne-Adèle Bernard (1872–1962), known as Jenny. Her works were elegant but simple and cozy to wear. Skillful management brought the house worldwide fame. The house was still popular during World War I, but in the 1930s, its prosperity declined. It closed in 1940.

Kawakubo, Rei (b. 1942)
Born in Japan. In 1975, Kawakubo presented her collection labeled Comme des Garçons in Tokyo. 1981 saw the debut of her first Paris Collection. At the Spring/Summer Paris Collection in 1983, her "rag-picker" look caused a global sensation. Her method of creating clothes is different from her predecessors, and embodies a uniquely Japanese aesthetic: she uses bare materials, and creates by removing decoration from clothes rather than adding it She has continued to question fashion, which is a constantly flowing, non-stop fluid phenomena (i. e. our unconscious acceptance of the current aesthetic sense), and creates new things which have been seen before. Kawakubo's works violently destabilize the fixed ideas of viewers, and exerted a great influence on the younger generations of designers who emerged after the 1980's.

Khanh, Emmanuelle (b. 1937)
Born in Paris. After working as a fashion model, she started her designing career in 1961. She worked for many shops as a designer, and presented her own *prêt-à-porter* collection for the first time in 1964. She established her own label in 1970. She intentionally went against haute couture, and led *prêt-à-porter* by taking the initiative in offering cheaper, more casual, ready-to-wear clothes for young people. She is well known for works that make use of handicraft techniques like appliqué and embroidery.

Kumagai, Tokio (1947–1987)
Born in Japan. After 1970 he worked mainly in Paris. He presented his first men's collection in 1980, and then went on to work as a shoe designer on a large scale. Characteristically, his works were unique designs, like fine works of art created with great freedom of imagination. He proposed the concept of shoes as artworks that can actually be used in daily life.

Lacroix, Christian (b. 1951)
Born in France. After working at Patou and other companies, he opened his own haute couture house in 1987. In the late 1980s, when simple or minimalist styles overwhelmed fashion circles, his daring, flamboyant decoration and vivid colors breathed new life into fashion. Since 1989, he has presented *prêt-à-porter*.

Laforcade (dates unknown)
Details unknown. A house active in the 1880s at 59 Fifth Avenue, New York City.

Lagerfeld, Karl (b. 1938)
Born in Hamburg, Germany and moved to Paris in 1952. After working at haute couture *maisons* such as Pierre Balmain, he was active as a designer for the houses of Fendi, Chloé and others from the 1960s onwards. He is known for his edgy sense that always catches the latest trends. He became the design director at the house of Chanel in 1983 and reformed its traditional image. In 1984, he launched a collection under his own name for the first time.

Lanvin, Jeanne (1867–1946)
Born in France. She opened a millinery store in Paris in 1888 and a shop specializing in matching mother-and-daughter garments in 1890, and this latter shop developed into a house of haute couture. She presented "robes de style," with flowing skirts and small waists inspired by eighteenth-century designs, and "picture dresses" based on Victorian shapes with lavish embroideries. At a time when other designers were heading towards modernism, her romantic creations were highly appreciated. Her works feature an elegant, sophisticated style supported by fine craftsmanship and magnificent embroidery. Her recurring use of a specific shade of blue led to it eventually bearing her name, and being known as "Lanvin blue." The house is still active today.

Le Monnier (1921–?)
A millinery shop opened in 1921 by Jeanne Le Monnier, who was born in Paris in 1887. It was at 231, Rue St Honoré, Paris. Le Monnier's beautiful embroideries and cutouts had an excellent reputation, and they had many customers, especially in the 1930s.

Lelong, Lucien (1889–1958)
Born in Paris, he set up his house in 1919. He was highly admired for his technique, and works that emphasized the beauty of the material rather than the originality of the design. He began to produce *prêt-à-porter* clothing in 1934. He was the president of the Chambre Syndicale de la Couture from 1937 to 1947, and made great efforts to ensure the survival of Parisian couture during World War II.

Herbert Levine, Inc. (1948–1975)
A shoe production company founded in the United States in 1948 by the husband and wife team of Herbert and Beth Levine. The fantastic and unique designs which Beth Levine created with joy and pop inspiration were very popular, especially in the United States.

Liberty & Co. (1875)
In 1875, Arthur L. Liberty (1843–1917) opened East India House, dealing in oriental silk and handicrafts in London. He later changed its name to Liberty & Co. In 1884, Liberty set up a new section for women's clothing, and promoted fashion that sought universal beauty. In 1889, they participated in the Great Exhibition in Paris and acquired great popularity; they exerted a strong influence on the formation of Art Nouveau. They were the first in the world to propose the concept of "life style," and established the brand-new "Liberty style," imparting artistic

quality to everyday commodities. In the twentieth century, the company was at the forefront of textile technology, using for example wood-block printing to produce paisley patterns.

Likarz, Maria (1893–1971)
She studied under Josef Hoffmann and other professors at the School of Arts and Crafts in Vienna (Akademie der bildenden Künste), and joined the Wiener Werkstätte during 1912–1914 and again during 1920–1931. She created works of graphic design, pottery and *cloisonné* ware. She also participated in the production of a book of fashion sketches, *Die Mode 1914/15*.

Linker, Amy (dates unknown)
Details unknown. Her house was in Rue Auber, Paris. Her works and advertisements appeared in fashion magazines between the 1910s and the 1950s.

Lucile (Lady Duff Gordon) (1863–1935)
Born in London. Lucille opened a shop for women's clothing with her mother in the 1890s, and went on to open branches in New York, Paris, and other cities. Her shops had many high-class customers. The style of her works was romantic and dramatic.

Maki, Hiroshige (b. 1957)
In 1989, he started his own label, Gomme, after working at Y's, a Japanese label by Yohji Yamamoto. *Gomme*, the French term for "rubber," represents the theme of his designs: his aim is to produce clothes that fit as closely as rubber body-wraps. He debuted in the Tokyo Collection in 1993, and in the Paris Collections in 1998. He tries to produce clothes that express reactions to body movements, and show the beauty of the body without hiding its individual characteristics.

Margiela, Martin (b. 1957)
Born in Belgium. After graduating from the Antwerp Royal Academy of Arts, he worked under Jean-Paul Gaultier as an assistant designer beginning in 1984. He then made his own debut at the Spring/Summer Paris Collections in 1988. His style took the lead in the movement to the grunge look in the early 1990s. For example, he made clothes of deconstructed items bought at flea markets or roughly painted clothes, and showed them loosely worn in layers. His work is a challenge to the fashion system, which continually produces new things; he creates clothes from his unique point of view, and he recycles used garments and remakes his own former works. Nor does he follow the traditional style of the catwalk, but presents his own works with innovative stage direction. As he consistently maintains his own unique, avant-garde style, Belgian fashion has acquired new global respectability. Since the Autumn/Winter Collections in 1998, he has concurrently been a creative director for women's *prêt-à-porter* line of Hermès.

Marni (1994)
A brand established in 1994 by the Swiss-born designer Consuelo Castiglioni, who had worked in her father-in-law's fur company. The style of Marni is romantic with soft colors. In opposition to contemporary urban minimalist fashion, they have created clothes with a handcrafted look, expressed with frills, patchwork, embroidery, etc., and their styles have drawn much attention.

Jane Mason & Co. (dates unknown)
Details unknown. The house was at 159 & 160 Oxford Street, London.

Matsushima, Masaki (b. 1963)
Born in Japan. In 1985, Matsushima joined Tokio Kumagai International Co. Ltd. After taking over the late Kumagai's position as a designer, he presented his own label's collection in Spring/Summer 1993. Since Spring/Summer 1995, he has participated in the Paris Collections. He always tries to seek out innovative and unique materials.

McCardell, Claire (1905–1958)
Born in the US. In 1940, she began to design clothes for her own label at Townley Frocks Inc., a ready-to-wear company in New York. She sought to create comfortable clothes that made body movements seem beautiful. The diaper-wrap swimsuit presented in 1937 became her basic style and developed into a romper-shaped one. Her style was simple and purposeful, making use of then-neglected materials like cotton, denim, gingham, jersey, and so on. In the 1950s, she blurred the boundaries between day and night clothes, and created evening dresses made of calico and playsuits of silk. Her works cultivated the concept of casual wear and established the fresh and innovative young "American Look." Her practical and simple wear with its plain construction was a great influence on the later development of ready-to-wear clothing.

McQueen, Alexander (b. 1969)
Born in England. After learning tailoring on Savile Row, he debuted with his own label at the collections in 1993. At the age of 27, McQueen took over the house of Givenchy, beginning with the Spring/Summer Collection in 1997, and continued through the Autumn/Winter Collection in 2001. McQueen's unique and innovative creations led to a Givenchy revival. His works feature structural silhouettes, such as his crisply tailored suit.

Miu Miu (1994)
Prada's label started for the younger generation as a diffusion line in 1994.

Miyake, Issey (b. 1938)
Born in Japan. Miyake presented his first collections in New York in 1971 and in Paris in 1972. Since the presentation of "A Piece of Cloth" in 1976, where Miyake first showed his trademark grasp of the relationship between two-dimensional fabrics and the three-dimensional human body, this has been the major concept behind his design. Since 1988, he has been creating clothes with pleats. His "Pleats Please" can be regarded as high-quality industrial products that combine material, form, and function in a uniquely organic manner. The works of Pleats Please combine practicality and artistic quality, and suit the lifestyles of contemporary women. At the Spring/Summer Collection in 1999, he presented "A-POC," which fuses state-of-the-art computer technology with knitting, a traditional technique of clothing creation. Miyake considers the T-shirt and jeans to be an ideal type of clothes, and is committed to clothes that function in our daily lives and can be mass-produced. Because of this his work is admirably suited to contemporary life.

Molyneux, Edward (1891–1974)
Born in England. In 1919, Molyneux opened his house in Paris. In the late 1930s he was based in London but he returned to Paris after 1945. His high-class clientele, which included many actresses, were attracted by his simple forms and elegant and sophisticated styles. Although he retired in 1950, he reopened his shop in Paris in 1965 and dealt in ready-to-wear in the United States.

Montana, Claude (b. 1949)
Born in France. After a career that included working as a designer for a leather production company, he presented his first collection in 1977. He produced dynamic and powerful work for working women, who were making inroads into business in the 1980s. His strong silhouette with large square shoulders led contemporary fashion, with other designers such as Thierry Mugler.

Mugler, Thierry (b. 1948)
Born in France. Mugler made his debut at the Spring/Summer Paris Collections in 1975. His works feature a sexy, body-conscious style and emphasize women's bodies. Mugler's sharp and powerful silhouette, typically featuring broad shoulders and a shaped waist, was overwhelmingly popular in the 1980s, a time that demanded a strong image of women. His creations are also famous for their vivid colors, daring cutting, and frequent use of unusual hard-edged materials like metal or reptile skin.

Paquin, Jeanne (1869–1936)
Born in France. After training at Rouff, she opened her house in Paris in 1891. Her luxurious, romantic, well-tailored dresses with drapes were highly prized by rich women and actresses in fashionable circles in the early twentieth century. Her house was typical of the time. She was the chief director of the clothing division in the Great Exhibition in Paris in 1900. In advance of other designers, she opened branches in many cities across the world, starting in London. Her house was also famous for its lingerie division and its large-scale fur section. The house continued after her retirement in 1920, and closed in 1954.

Patou, Jean (1880–1936)
Born in France. In 1912, he opened Maison Parry, his women's clothing shop in Paris. After serving in World War I, he opened his salon, called Jean Patou, in 1919. He designed clothes for the tennis star Suzanne Lenglen in the early 1920s, and pioneered the field of fashionable sportswear. His dresses and suits designed in the spirit of sportswear were embraced by active women in the 1920s, who were known as *garçonnes*. He worked with the French textile manufacturer Bianchini-Férier and others to develop new materials for swimsuits and sportswear.

Peche, Dagobert (1887–1923)
Born in Austria. Peche began to work at the Wiener Werkstätte in 1915, and went on to be on of the most important designers of the late period there. Peche created in a variety of areas – interior decoration, stage arts, silverware, embroideries, clothes, etc, and nowadays his unique and energetic decorative style is once again highly appreciated.

Perugia, André (1895–1977)
Born in Italy and grew up in Nice, France. He trained under his father, who was a shoemaker, until the age of 16. Early in his career, he designed shoes for Poiret, and was well regarded. In 1920, he became independent in Paris and provided his artistically designed shoes for Chanel, Schiaparelli, and so on. After World War II, he continued to make shoes for top couturiers.

Piguet, Robert (1901–1953)
Born in Switzerland. After training in Paris from 1918, he became independent in 1933. He was active mainly in the 1930s, and created romantic-styled and slim-shaped long dresses and suits. He was intimate with writers and artists, and made many clothes for theatrical dramas.

Pingat, Emile (dates unknown)
Details unknown. He opened his house in the 1860s. His main period of activity was between 1860 and 1896, which coincided with the peak period of Worth, another prominent designer. His elegant works, expressions of his delicate sensibilities, were popular with Americans.

Poiret, Paul (1879–1944)
Born in Paris, he worked at Doucet and Worth, before setting up his own house in 1903. In 1906, he presented a straight-shaped, high-waisted dress, which released women from the bondage of corsets. Influenced by *Japonisme* and the Ballets Russes, he created a succession of oriental fashions – the kimono coat, hobble dress, lampshade style and so on. Due to his extravagant, dramatic works in bold colors, he earned the nickname "The Sultan of Fashion." In the early twentieth century, he keenly grasped the trends of the age, and led fashion in a new direction. He was also known as the founder of the Ecole Martine, a textile workshop for young girls, and was a great supporter of many young artists such as Raoul Dufy. His influence rapidly declined after World War I.

Porter, Thea (b. 1927)
Born in Syria, she moved from place to place in the Middle East, before finally arriving in London in 1966. Porter's well-known style contains elements of various tastes, such as oriental, Gothic, Victorian, etc. In particular, her work with ethnic embroidery and decorations and soft silhouettes synchronized with the hippie movement of the late 1960s, and became especially popular in the United States.

Prada (1913)
Prada, an Italian fashion house that originally dealt in leather products, took on a new lease of life when Miuccia Prada (b. 1949) took over in 1978 and presented functional nylon bags. In 1988, she introduced her first *prêt-à-porter* line. Her clothes are modern remixes that retain the essence of traditional garments, and her work has met with global success thanks to its typically minimalist style, which has transformed the previous image of Milanese fashion.

Pucci, Emilio (1914–1992)
Born in Italy. In the 1950s, his sportswear was highly valued. In the 1960s, his printed works with vivid psychedelic colors and bold patterns became a worldwide trend in fashion. At the end of the twentieth century, his unique, unmistakable works were revived for a new, post-modern age.

Rabanne, Paco (b. 1934)
Born in Spain. At the Spring/Summer Collections in Paris in 1966, he made a striking debut with dresses of plastic discs linked with fine wire rings. His revolutionary "sewing" technique without fabric, thread, or needles was called "the clothing of bolts and pliers." The 1960s was a period when many artists abandoned the traditional techniques and materials and began new experiments. Rabanne created a succession of entirely new garments that caused a sensation.

Reboux, Caroline (1837–1927)
A hat designer born in Paris. She opened her shop in Paris in about 1870. She became one of top figures in Parisian millinery in the 1920s with her simple works, which were often made of felt. She provided hats for Vionnet and other designers.

Redfern (?–1920s)
A couture shop famous for its tailored suits. An Englishman, John Redfern (1853–1929), had worked as a drapers on the Isle of Wight since the 1850s. In 1881 he established his business in London and Paris, followed later by branches in New York and other cities. In 1888 he was appointed the dressmaker to Queen Victoria, and the fame of his shop dealing in tailored suits and sportswear was established. He opened branches in Paris, New York, and other cities. In 1916, he designed the first women's uniform for the Red Cross.

Rix (-Ueno), Felice (1893–1967)
Born in Vienna. After studying under Josef Hoffmann and others, Rix worked on decorative designs for wallpapers, textiles, etc. at the Wiener Werkstätte. Her forte was two-dimensional design featuring bright colors and thin lines. After marrying a Japanese husband, she settled in Kyoto, Japan in 1935. She continued to design, mainly interior decorations, and established the Kyoto Municipal School of Art.

Peter Robinson Ltd. (date unknown)
Details unknown. A house active in the 1860s on Regent St., London.

Rodrigues, N. (date unknown)
Details unknown. A Parisian house active in the late 19th century.

Rouff (date unknown)
Details unknown. A house in Paris in the latter half of the nineteenth century, located on the Boulevard Haussmann. Jeanne Paquin is supposed to have trained there. (Not to be confused with Maggy Rouff, a well-known house of the early twentieth century.)

Rykiel, Sonia (b. 1930)
Born in Paris. In 1968, she opened her Paris boutique, and her unique and imaginative sweaters quickly became popular. Although knitwear was everyday wear at that time, she transformed it into fashionable clothing and was nicknamed "The Queen of Knitwear." She invented a revolutionary technique, called "Sans Couture," in which the seams and hems of clothes appeared on the outside by the use of inside-out fabric. The overall forms of her works are simple and feature muted shades based on black. She described her own creative activities as "démodé (out-dated)," and was supported by a great number of women because she encouraged them to wear clothes in their own way.

Saint Laurent, Yves (b. 1936)
A Frenchman born in Algeria. In 1954, he was hired by Christian Dior, who had high hopes for his young protégé, and when Dior died suddenly in 1957 he took over the house at the age of 21. In 1958, he presented the "Trapeze" line, a new concept demonstrating the abstraction of the human body. In 1961, he founded his own house and presented his first collection. In 1965, he applied geometric abstract paintings to his dresses, and his "Mondrian look" was highly influential. The next year, he used "Pop Art" as a subject, and he continued to create works involved with paintings in the 1970s and 1980s. With collections like the "Tuxedo look" in 1966, and the "Safari look" in 1968, he applied the style of men's clothing to women's fashion, and was a pioneer in expressing the concept of unisex. He also predicted that the body itself would be the subject of expression in the coming age in "See-Through," an extremely avant-garde style he presented in 1968. He was also aware of the drastic changes taking place in the mass-consumption world of the 1960s, and he opened a *prêt-à-porter* shop, Rive Gauche. He always exactly perceived the style demanded by each era, and clearly indicated the direction of late-twentieth-century fashion. In Spring/Summer of 2002, he presented his last collection.

Sander, Jil (b. 1943)
Born in Germany. After working in the fashion industry in Hamburg, Sander debuted at Fall/Winter Milan Collections in 1985. The key features of her work are the use of rich, high-quality materials, the choice of subdued colors such as dark blue and black, and the sharp minimalist design achieved by reducing superfluous decoration. After her company merged with Prada, she stopped working as a designer after the Fall/Winter Collection in 2000.

Sant' Angelo, Giorgio (1936–1988)
Born in Italy, he started a *prêt-à-porter* shop in New York. His folkloric style and Gypsy look, with bright colors and multiple layers were deeply influenced by the hippie movement, and drew considerable attention in the late 1960s and early 1970s. He started using artificial fibers, especially elastic fabrics, well in advance of other designers.

Schiaparelli, Elsa (1890–1973)
Born in Rome. In 1927, she opened a shop, Pour le Sport ("For Sports"), in Paris. She first drew public attention with a black sweater knitted with a *trompe-l'oeil* white bow. Her house, Schiaparelli, opened in 1935. She was active mainly in the 1930s, and enthusiastically absorbed artistic elements into fashion. She created witty clothes thanks to the effective use of new artificial materials. She was intimate with Dalí, who was the leading figure of surrealism, Cocteau, Picabia, Bérard and other contemporary artists, and she produced many works in collaboration with them. A shade of pink created with Bérard's help was named "Shocking Pink," and became well known. Her haute couture house closed in 1954, and for a while dealt exclusively in accessories and perfumes, but closed completely shortly afterwards.

Shiino Shobey Silk Store (1864–?)
A typical Japanese silk textile export company in Yokohama in the early part of

the Meiji period (1867–1912), started by Shiino Shobey (1839–1900). They sold silk fabrics to foreign residents in Japan. After their participation in the Vienna World Exhibition in 1873, they created and exported silk commodities targeted at the European market.

Takada, Kenzo (b. 1939)
Born in Japan. In 1965, Takada moved to France. In 1970, he opened his own *prêt-à-porter* shop, Jungle Jap, in Paris. He was inspired by Japanese traditional wear like everyday kimonos and farmers' garments, and arranged them into unique Western clothes, which caused a sensation and appeared on the cover of *Elle* in 1970. His provocative layered clothes, freely combining a variety of patterns, colors, and forms, had a great impact on the more constructed Western fashion. Matching the trend of easy-going and loose fashion, so-called "déstructuré," his works showed the way for the fashion of the 1970s. Later, he sought inspiration in ethnic clothes from all over the world, and acquired an assured position as a Paris designer thanks to his skillfully harmonized and colorful works. Takada retired as a fashion designer after the Spring/Summer Collection in 2000. The Kenzo brand is still active as a subsidiary of LVMH.

Takahashi, Jun (b. 1969)
Born in Japan. Takahashi started Undercover, a Japanese label, with friends when he was still a fashion school student. They started out designing T-shirts, and then debuted in the Fall/Winter Tokyo Collection in 1994. Undercover presented wild and decorative street fashion with a punkish influence, which straightforwardly represented the interests of Takahashi, who had a deep knowledge and experience of music culture. (He had even been a member of an indie punk-rock band.) Their avant-garde works, expressions of their subcultural originality, have met with overwhelming support among the Japanese younger generations, and Takahashi has become a cult figure of "Ura-Harajuku" (the back streets of Harajyuku, Tokyo, the center of Japanese subcultural fashion). Their works seem very simple at first sight, but they abound with epoch-making ideas. Takahashi has been gaining a reputation as one of the top designers of the coming generation in Tokyo.

Tsumura, Kosuke (b. 1959)
Born in Japan. In 1983, Tsumura joined the Issey Miyake Design Studio. At the Autumn/Winter Paris Collections in 1994, he presented a nylon coat with dozens of pockets, called "Final Home." This work enables its possessor to survive in the city and is sold in a recycling-conscious system (it can be recycled at the store, rather than thrown away). He does not follow the rapid metamorphosis of the current fashion cycle, but aims to establish a contemporary realistic standard for the creation of clothes. He also engages in various other activities, e. g. the Venice Architecture Biennale in 2000.

Misses Turner (dates unknown)
Details unknown. The house was active in 1870s at 151 Sloane Street, London.

20 471 120 (1994)/Nakagawa, Masahiro (b. 1967) & Lica (b. 1967)
20 471 120 is a label launched in 1994 by two Japanese designers, Masahiro Nakagawa and Lica, who had been active in Osaka, Japan. They participated in the Tokyo Collection for the first time in Spring/Summer 1995. Their daring and extreme street fashion design, adopting the spririt of "today" from non-fashion fields such as subculture and art, is overwhelmingly supported among the young generation in Japan.

Vionnet, Madeleine (1876–1975)
Born in France. She worked at the houses of Callot Sœurs and Doucet, then opened her own house in Paris in 1912. The house reopened after World War I, and by the 1920s it was regarded as one of the most successful houses. She explored the body as captured by her own point of view, and could bring out the beauty of the female figure with her innovative forms and unique cutting skills. In the early 1920s, she presented dresses with a simple structure that was influenced by the Japanese kimono. Later, she established the "bias cut," a brand-new technique in the creation of clothes. She created all of her original designs by her unique draping method on a half-sized miniature model. She retired from designing in 1939. The works that Vionnet created, drastically reconsidering the relationship between the body and clothes, exerted a tremendous influence on twentieth-century fashion.

Vivier, Roger (1913–1998)
Born in Paris. He became a shoe designer after studying sculpture. He started his own business around 1936. In 1953, he started working as a designer for the shoe division at Dior. He was famous for his unique style: his works featured original shapes and unusual materials, brightly colored embroidery, and jewels and fur for decoration.

Watanabe, Junya (b. 1961)
Born in Japan. Watanabe joined Comme des Garçons in 1984, having been in charge of Comme des Garçons Tricot since 1982. He made a debut under the label of Comme des Garçons Junya Watanabe at the Tokyo Collections in Autumn/Winter 1992, and then at the Paris Collection in Spring/Summer 1994. Since then, he has kept refining his own cutting techniques and reconsidering materials for his clothes. Particularly notable has been his successful use of high-quality and high-tech fabrics in recent years. His innovative ideas are apparent in all his clothing creations, and his works are globally appreciated.

Westwood, Vivienne (b. 1941)
Born in England. In 1971, she opened a shop in London with Malcolm McLaren (b. 1946) called Let It Rock. Their punk style, expressing the culture of urban young people who found society repulsive, led contemporary street fashion. In 1982 she participated in the Paris Collections for the first time. Inspired by garments of the past, paintings, and literature, she designed her clothing from her own original viewpoint. The sexy and avant-garde clothes that she produces do not go along with contemporary easy-to-wear, comfortable and functional fashion. She pursues her original concept of elegance, even occasionally forcing the body into bondage.

Worth, Charles-Frederick (1825–1895)
Born in England. He moved to Paris in 1845, and worked at Maison Gagelin, an exclusive fabric emporium, as a sales clerk. Later, he was put in charge of

a dressmaking department making women's clothes. His work in this period was highly praised at the Great Exhibitions in both London and Paris. In 1857, he opened his own haute couture house in Paris. He was a talented businessman and was the first to present his works by means of a fashion show, as couture is shown today. He established the basis for the present system of haute couture. The most notable feature of his works was the abundant use of expensive silk fabrics made in Lyons. He was a favorite couturier of Eugénie, Empress of Napoleon III. He also worked for other royal families around the world, noble ladies, actresses, and the *demi-monde* of high-class prostitutes. In the late nineteenth century he dominated fashion circles and gained popularity among the rich in the United States. After his death, his two sons, Gaston and Jean-Philippe, succeeded him in the business. Although the house lasted for four generations, it finally closed in 1954.

YAMAMOTO, YOHJI (b. 1943)
Yamamoto presented his first collections in Tokyo in 1977 and in Paris in 1981. In his Spring/Summer 1983 Collection, he presented loose and rugged clothes. His style, which arbitrarily leaves clothes unfinished, was supposed to express a very Japanese aesthetic. His works, along with those of Rei Kawakubo, caused "Japan Shock" in Europe and the United States. In opposition to the Western way of making clothes, he plainly expressed a new intent to find the beauty in the movement of human bodies wrapped loosely by garments. Although his later works are based on traditional Western clothes, he has brought out the maximum possibilities that can occur between two-dimensional cloth and the three-dimensional body, and has skillfully given form to his ideas by his own unique technique. He has given special attention to silhouette, and cuts like an artisan according to his own aesthetics.

ZIMMERMANN (dates unknown)
Details unknown. A house in Paris, at 10, Rue des Pyramides. The name appeared in *Vogue* around 1910.

Glossary

(D): Dutch, (F): French, (J): Japanese term.
Terms in capital letters are explained elsewhere in the Glossary

ALENÇON (F)
see NEEDLEPOINT LACE

ALL-IN-ONE
A name for a foundation with bra and girdle combined into a one-piece garment.

AMAZONE (F)
Women's riding wear, popularized during the nineteenth century. Named after the Amazons, the female warriors of Greek mythology.

ARGENTAN (F)
see NEEDLEPOINT LACE

ARTIFICIAL SILK
Term used to describe rayon before 1925.

AUMÔNIÈRE (F)
Originally a small bag for alms carried by men and women in the Middle Ages; women carried it as a fashionable and practical accessory in the eighteenth century. It is the forerunner of the RÉTICULE and later the handbag.

BABY DOLL
Mini nightwear or dress with short puffed sleeves and an undefined waistline; named after the film *Baby Doll,* produced in 1956.

BANYAN
Men's indoor garment of the seventeenth and eighteenth centuries in England, originally worn by the Hindi in India.

BARE-MIDRIFF TOP
Style exposing the body from the rib cage under the bust to the waist or hips. Popularized in the 1970s.

BEACH PAJAMAS
Full-length trouser ensemble worn as women's sportswear in the 1920s and 1930s.

BERTHE (F)
Large cape-like collar for women, covering their décolleté neckline, introduced in the nineteenth century.

BIAS CUT
Manner of cutting diagonally across the grain of the fabric. Madeleine Vionnet was famous for bias-cut dresses.

BICORNE (F)
Men's hat in the shape of a crescent worn during the Napoleonic period. Worn by the *Incroyables* as a substitute for the tricorne. It was also favored by Napoleon I.

BINCHE (F)
see BOBBIN LACE

BIZARRE SILK
Silk fabric woven with strange and exotic patterns often combining Oriental and baroque motifs, popular from the end of the seventeenth to the early eighteenth century.

BLONDE LACE
A very fine silk BOBBIN LACE, made in Bayeux, Caen, and Chantilly in France. Popular from the mid-eighteenth to the nineteenth century. Originally made with cream-colored, unbleached China silk thread.

BLOOMERS
Underpants with loose legs gathered at the bottom, around knee length. In 1851, Amelia Bloomer designed them to promote dress reform for women, but they gained very little acceptance. Bloomers became popular as specialized clothing worn for bicycle riding in the 1880s. Later, they were commonly worn as gym clothes for girls.

Bobbin lace
A general name for lace made on a pillow in which the designs are marked out by pins, and the bobbins or bones crossed back and forth over the positioned pins. Specific types include Brussels, Binche, Chantilly, and Mechlin.

Bonding
Textile process involving the joining of two fabrics into one by backing with adhesive or foam.

'Boro' look (J) Ragged look
Name coined for Rei Kawakubo and Yohji Yamamoto's collections in 1982. *Boro* means "ragged" in Japanese. Their monochromatic, torn and non-decorative clothes brought shabbiness into fashion, and intentionally expressed a sense of absence rather than presence.

Bustle
Pad or arrangement of steel springs worn under a skirt to create a projecting derrière, popular in various forms in the latter half of nineteenth century.

Cannelé (F)
A weave with a channeled or fluted surface produced by continuous loops of warp thread; a typical French fabric of the eighteenth century.

Cardigan
Knit jacket, open in front, named after James Thomas Brudenell, Earl of Cardigan (1797–1868) of the British army. Gabrielle Chanel introduced her famous cardigan suits in the 1920s.

Carmagnole (F)
Jacket with wide lapels and gold buttons worn by *sans culottes*, the French Revolutionaries. Originally worn by workers in France from Carmagnola, Italy.

Chambre Syndicale de la Couture Parisienne (F)
An association to promote Parisian high fashion founded in 1910. Its activities are the organization of collections, press relations, the defense of copyright and the operation of vocational schools.

Chantilly (F)
see Bobbin lace

Chemise à la reine (F)
The style of dress worn by Marie-Antoinette, queen of Louis XVI of France, in the 1780s. It was the origin of the chemise dress.

Chemise dress
Muslin dress of the Empire period, styled with high waistline and slim skirt, worn without a corset or a pannier.

Chenille (F)
Yarn with fuzzy pile protruding from all sides. Derived from the French for "caterpillar."

China silk
Shiny, lightweight plain-weave silk, made in China or Japan.

Chiné, Chiné à la branche (F)
Technique of printing a pattern onto the warp before weaving; the finished fabric has a pattern with a blurred outline. It is same as the Japanese *hogushi*, one of the *kasuri* techniques.

Chintz
see Indienne

Cloche (F)
Deep-crowned hat, fashionable in the 1920s. Derived from the French word for "bell."

Cockade, Cocarde (F)
A rosette of pleated ribbon, originally a military insignia.

Compères (F)
Two cloth panels for women's open robes in the mid-eighteenth century, attached to the inside front bodice and fastened by hooks or buttons. Compared to the stomacher, which had to be pinned to the dress each time it was worn, *compères* were much more functional.

Confection (F)
French term for the mass-produced, inexpensive ready-made clothing that appeared in the mid-nineteenth century.

Corps, Corps à baleines (F)
see Corset

Corset (F)
Closely fitting inner bodice stiffened with whalebone, metal, or wood, and fastened by lacing. The term "corset" did not appear until the nineteenth century, but referred to an undergarment that had been called stays (in English), and *corps*, or *corps à baleines* (in French) in the eighteenth century.

Costume jewelry
Jewelry made either of gemstones that resemble precious stones or of imitation stones. It came into fashion thanks to Gabrielle Chanel, who showed imitation jewels in the 1920s. It then developed into a genuine accessory and was thought of more highly, rather than being considered merely as an imitation.

Coutil (F)
Durable, firm cotton or linen with a herringbone twill weave, used for undergarments like corsets.

Cowl neckline
Draped collar that extends nearly to shoulders in a circular style, like the cowls worn by monastic orders.

Cravat
A neckcloth or tie. Originally men's neckwear of muslin or silk worn in the seventeenth century, which developed into the neckties of today in the nineteenth century.

Crinoline (F)
A petticoat made to produce skirts of extraordinary volume in the mid-nineteenth century. *Crinoline* was the term for a petticoat made of a fabric woven from horsehair (*crin*) and linen (*lin*). During the 1850s the cage frame crinoline, made of steel hoops or whale bones, was introduced.

Culottes (F)
See Knee-breeches

Dandy
Term used from the early nineteenth century onwards, for men who were deeply concerned about the smartness of their clothes and appearance.

Dolly Varden style
Women's fashion popular in the 1870–1880s, a revival of the Robe à la polonaise style. Named after the heroine of Charles Dickens' novel *Barnaby Rudge* (1841).

Drawers
Underpants worn by women from the early nineteenth century onwards.

Drawn work
Openwork embroidery made by removing some threads in each direction in the fabric and interlacing the remaining yarns with embroidery stitches.

Drugget, Droguet (F)
Fancy eighteenth-century silk fabric woven with intricate small patterns.

Dust ruffle
Ruffle added on the inside of the hem of a full-length dress or petticoat in the late nineteenth and early twentieth century, to protect the dress from becoming soiled when walking outdoors.

Echelle (F)
Decorative ladder-like lacing of ribbons on the front of a STOMACHER, popular from the late seventeenth to late eighteenth century, derived from French for "ladder."

Empire styles
Dresses worn during the First Empire in France (1804–1815), characterized by a high waistline, straight skirt and puffed sleeves.

Engageantes (F)
Sleeve ruffles made of fine lace or DRAWN WORK in double and triple layers, worn in the seventeenth and eighteenth centuries.

Fichu (F)
Women's scarves, usually made of muslin, worn in the eighteenth and nineteenth centuries.

Fly-fringe
A silk fringe consisting of tufts or small tassels, often used for trimming women's gowns during the eighteenth century.

Frac (F)
French term for the English FROCK COAT.

Frock coat
Single- or double-breasted men's coat with fold-back lapels, worn from the late eighteenth through the nineteenth century.

Fuki (J)
Protruding lining at the hem and sleeve openings in the Japanese KIMONO, often in a contrasting color, occasionally heavily padded.

Garçonne (F)
The name that came into use after World War I to describe women who dressed and looked like boys. A French word that originated from the novel of the same title by Victor Margueritte, published in 1922.

Gazar (F)
Silk gauze with a crisp and smooth texture made by Abraham, a textile manufactory founded in Switzerland.

Gibson Girl
Character created by the American illustrator Charles Dana Gibson, who appeared in his drawings from 1895 until 1910.

Gigot (F) sleeve, Leg of mutton sleeve
Sleeve shaped like a leg of mutton: full and rounded from the shoulder to the elbow, and then tapered to the wrist. Very full sleeves were popular around 1835, and were revived in the 1890s.

Gilet (F), Vest, Waistcoat
Men's waist-length, sleeveless garment worn under a jacket and over a shirt.

Girdle
Women's undergarment designed to mold the lower torso and sometimes the legs.

Glass beads
Made since ancient times in various places such as Venice. Mariano Fortuny favored their use in his designs.

Habit (F)
Name applied to a men's jacket, used from the latter half of the eighteenth century, replacing the *justaucorps*.

Habit à la française (F)
Men's formal attire in the eighteenth century; it consisted of a jacket, waistcoat and knee-breeches.

Habutae (J)
A soft, lightweight, plain-weave silk fabric of Japan, sometimes called *hiraginu* in Japanese.

Harem pants
Bouffant pants gathered into bands at the ankles, copied from the Middle Eastern style.

Haute couture (F)
Parisian high-quality clothing and its exclusive creation system. In the late nineteenth century, Charles Frederick Worth established the basis of the industry of haute couture that developed into today's manner.
see CHAMBRE SYNDICALE DE LA COUTURE PARISIENNE

Hobble skirt
Skirt rounded over the hips and tapered to the ankles, so narrow that walking was impeded. A fashion introduced by Paul Poiret in 1910.

Hostess gown
Women's informal gown worn at home while entertaining.

Hot pants
Slang term to describe women's short pants; the name was coined by the fashion industry newspaper *Women's Wear Daily* in 1971.

Hussar, Hussard, à la hussarde (F)
The light cavalry of the French army. Their uniform was derived from the cavalry units of Hungary. From the end of the eighteenth century the Hussar style, *à la hussarde* in French, spread to become a popular trend.

Incroyable (F)
Used instead of "DANDY" or "fop" for men who wore extreme fashions during the Directoire period (1795–1799); from the French word for "incredible."

Indienne (F)
French term for painted or printed muslin from India; the English name is CHINTZ.

Irish crochet lace
Handmade lace made with the chain stitch, copying the style of needlepoint lace made originally in Ireland. Popular in the late nineteenth to early twentieth century.

Jabot (F)
Cloth or lace ornament worn at the neck and over the chest. Originally for men; became popular among women from the mid-nineteenth century.

Japonsche rock (D)
Dutch term for the Japanese kimono with cotton padding which was imported by the East India Company, worn by European men as an indoor gown in the seventeenth and eighteenth centuries. Since there was a shortage in the number of imported Japanese KIMONOS, oriental gowns made out of INDIENNE appeared to supply the demand. All of these were called *Japonsche rocken* ('Japanese robe') in Holland.

Jumps
Women's soft bodice without stiffening bones, usually worn at home instead of a corset in the eighteenth century.

Jouy print, Toile de Jouy (F)
Printed fabrics by Christophe P. Oberkampf, who established a factory in Jouy near Versailles. When the ban on importing or producing indienne was removed in 1759, the printing industry immediately grew, and Jouy developed into a major center for the printing industry in France.

Kimono (J)
A traditional costume from Japan. In the West, it meant a dressing gown, since Western women wore the Japanese kimono as an exotic at-home gown in the late nineteenth century. In the early twentieth century, the kimono sleeve and kimono coat were adapted from the Japanese kimono into Western clothing.

Knee-breeches, Culottes (F)
Typical knee-length pants worn by men in the eighteenth century, made to fit the leg.

Lappet
Drapery or long ribbon-like fabric, often lace-trimmed, hanging from the cap or bonnet during the seventeenth, eighteenth, and nineteenth centuries.

Leg of mutton sleeve
see Gigot sleeve

Lingerie (F)
Collective term for women's underwear. Derived from the French word, *linge*, for linen, which was the most common material for underwear from the Middle Ages to the twentieth century.

Little black dress
Emerging in the 1920s, the "little black dress" was based on the simple lines of the chemise. Heavily promoted by Gabrielle Chanel and Edward Molyneux.

Lycra®
see Spandex

Mameluke sleeve, à la mamelouk (F)
A woman's sleeve with a series of puffs, large at the top and diminishing in size to the wrist, finishing with frills. A fashion of the early nineteenth century, named after the Egyptian cavalry squadron of Mamelukes created by Napoleon I.

Manteau de cour (F)
Court dress with a long train. Empress Joséphine introduced this fashion of court dress at the coronation ceremony of Napoleon I.

Marchand de mode (F)
French haberdasher. A term recognized through an association formed in 1776.

Marseilles quilting
Woven fabric with a quilted effect on both sides. Named after the city in France.

Mechlin lace, Malines (F)
see Bobbin lace

Merveilleuse (F)
Term used for women who wore extreme fashions during the Directoire period, 1795–1799; from the French word for "marvelous."

Microfiber
Extremely fine filament or staple fiber, generally less than 1.0 denier per filament. Since a Japanese textile manufacture developed it from polyester in 1970, microfiber fabrics with high volatilization and ventilation have been produced.

Mini (F)
A skirt length reaching to mid-thigh, popular from the early 1960s.

Mitts, Mittens, Mitaines (F)
Fingerless gloves.

Monokini
Topless bathing suit introduced by Rudi Gernreich in 1964. The name derived from the word "bikini."

Morocco, Morocco leather
A soft goatskin, usually dyed red; originally produced in Morocco.

Muff
Warm tubular covering for the hands, open at each end.

Mules
Open-backed slippers.

Muscadin (F)
Name given to the flamboyant young loyalists of the French Revolutionary period who favored extreme fashions.

Nankeen, Nankin (F)
A strong, brownish-yellow Chinese cotton woven from hand-spun threads.

Needlepoint lace
A lace made entirely with a sewing needle instead of bobbins, and worked on a paper pattern with buttonhole and blanket stitches. Types include: Point de Venise, Alençon, and Argentan.

Netsuke (J)
Japanese decorative toggle, 3-4 centimeters in size, worn hanging from the *obi* (sash), with an *inro* (seal basket) or cigarette case. Popular from the late Edo period to the Meiji period, and also exported to the West.

New Look
Style introduced by Christian Dior in 1947. The "New Look" style was nostalgic and elegant, characterized by a thin waist and a longish bouffant skirt.

Norfolk jacket
Belted jacket with two box pleats from the shoulders to the hem in front and behind. Worn by men for sports and travel in the latter half of the nineteenth century.

Nylon
A generic term for a manufactured fiber in which the fiber-forming substance is a long-chain synthetic polyamide with recurring amide groups. It was invented in 1937 and industrially produced in 1939 by the Du Pont company. In 1940, Du Pont made the first nylon stockings, and nylon has been used extensively in underwear and dress manufacture ever since.

Pagoda sleeve
Funnel-shaped outer sleeve flaring at the wrist. Named for its shape, which resembles the flared roof of an Asian pagoda.

Paisley
In the 1840s, imitation printed cashmere shawls were mass-produced in the Scottish town of Paisley. The name "Paisley" was used so widely that it became a synonym for the cone pattern found on cashmeres.

Pajama
Originally inspired by Persian or Indian pants. Popular as men's sleepwear instead of nightgowns in the late nineteenth century. Introduced for women in the 1920s.

Pannier, Panier (F)
Hoop made of reed or whalebone to support a wide skirt; it was bell-shaped during the early eighteenth century but sometimes divided into two side basket shapes after the middle of the century.

Pantalon (F)
Long trousers worn instead of knee-breeches by French Revolutionaries.

Pants suit, Pants style
A suit with trousers, presented by Yves Saint Laurent and André Courrèges for women as fashionable town wear in 1960s. Although women had already adopted trousers, they had previously been worn only indoors or on the beach.

Patchwork
A method of sewing small pieces together to form a fabric or quilt. Fashionable in the 1970s.

Pattens, Patins (F)
Overshoes worn over regular shoes to raise the feet to protect them from muddy streets.

Peacock Revolution
A term used to signify the radical changes in men's wear in 1960s.

Pekin stripe
Stripes with even widths made in Peking, China.

Pèlerine (F)
A short cape that covers the shoulder, used from the mid-eighteenth until the late nineteenth century.

Percale
Plain-weave cotton fabric with a firm, smooth finish.

Pet-en-l'air (F)
A type of woman's jacket in the eighteenth century.

Phrygian cap, Bonnet phrygien, Bonnet rouge (F)
Ancient Greek soft cap or bonnet of felt or leather with a high crown, forward-curving peak, and chin strap, adopted by the French Revolutionaries as an emblem of liberty.

Pièce d'estomac (F)
see Stomacher

Pierrot (F)
Women's short fitted jacket with tails, popular from the mid 1780s to the 1790s.

Platform shoes
Shoes with thick mid-sole, usually made of cork. Popular for women in the 1940s and 1970s.

Pocket
Small bag for carrying small items. Wearing a pocket under the dress was the appropriate solution for the layered structure of rococo clothing. Replaced by the réticule when the chemise dress with its simple lines became fashionable at the end of the eighteenth century. From the late nineteenth century pockets were sewn into dresses and shirtwaists.

Point de France (F)
Needlepoint lace made at the Royal Manufactory in France in the late seventeenth and eighteenth centuries.

Polyester
Generic name for man-made fibers made of ethylene glycol and terephthalic acid. A company called Imperial Chemical Industries (ICI) was the first to market polyester, in 1946.

Prêt-à-porter (F)
see Ready-to-wear

Princess line, Princess style
Sleek-fitting dress line achieved by making a garment without a waist seam, popular in the 1870s. Named in honor of Alexandra, Princess of Wales, by Worth.

Quill, Quille (F)
A type of trim put all around the front opening of a women's robe in the eighteenth century.

Racquet sleeve
Sleeve shaped like a racquet. A type of women's sleeve in the eighteenth century.

Raffia
Fiber from the leaves of a species of Madagascar palm.

Ramoneur (F)
A dark brown print popular in the late eighteenth century. *Ramoneur* is the French term for "chimney-sweep."

Rayon
Generic term for man-made fibers created from cellulose, used after 1927. First produced by Count Hilaire de Chardonnet in 1889.

Ready-to-wear, Prêt-à-porter (F)
Clothes that are produced in standard sizes. Since the 1960s, with the rise of mass production, it has fostered the popularization of fashion.

Redingote (F)
A coat for men in the eighteenth and nineteenth century, or a women's dress or coat derived from the men's style. The English "riding coat" was used by the French army, and came to be called a *redingote* in French around the end of the eighteenth century.

Réticule (F), Ridicule
Women's small handbag, which appeared from the late eighteenth century to take the place of a pocket.

Retroussée dans les poches (F)
The style of dressing popular in France throughout the eighteenth century. The skirt was pulled out from the pocket slits on either side of the dress, creating full drapes at the back.

Robe à l'anglaise (F)
Style of women's dress in the late eighteenth century without panniers. It consisted of a front-closing robe and a jupe (skirt); the bottom part of the bodice back was pointed and sewn to the jupe. It appeared in France as the "English-style gown" in the 1770s.

Robe à la française (F)
The typical women's dress in France in the eighteenth century. It consisted of a front-opening robe pleated in the back, a jupe (skirt), and a stomacher (*pièce d'estomac*). Worn as a formal dress throughout the Revolutionary period.

Robe à la polonaise (F)
Style of women's dress in the late eighteenth century; the back of skirt was held up by cords and divided into three draped parts. It is said that the term derived from a political event, in which Poland was first divided among three countries, in 1772.

Robe volante (F)
A popular style of women's flowing gown in the early eighteenth century, with large

pleats and a round skirt. Derived from the negligee in the later reign of Louis XIV.

ROMPERS
One-piece suit with shirt and bloomers, joined by a waistline seam. Rompers were originally introduced for children's wear in the early twentieth century.

ROUND GOWN
One-piece dress with rising waistline reaching just below the bust, worn in the late eighteenth century.

SABOT (F)
Shoe carved from one piece of wood.

SABOT SLEEVE
Women's sleeve in the eighteenth century with a SABOT-like shape, tight-fitting to the elbow then flared, trimmed with ruffles.

SACK DRESS
Loose dress without emphasis on the waist, introduced by Cristobal Balenciaga in the 1950s.

SANS-CULOTTES (F)
A name given to the French Revolutionaries or Jacobins to distinguish them from the aristocrats. The term referred to the fact that the men of the people wore trousers rather than the KNEE-BREECHES (*culottes*) of the nobility.

SAROUEL (F)
Very full ankle-length pants gathered into a band at the ankle, similar to HAREM PANTS.

S-CURVE SILHOUETTE
An artificial S-curve silhouette which was most popular around 1900. The shape was created by the CORSET, which tightened the waist and pushed out the bust and hips.

SEE-THROUGH
Style with a sheer textile worn over bare skin. Heavily promoted by Yves Saint Laurent in the 1960s.

SEIGAIHA (J)
Blue wave pattern in Japan or China. In the West the pattern is seen as fish scales.

SHIRTWAIST
Term originating in the 1890s for women's blouses styled like men's shirts.

SHOCKING PINK
A bright pink color named by Elsa Schiaparelli.

SLIP
Undergarment worn by women beginning above the bust usually with shoulder straps; acts as a lining.

SMOKING (F)
French version of what is known in America as a tuxedo. A semi-formal dinner jacket.

SPANDEX
Generic term for man-made fibers, composed largely of segmented polyurethane, that are stretchable and lightweight. LYCRA is a trademark of Du Pont for filament spandex fiber.

SPENCER (F)
Men's waist-length jacket named after the second Earl of Spencer (1758–1834). Popular from the late eighteenth century until the 1820s as a women's jacket.

STAYS
see CORSET

STENCILED PRINT
Design made by placing cardboard or metal cut-outs over fabric and then spraying paint or roller printing over them. It is the same technique as the Japanese *katagami-zome*.

STOMACHER, PIÈCE D'ESTOMAC (F)
V-shaped panel worn over the chest area of a women's open robe in the eighteenth century. The decoration of the stomacher was frequently most elaborate as it covered an erogenous zone.

TAIL COAT
Men's formal black suit coat, open to the waist in the front and cut away to the back of the knees, the long vent to the waist behind resembling a swallow's tail.

TAILORED SUITS, TAILORED, TAILLEUR (F)
Women's suit consisting of a jacket and skirt made by a tailor rather than a dressmaker, from the latter half of the nineteenth century.

TARLATAN
Net-like transparent cotton fabric, generally dyed in solid colors, and given a stiff finish; popular in the 1860s.

TARTAN
Closely woven woolen cloth that originated in Scotland, where different patterns are used to identify individual clans. The fabric is cross-banded with colored stripes. From the mid-nineteenth century, Queen Victoria's frequent visits to her estate in Balmoral, Scotland stimulated the popularity of tartan garments.

TEA GOWN
Worn without a CORSET as an informal hostess gown from the late nineteenth to early twentieth century.

TEDDY
An undergarment combining a chemise with drawers. First introduced in the 1920s.

THEATER COAT
Loose outer garment for evening theater visits, popular in the early twentieth century. Some theater coats of Chinese mandarin robe-style were made in Japan.

TOQUE (F)
A style of brimless hat fitting close to the head. Popular in the latter half of the nineteenth century and revived in the 1950s.

TOURNURE (F)
see BUSTLE

TRAPEZE, TRAPÈZE (F)
A dress with narrow shoulders and a wide swing at the hem; designed by Yves Saint Laurent for the House of Dior in 1958.

TRICORNE (F)
Cocked three-cornered hat with the brim turned up on all three sides.

TUBULAR DRESS
Women's tube-shaped dress, popular in the 1920s.

TUNIC DRESS
Two-piece dress with a tunic (a long overblouse).

TURBAN (F)
Originally men's headdress of the Near East; a long piece of fabric wrapped around a hat without a brim. Draped women's hats like the Eastern turban appeared in Western fashion during the many periods when Orientalism was in style.

Ungen (J)
Originally Chinese coloring technique that creates a three-dimensional look by placing bands of different colors horizontally one after another.

Unisex fashion
A style that can be worn by both men and women, introduced in the late 1960s.

Utility garment
Functional clothes designed in the UK under the Utility Clothing Scheme, a rationing system developed by the British Board of Trade during World War II. Many well-known designers cooperated in designing Utility clothing.

Valenciennes (F)
see Bobbin lace

Velveteen
Cotton or rayon pile fabric on a plain or twill backing; woven singly, the loops are cut to make a soft and velvety surface.

Visite (F)
Woman's cape-like outdoor garment, worn in the latter half of the nineteenth century.

Index of Names

Acknowledgements & Photo Credits

Many people and institutions have been extraordinarily helpful in providing information and facilitating introductions. We would thank, collectively and individually, the following:

Comme des Garçons Co., Ltd. / Fashion Institute of Technology, SUNY. / Mr. Maurizio GALANTE / Mr. Yoshitaka HASHIZUME / Mr. Tokutaro HIRANO / Ms. Shoko HISADA / Mr. Martin KAMER / Ms. Sumiyo KOYAMA / Maki Hiroshige Atelier Co., Ltd. / Masaki Matsushima Japan Co., Ltd. / Miyake Design Studio / Ms. Mona M. LUTZ / Ms. Fusako NISHIBE / Ms. Yoshiko OKAMURA / Ms. Yoko OTSUKA / UNDER COVER Co., Ltd. / Mr. Hiroshi TANAKA / Teijin Limited / Mr. Richard Weller / Yohji Yamamoto Inc. / Ms. Mari YOSHIMURA

The editor and the publisher have made every effort to ensure that all copyrights were respected for the works illustrated and that the necessary permission was obtained from the artists, their heirs, representatives or estates. Given the large number of artists involved, this was not possible in every case, in spite of intensive research. Should any claims remain outstanding, the copyright holders or their representatives are requested to contact the publisher.

t = top, b = bottom, c = center, l = left, r = right, tl = top left, tr = top right, bl = bottom left, br = bottom right

Photo: **AKG Berlin**, 39, 54/55, 79
Photo: **AKG Berlin**/Erich Lessing: 243r
Peter Willi – **Artothek**, 96l
Westermann – **Artothek**, 222
© **Bianchini Férier**, 433
UK/**Bridgeman Art Library**, 36l, 42l, 56, 76l, 102b, 106/107, 217, 284
Jean Pagès © Vogue **The Condé Nast Publications Ltd**, 482
© **Timothy Greenfield-Sanders**, New York, 646/647
© **Naoya Hatakeyama** / © **KCI**: 2–7, 196b, 201, 434, 443, 630, 698
© **Takashi Hatakeyama** / © **KCI**: 18, 19, 38, 44, 46, 47, 58, 59, 64, 67, 77, 101, 120t, 121–123, 127, 140, 141, 156, 157, 166, 180, 184, 185, 199, 202–205, 210, 216, 226, 227, 234–237, 240, 252, 253, 256, 257, 260, 261, 269, 270, 272–275, 278, 280–283, 308, 316r–319, 332, 336, 337, 339, 340, 343, 347, 349l, 363, 373, 384, 385, 387, 389, 392, 393, 395, 398, 401, 407, 410, 418, 419, 432, 438, 441, 442, 445t, 446, 449, 452, 456–458, 460, 461, 463, 466, 467, 469, 470, 471, 474, 475, 481, 483, 484, 488, 490, 494–497, 507–509, 511, 514, 515, 518l, 519r, 523, 524, 526–532, 534, 536–541, 543–547, 549–552, 555, 556, 557, 562, 563, 566–571, 573, 576–579, 586–591, 593, 596–604, 606–612, 614–619, 622, 624, 625, 627, 628, 631, 634, 635, 639l, 640–645, 648–653, 656, 662, 663, 665, 666, 668–671, 673–677, 680, 681, 683, 684, 686–688, 690–693, 696, 697
© **Richard Haughton** / © **KCI**: 268, 285, 286l, 288, 289, 294, 295, 297, 302, 303, 306, 307, 344, 348, 359, 361, 366–368, 369r, 402–404l, 422r, 423l, 424r, 425–430, 437, 448r, 453r, 454, 658
© **Masayuki Hayashi** / © **KCI**: 70b, 178, 179r, 197, 286r, 346c, 346b, 444b, 478, 479, 492, 512t, 512b, 558, 580, 581, 620, 621
© **Taishi Hirokawa** / © **KCI**: 15, 17, 23, 35l, 45, 63, 72t, 93l, 116l, 120b, 142–145, 179l, 182, 183, 186–196t, 206–209, 212–215, 218, 219, 223, 224, 225, 228–232, 238, 241–243l, 244–249, 254, 255, 258, 259, 262–267, 276, 277, 287, 291, 304, 305, 309, 312–314, 333–335, 338r, 341, 346t, 349r, 362, 364, 365, 370, 376, 377, 380, 386, 390, 391, 396, 397, 409, 412–417, 420, 421, 440, 444t, 445b, 447, 459, 464, 465, 468t, 472, 473, 480, 486, 487, 489, 493, 510, 512c, 521, 522, 533, 535, 554, 561, 572, 582, 583, 613, 623, 654, 667, 678
© **Taishi Hirokawa** © **Yoshitaka Hashizume**, 682, 685
Horst P. Horst Estate, 462
© **Tohru Kogure** / © **KCI**: 32–34, 35r, 37, 40, 41, 43, 48–50t, 51, 52–54l, 55r, 57, 60–62, 66, 68–70t, 71, 72b, 73–75, 78, 79r, 80–84, 87, 88, 90–92, 93r, 94, 95, 97, 98, 101, 102t, 103–105, 108, 109, 111–115, 117–119, 124, 129–131, 134–137, 139, 154, 158–163, 164r, 165, 168–171, 173–175l, 176, 198, 220
© **Kazumi Kurigami** / © **KCI**: 292, 298–301, 350r, 351r, 352r, 354, 357, 399, 405, 436, 439, 455, 516, 517, 629, 636, 637, 655, 657, 659–661, 679
© **Kyoto Costume Institute (KCI)**, 72tl, 76br, 110t, 116br, 118br, 126b, 138, 176br, 181, 200, 290, 345, 351bl, 353, 356, 360, 369bl, 400, 404br, 406t, 406c, 406b, 411, 424bl, 450, 451, 506, 605, 698/699
© **Man Ray Trust, Paris / VG Bild-Kunst**, Bonn 2006, 382
© **Francis G. Mayer, Picture Press Hamburg**, 315
© **Mondrian/Holtzman Trust, c/o hcr@hcrinternational.com**, 560/561
© **Morimura Yasumasa**, 638/639
© **Musée d'art et d'histoire**, Ville de Genève, 50b
Musées royaux des Beaux-Arts de Belgique / Photo Speltdoorn, 310/311
Galerie Sylvie Nissen / www.renegruau.com, 525
© Photo **RMN** – Gérard Blot, 172
Cecil Beaton Photograph/Courtesy of **Sotheby's London**, 491
Louise Dahl-Wolfe/Courtesy **Staley-Wise Gallery**, New York, 542
© **Steichen Carousel**, New York, 408, 435
© **Minsei Tominaga** / © **KCI**: 374, 378, 381, 383
© **Shoji Ueda Office**, 632/633
© **VG Bild-Kunst**, Bonn 2006, 388, 468bl, 480bl, 506, 574/575

The authors

Akiko Fukai (Chief Curator of The Kyoto Costume Institute), Tamami Suoh (Curator of The Kyoto Costume Institute), Miki Iwagami (Lecturer of fashion history at Sugino Fashion College, Tokyo), Reiko Koga (Professor of fashion history at Bunka Women's University) and Rii Nie (Assistant Curator of The Kyoto Costume Institute).

Imprint

To stay informed about upcoming TASCHEN titles, please request our magazine at www.taschen.com/magazine or write to TASCHEN America, 6671 Sunset Boulevard, Suite 1508, USA-Los Angeles, CA 90028, contact-us@taschen.com, Fax: +1-323-463.4442. We will be happy to send you a free copy of our magazine which is filled with information about all of our books.

Hohenzollernring 53, D–50672 Köln
www.taschen.com

103, Shichi-jo Goshonouchi Minamimachi, Shimogyo-ku, Kyoto
www.kci.or.jp

Chief Editor: Akiko Fukai (KCI)
Photographers: Tohru Kogure, Kazumi Kurigami, Naoya Hatakeyama, Takashi Hatakeyama, Richard Haughton, Masayuki Hayashi, Taishi Hirokawa, Minsei Tominaga
Editor: Tamami Suoh (KCI)
Editorial Coordination: Ute Kieseyer and Thierry Nebois (TASCHEN)
Design: Tsutomu Nishioka
Cover Design: Sense/Net, Andy Disl and Birgit Reber, Cologne
Production: Ute Wachendorf (TASCHEN)
Texts: Akiko Fukai, Tamami Suoh, Miki Iwagami, Reiko Koga, Rie Nii, Junko Nishiyama
Editorial Assistants: Naoko Tsutsui, Yumiko Yata (KCI)
Costume Fitters: Atsuko Miyoshi, Keiko Goto, Reiko Goto, Yuchiko Ito, Chiemi Tani
Translation: Dominic Cheetham, Yuko Fukatsu-Fukuoka, Chiharu Hayashi, Ai Inoue, Akio Kobayashi, Maki Morimura, Masaya Shimokusu, Chikako Shimokusu, Miwa Susuda
Proofreading: Ai Inoue, Kit Nagamura, Susan Ward, Jonathan Murphy, Michele A. Schons-Foster, Malcolm Green

Printed in China
ISBN 978–3–8228–2763–5